The Strategic Management of Large Engineering Projects

The Strategic Management of Large Engineering Projects

Shaping Institutions, Risks, and Governance

Roger Miller and
Donald Lessard

with the participation of
Serghei Floricel and the
IMEC Research Group

This book was set in Palatino in 'QuarkXpress' by Asco Typesetters, Hong Kong.

Printed and bound in the United States of America.

Library of Congress Cataloging-in-Publication Data

Miller, Roger, 1938–
The strategic management of large engineering projects : shaping institutions, risks, and governance / Roger Miller and Donald Lessard ; with the participation of Serghei Floricel and the IMEC Research Group.
p. cm.
Includes bibliographical references and index.
ISBN 0-262-12236-7 (hc. : alk. paper)
1. Engineering—Management. 2. Construction industry—Management. I. Lessard, Donald R. II. Serghei Floricel and the IMEC Research Group. III. Title.
TA190 .M55 2001
658.5—dc21 00-056867

Contents

Tables

Figures

The IMEC Research Group

Bjorn Andersen is an associate professor of industrial engineering at the Norwegian University of Science, in Trondheim, Norway.

Richard Brealey is adviser to the governor of the Bank of England and a professor of finance at the London Business School, United Kingdom.

Ian Cooper is a professor of finance and director of the Institute of Finance at the London Business School, United Kingdom.

Serghei Floricel is an associate professor of project management at Université du Québec à Trois-Rivières, Canada.

Michel Habib is an associate professor of finance at the London Business School, United Kingdom.

Brian Hobbs is a professor of project management at Université du Québec à Montréal, Canada.

Donald Lessard is the EPOCH Foundation professor of strategy and international business and deputy dean of MIT's Sloan School of Management, United States.

Pascale Michaud is a partner in SECOR, a Montreal-based international consulting firm. Her area of expertise is the piloting of change projects.

Roger Miller is the Hydro-Québec/CAE Professor of Technology Management at Université du Québec à Montréal, Canada, a fellow at SPRU, University of Sussex, U.K., and a founding partner of SECOR.

Francisco Xavier Olleros is a professor of technology management at Université du Québec à Montréal, Canada.

The IMEC Research Program

The IMEC Research Program was launched in Montreal in 1995 by the Hydro-Québec/CAE chair in the Management of Technology at Université du Québec à Montréal, and SECOR. The World EDI Institute and SNC-Lavalin were initial partners. As the concept began to take shape, EDF, Ontario Hydro, Cofiroute, and CAE agreed to provide additional sponsorship for three years. Later, support was extended by the Project Management Institute, Norsk-Hydro, Inter-American Bank, EDC, PM 2000 of Norway, and the Quebec and Canadian government departments of industry. The Natural Science and Engineering Research Council and the Social Science Research and Humanities Council of Canada matched industrial contributions, thus making the venture possible. Patrick Rich, of Geneva, agreed to chair the IMEC program to ensure a real industry focus.

An international team led by research director Roger Miller was formed; Pascale Michaud was the program manager. The purpose was to benchmark sixty projects to identify best practices. The research team was divided into five groups: benchmarking (Roger Miller, Pascale Michaud, and Tracey Ernsting); institutions and strategy (Donald Lessard and Xavier Olleros); engineering, procurement, and construction (Brian Hobbs and Bjorn Andersen); the Japanese team (led by S. Furosaka of the University of Kyoto); and data analysis (Roger Miller and Serghei Floricel).

Three forums with the sponsors were held as the project evolved. A launch meeting was held in Montreal in September 1995. A midcourse review was held in Poitiers, France, with extensive sponsor participation. A final forum was hosted at James Bay, Canada. (Appendix A lists the forum attendees.) The primary purpose was to provide a context for exchange among industry, government, and academic representatives to shape research issues and share learning on large-scale engineering projects.

Abbreviations

ADB	Asian Development Bank
BOO	build–own–operate
BOT	build-operate-transfer
EEC	European Economic Community
EPACT	Energy Policy Act
EPC	engineering, procurement, and construction
FERC	Federal Energy Regulatory Commission (United States)
IFC	International Finance Corporation
IMEC	International Program in the Management of Engineering and Construction
IMF	International Monetary Fund
IPP	independent power plant
LEP	large engineering project
PFI	Private Finance Initiative (United Kingdom)
PPA	power purchase agreement
PUHCA	Public Utility Holding Company Act
PURPA	Public Utilities Regulatory Policies Act (United States)

Preface

Why This Book?

Managers who want to learn about large projects can draw on a fair amount of literature dealing with the subject. I have always found these books disappointing, however. For one thing, they are mainly descriptive or anecdotal; such projects are described as so many self-contained, one-off undertakings, and few serious attempts are made to uncover commonalities and think through their meaning.

Most of this literature, whenever it attempts to be narrative, focuses on internal management mechanisms such as engineering estimates, choices of technology, performance, and control of contractors. This is useful material, but it hardly provides managers with a sound theoretical framework based on real life that can be of concrete help in tackling the complex challenges offered by today's megaproject developments.

I believe we are at the threshold of an explosion in large projects—in numbers, size, and diversity. The development and diversification of new worldwide technologies, the relentless search for energy sources and raw materials, and the huge infrastructure requirements of countries such as China, India, and Brazil are some of the drivers that will stimulate the expansion of project activity in a growing, globalizing world. The huge stakes involved will endanger the survival of corporations and threaten the economic stability of countries that embark too recklessly on megaprojects.

As risks and uncertainties increase steeply, project ventures will move more toward elaborate coalition arrangements. This will enable them to pool their know-how and skills to deal with the multiplicity of issues surrounding project implementation. Public-private coalitions often will be chosen as a way to solve societal externalities more efficiently. All of these new models of participation and partnership will, one hopes, lead to better management of risks, in which each participant assumes the part of the project risk that it is particularly well qualified to handle.

The authors of *The Strategic Management of Large Engineering Projects* address all of these questions and therefore fill a real need. They have combined theory and practice in a brilliant way. They started by analyzing in depth sixty major projects in different industries and parts of the world to build a unique, robust database on large projects. Based on this work, they were able to build an experience-based theoretical framework that is of great help to managers who have to understand and respond to the uncertainty and complexity inherent in large projects.

This is not a book of recipes but rather one that provides managers who study the involvement of their corporation in a megaproject with a larger vision and a greater depth of understanding. I particularly recommend this book to CEOs and senior managers who have to make decisions that may gamble with their corporation's future. Those who have been heavily involved in conceiving, managing, or governing large projects will, time and again, hear the unmistakable ring of truth and find at last a satisfactory theoretical explanation for so many of their past experiences.

Managers need to acquire novel know-how and skills to produce successful outcomes. Project failure is often the result of bad handling of externalities, superficial analysis of the institutional and social milieu that surrounds the project, or a lack of understanding of complex coalition dynamics rather than, say, how you control your contractors or do your estimating.

The authors emphasize the importance of solid front-end work as a crucial success factor. As much as 25 percent of total project cost might be spent on the exploration of issues pertaining to coalition building, governance, adequacy of institutional framework, the role of the state, population support, and the ecological, social, and economic impacts of the project.

This book offers a thorough understanding of the nature and consequences of the many trade-offs that need to be resolved when entering a large project coalition and the recognition that they all have costs as well as benefits. All in all, the authors have made an original contribution to the art of project management. They have designed a road map to guide managers through the complex processes that might lead to a successful project. One hopes that this work will lead to the development of executive learning programs to transmit this body of knowledge to managers, while also helping to reduce the stress, urgency, and unforeseen difficulties that are so much a part of life for managers involved in large projects.

Patrick Rich
Chairman, IMEC Research Program

Acknowledgments

Development of the IMEC program required contributions from many people. Pierre Lortie, president of Bombardier International; Richard Drouin, senior partner in McCarthy Tétrault; and Marcel Côté, founding partner of SECOR, all of Montreal, Canada, were initial supporters. Daniel Roos and Fred Moavenzadeh, both of MIT's School of Engineering, introduced us to the world of international research program development. Our early pump-priming sponsors were Terry Kerwin, of CAE; Henri Cyna, of Cofiroute; and Guy St-Pierre, of SNC-Lavalin.

Pascale Michaud, a partner in SECOR and the IMEC program manager, deserves credit for skillfully coordinating resources and undertaking a number of project studies. Joe Lampel, of the Nottingham Business School, participated in many brainstorming sessions. Käthe Roth, our editor, transformed our text with celerity. We are grateful to them and to all of our sponsors.

Kaiko and Pauline, our respective spouses, had to cope with the frenzy involved in this project. We would also like to thank all of the executives in the sixty projects we studied, who gave their time generously, thus grounding our theorizing. Finally, Patrick Rich of Geneva, Switzerland, former chairman of BOC Limited, shared with us—in a tactful and direct manner—his extensive international experience in the strategic management of large engineering projects.

Introduction

Large engineering projects (LEPs), such as airports, urban-transport systems, oil fields, and power systems, constitute one of the most important business sectors in the world. These projects tend to be massive, indivisible, and long-term artifacts, with investments taking place in waves. Their effects are felt over many years, especially as auxiliary and complementary additions are made. As an indication of the demand for capital investment in infrastructure, in 1999 more than 1,500 LEPs in the world were at different stages of financing or construction—each worth over US$1 billion—in sectors such as oil, power, transportation, and manufacturing (Conway Data 1999). These projects transform daring utopias into reality, such as a dam to produce 8,000 megawatts in the Brazilian Amazon, an oil platform in the stormy North Sea, multicountry simulation systems for air-traffic management, networks of roads and tunnels, and so forth. The number, complexity, and scope of such projects have been growing rapidly over the last few decades.

LEPs are important not only because they transform the physical landscape and change the quality of human life, but because they are the crucibles in which new forms of collaboration are developed. The study of LEPs provides insights into the workings of human organizations, both large and small. The shaping of institutional arrangements, the creation of partnerships that focus on a single project yet form the fabric for the transfer of knowledge across projects, and the competency required to execute LEPs are the major concerns of this book. We will see that front-end engineering of institutional arrangements and strategic systems is a far greater determinant of the success or failure of LEPs than are the more tangible aspects of project engineering and management.

The Demand for Infrastructure and Capital Investment

In spite of economic setbacks in Asia, policymakers continue to see a link among productivity growth, national competitiveness, and infrastructure investments. The connection that was apparent during the industrial revolution became veiled in the twentieth century, largely because advanced industrial societies in the West dealt with their infrastructure needs through a mixture of centralized public bureaucracies, regional governments, and private firms. As modernization in emerging economies accelerates and basic infrastructure in the West begins to age, however, a gap is opening between current and needed infrastructure.

The ability of a nation to deliver LEPs, as well as the concomitant investments in research facilities, education, and communications, contributes greatly to the quality of life of its citizens. In developed countries, investments in infrastructure represent, on average, one-tenth of total capital investments. In developing countries, the role of infrastructure investment in modernization makes it even more important. Net public investment in infrastructure as a proportion of GNP ranges from 2 percent in the United States to 4 percent in France and 6 percent in Japan (Mintz and Preston 1994). Declines were experienced in the 1990s, but bouncebacks have been occurring as the links among productivity, growth, and infrastructure investment have become clear.

Projections on the demand for infrastructure in power, transportation, telecommunications, and other systems are often hyperbolic: estimates of $500 billion yearly investment worldwide are high but not exaggerated. Although economists still debate the links between infrastructure investments and productivity, private investments in infrastructure are growing because many projects are expected to bring good returns. Economic and institutional reforms are being made to induce private investors to become project sponsors.

Modernization of infrastructure in terms of transportation, energy, and telecommunications is viewed as a major factor in improving competitiveness in Europe. In North America, investment in capital infrastructure (construction, machinery, and equipment) fell as a proportion of GDP in the 1970s and 1980s, but it is on the rise again. In the Middle East and North Africa, US$350 billion will be invested in infrastructure over the next decade, according to World Bank officials. Asia, in spite of recent difficulties, will continue to invest in infrastructure as economic growth returns. The need for power in Asia is such that capacity has to grow by at least 10 percent per year simply to prevent blackouts. Latin America has once again become a place to invest; Brazil alone has to add at least 3,000 megawatts per year to keep up with the growing demand for electricity.

The continued demand for infrastructure investment directly poses the question of effective and efficient ways of delivering LEPs. Public investments and international agencies finance only a small fraction of needed investments, thus opening the field to private investors. The private share in infrastructure investments now ranges from lows of 9 percent and 13 percent in Germany and France to highs of 47 percent and 71 percent in the United States and the United Kingdom (Roger 1998).

Amid this effervescence, a major transformation is taking place as new ways of delivering projects compete with established ones in which project shaping and delivery create value through expert design and competitive bidding. This mode was stable for almost seventy years, but new conditions are challenging this way of doing things, as ecological and community activists assert new rights, regulators promote competition, and politicians and bankers reassess the methods by which risks are analyzed in loan decisions.

As projects shift from sponsorship by large public or private firms to alliances spearheaded by developers, engineering firms, or entrepreneurs, the relevance of the traditional planning paradigm becomes increasingly questionable. The gap between the realities of projects and theories for managing them is widening. The metaphor of rational planning, beginning with a complete project description that is broken down into a myriad of prespecified tasks, is largely inadequate for describing what is now happening in LEPs.

In IMEC's research, discussions with a wide variety of executives pointed everywhere to change. We were fortunate to study LEPs at a time when major transformations in modes of management were taking place. Managers are asking themselves whether established beliefs and standard prescriptions still hold true. What we found was a considerable gap between accepted views of how to manage large projects and the practices being observed. The traditional model has been modified to deal with an increased array of stakeholders, yet uneasiness remains pervasive. Several verbatim observations made to IMEC researchers by those who are experiencing the challenge first-hand illustrate the magnitude of the change better than statistics alone could:

> Many decades of established contracting practices are coming to an end. Instead of responding to bids from creditworthy sponsors, we have to initiate projects, become investors, and learn to become concessionaires.

> Things used to be clear. As engineering consultants, we met ABB as equipment suppliers; we specified on behalf of our clients and ABB supplied competitively. Now we meet them sometimes as partners, sometimes as investors, and sometimes as contractors. We each have to wear many hats and play different roles in many projects to get business.

> Politics used to be at the fringe of project management; now, it seems as if the fringe has become the core. Politics is at the center of discussions, and engineering has moved to the periphery. We seem, as an engineering firm, to have lost control over the factors that influence our future.

> As equipment suppliers, it is challenging for us to work with innovative sponsors, as opposed to responding to detailed bidding documents. Innovative buyers value our competence and stretch our creativity. What a change from the times when we had to deal with traditional clients who preferred detailed specifications and required us to design old-fashioned solutions.

> Public agencies used to get involved as independent regulators protecting the public, the environment, the fisheries, and so on. Increasingly, we have to participate in the design and prior approval of sponsors' plans and agree not to interfere as long as sponsors respect their commitments. We have to navigate between the state, the public, and the developer. We have to become partners while remaining regulators accountable to elected officials.

In this climate, the limitations of established bodies of knowledge are being felt. The assumption that LEPs can be scoped, planned, and managed with existing planning techniques cannot prevent problems, which are then seen as managerial failures. Prior empirical studies of large-scale projects have generally focused on technical and economic factors, but a few have suggested that the model of prespecified rational planning is increasingly in trouble.

Analyses of LEPs in fields as diverse as arms, energy, petrochemicals, power, and nuclear-electricity production identified cost overruns ranging from 30 to 700 percent. The causes cited were inflation, poorly defined contract terms, technical advances, scope changes, and incentives to underestimate costs (Merrow, McDonwell, and Arguden 1988).

A World Bank team, led by Gregory Ingram, observed that the cause of poor performance lies not in planning errors but in the incentives facing sponsors and users. Higher performance requires commercial rather than bureaucratic management, competition instead of monopoly, and regulatory frameworks that favor entry by new players. Collaboration with international agencies to support the development of new institutional frameworks was strongly suggested (Ingram et al. 1994).

In their study of the NASA program, Leonard R. Sayles and Margaret K. Chandler concluded that to manage complex systems better, the separate strands of management science, organizational behavior, and policy must be woven together. Managing LEPs involves political issues that lead to breakdowns of rational management techniques (Sayles and Chandler 1971).

A study of factors accounting for innovation in power projects indicated that novel projects were sponsored by entrepreneurial developers and not by large firms. Although utilities built projects on time and on schedule, collaborative relationships between entrepreneurs and engineering suppliers were associated with innovation (Lampel and Miller 1996).

Peter Morris and his associates, in two pathbreaking studies, proposed a new perspective for project management (Morris 1994; Morris and Hough 1987). Morris observed that procedural approaches cannot deal with externalities, institutions, and strategic issues (Morris 1994).

In the 1970s, the Macro-Engineering Program at MIT used industrial dynamics to focus on project oscillations. Observed nonlinear relationships were modeled and simulations were performed using Dynamo to identify the management levers that could help control delays, cost overruns, and loss of reputation (Diehl and Sterman 1995; Forrester 1987, 1992; Richardson 1992).

Albert O. Hirschman developed the key concepts of "hiding hand" and "voice" when he studied development projects in the 1960s. The principle of the hiding hand states that projects survive their difficulties as parties face issues that were unforeseen in economic planning. The principle of voice highlights the need to embody participation in the planning of projects (Hirschman 1975).

Jeffrey L. Pressman and Aaron Wildavsky tried to understand why great planning expectations are so often dashed. They concluded that policy and implementation have to be brought into closer correspondence with one another by contrasting the planning model with the realities of interactions (Pressman and Wildavsky 1973).

A quantitative study of publicly available project case studies by John M. Bryson and Philip Bromiley attempted to understand the value of strategic planning. Their results indicate that the numerical adequacy of the planning staff strongly influences project outcome (Bryson and Bromiley 1990).

Studying oil projects in Norway, Arthur Stinchcombe observed that contracts are hierarchical documents through which firms extend their control to suppliers. Administrative ingenuity also turns markets and networks into quasi-hierarchies (Stinchcombe 1990; Stinchcombe and Heimer 1985).

The IMEC Program

IMEC's mandate grew out of the increasing difficulties that project delivery encountered in meeting targets in the early 1980s. As long as demand for infrastructure pulled supply in a manageable way, governments and businesses were content to rely on delivery methods perfected during the first part of the twentieth century. As demand for competition increased and public financing became tight, however, methods that had served their purpose in the past were no longer sufficient. Simply put, the bar had been raised and innovations were required.

New arrangements thus emerged; practices and methods were developed to deal with challenges. Tapping into this collective body of knowledge is an important part of what managers and decision makers must do to be effective. IMEC was set up to understand the changes that were occurring.

Much has been written about the execution of large projects, but little about their management. To our knowledge, there has been no attempt to study, evaluate, and present a systematic analysis of the new approaches to large projects except the book by Thomas Hughes (1998), *Rescuing Prometheus.*

To meet the objection that each project is unique and that generalizations are therefore impossible, we decided to undertake practical, grounded research to understand what leads to success or failure, using a sample of sixty LEPs. The goal was to identify the practices that, in the experience of executives involved in projects, made a difference. Here are the distinctive features of the IMEC research program.

International field study. The study sums up 450 years of collective experience. In general, seven to eight players—sponsors, bankers, contractors, regulators, lawyers, analysts, and others—were interviewed for each of the sixty projects. Few individuals can acquire such variety and depth of practical experience in a lifetime.

Projects were selected to arrive at a structured international sample. A range of sectors was covered: electricity production, oil and gas, public transportation, and complex technical systems. (See appendix A for short descriptions of the sixty projects.)

Systemic and strategic perspectives. Particular emphasis was placed on front-end development decisions, but execution and initial operation periods were also studied. Calling upon a range of disciplines, the IMEC study focused on themes such as coping with uncertainty through risk analysis, institution shaping, and strategies.

Executive forums for reality checks. Reality checks were built into the IMEC program by interactions with sponsors. Three forums were hosted by Electricité de France in Poitiers, France, and by Hydro-Québec in Montreal and James Bay, Canada. Senior executives from sponsoring firms, banks, law firms, and international agencies attended: their contributions steered research in fruitful directions (see appendix B).

The Hallmarks of LEPs

Engineering projects have little in common with mass-production or high-technology entrepreneurship. Figure I.1 positions various types of industries according to three axes: volume of production (small runs versus mass production); product specificity (dedicated to a particular customer or standard); and interactions between clients and suppliers (continuous or arm's-length). LEPs are unique, dedicated, and usually one-off products with intensive interactions between sponsors and contractors. They form an engineering craft business as opposed to mass production. Here are the major hallmarks of LEPs in the IMEC sample (see table I.1).

Negotiated Innovations

The entrepreneurial function in LEPs is shared among sponsors, bankers, and complementary organizations. Sponsors alone do not determine the attributes of projects, which are shaped in a long process of negotiation. The design, financing, and building of these projects thus shares many similarities with producing operas, movies, or new

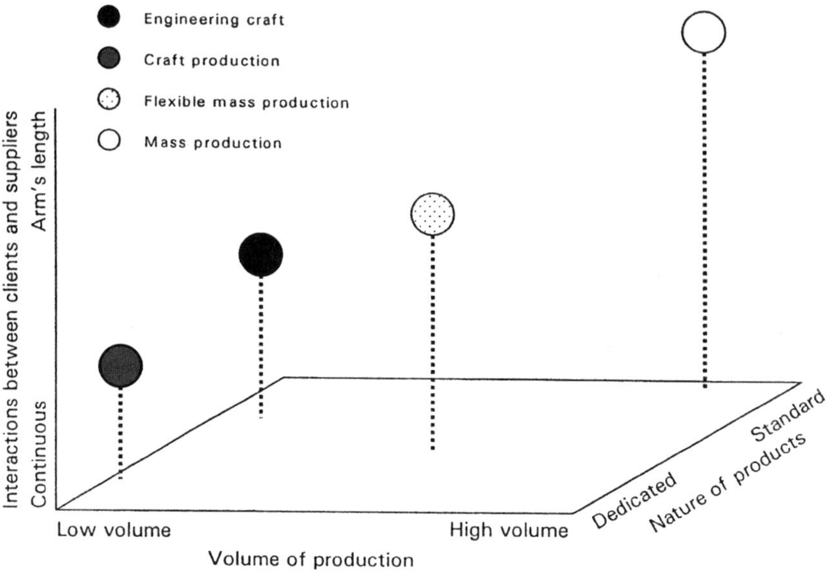

Figure I.1
Engineering craft and other types of industries

generations of aircraft. As informed and forceful decision makers, sponsors expect to influence design choices through internal staff or agents, but they need the innovative ideas of cospecialized players. Four types of issues arise from strategic interdependencies involved in sponsorship.

The infancy trap. Projects grow to maturity because they are fortunate enough to have sponsors that stand up to their commitments and coordinate their efforts with others in a coherent manner. They fail not so much because of planning errors, but because parties refuse to honor their commitments or do not undertake the auxiliary investments needed to make them viable. In other words, errors of omission, rather than commission, are the major cause of aborted projects. Sponsors and related parties often fail to understand the strategic linkages involved in bringing a project to a successful completion.

Producing electricity from a large dump is not a project that easily finds social favor. Bio-Thermica, a biomass engineering firm headquartered in Montreal, however, saw such an opportunity. The entrepreneur-owner initiated the idea, which was immediately rejected by all parties. He then invested his own funds, supplemented by a gas-drilling support program. Eventually, he established that there

Table I.1
Hallmarks of LEPs in the IMEC sample

Product of negotiated compromise	
Customized to meet client requirements	70.9%
Integrated parts of networks	64.4%
Contested externalities	
Facing extensive community opposition	40.3%
Facing international pressure groups	31.9%
Crafted over many years	
Average front-end period (search)	79 months
Average EPC period (sprint)	49 months
Exposed to political risk	
Political considerations influenced initiation	43.8%
Viewed as a vehicle for economic development	51.1%
Facing bureaucracy with strong expertise	69.8%
Facing coherent regulatory frameworks	
Facing highly developed regulatory frameworks	61.8%
Having to deal with multiple uncoordinated agencies	38.3%
Large, irreversible commitments	
Average cost	$985 million
Built ahead of demand	35.6%

was enough gas in a dump to produce peak-power electricity with some base load for twenty years. After five years of effort, he succeeded in forming an alliance with a gas company and engineering firms that successfully negotiated both a power-purchase agreement with a utility and funding from a pool of insurance firms. Shaping the project lasted eight years; building it took only two. Without relentless pursuit, the idea easily would have been dropped.

Partnerships with governments. These partnerships are important both for the subsidies they provide to make infrastructure projects possible and for ensuring the stability of contracts. Governments also build frameworks to structure negotiations with affected parties and create legitimacy. Consent may be gained through communication, compensation, or credible state commitment. When changes of leadership occur, the state may renege on its promises.

Regulatory difficulties. Such difficulties are bound to arise, as it is not atypical for a project to require 200 to 300 permits to conform to environmental, construction, and economic regulations. Officials are thus in a position to delay projects and exact various benefits to allow them to go forward. In most countries, permits are granted by uncoordinated agencies, each of which sees itself as a protector of the public good—but that good is defined in many different ways.

Sector rules. Regulations concerning pricing, entry, and other issues are now undergoing major changes in many countries; traditionally oriented toward price and profit control, they are moving toward the promotion of competition. Legislators are considering the unbundling and breaking up of integrated systems. The regulatory framework orients sponsors toward energy efficiency, cogeneration, merchant plants, and so forth. For instance, PLN, the Indonesian public power utility, was obliged by political authorities to sign purchase agreements to support private and foreign investments. Initial agreements were negotiated rapidly. In fact, the purchase agreements were signed at rates that were above PLN's own marginal costs. Gradually, PLN's financial position deteriorated and even though later agreements were signed at lower costs, it has been difficult for the utility to make its payments to independent power producers (IPPs).

Conversely, clients may become unwilling to respect agreements because projects work too well. The Toulouse Metro project was a success, but the organizing authority decided to renegotiate contracts, concessions, and property rights when the government changed because the upside had turned in favor of investors.

Real-Life Social Experiments

A large part of the untidiness of projects arises from debates over the creation and capture of value. Sponsors promote projects with the expectation that they will capture a significant proportion of the value they create. Others join with the same intent, each contributing to overall value creation, but also hoping to capture what they see as a fair share. The result is a constant seesaw between positive-sum collaboration, which creates value, and zero-sum gaming, which may destroy it. Value is the potential difference between expected future revenues or benefits and costs to be incurred. Benefits also accrue to clients, customers, sponsors, investors, regional interests, and governments, while sponsors, builders, affected parties, and governments incur costs.

Stakeholders expect that some of the value created will be distributed to parties negatively affected by the project. The social acceptability of a project is the result of consent by parties who bear the consequences of sponsors' choices without participating in residual profits—a consent gained through compensations and redesign. Tugs-of-war with governments are common. Sharing value with the state to gain public legitimacy means that sponsors deal with public authorities. Projects for which the state has to use coercive power to gain approval are likely to suffer from a lack of public legitimacy. Sharing the rent with both central and regional governments gives a political dimension to projects. Governments may grant sponsors concessions, rights, and opportunities because they are interested in job creation, provision of service, or the public good. Appropriation of the residual rent by the leader and its cosponsors often raises serious questions of legitimacy.

Deadlocks may result from the fact that affected parties use their power opportunistically to refuse collaboration. Projects, even some successful ones, may be subjected to strategic games that sponsors and project managers try to overcome through negotiations, timely interventions, court challenges, and so forth. Some parties increase their reputation if they can reorient or block a project; by doing so, they incur little cost and increase their prestige within their reference group.

Slow Clock-Speed Transactions

Conventional descriptions of decision making view choices as fully rational. The reality is quite different: projects are groomed and transformed by champions, while other actors downplay them. Sponsors invest resources and time to find partners, lobby intelligently to change rules, and participate in time-consuming public hearings to gain approval. Projects experience crises, omissions, or rejections because regulators, ministers, or affected parties have their own strategic agendas.

The time taken to complete the overall transaction for an LEP is long, compared to that for making a movie or issuing bonds. Designing a car may take a few years; investment-bank transactions and computer-chip production take little time. Engineering projects, in contrast, require more or less a decade to shape, build, and launch.

Conflicting logics of time commitment meet in these projects. The sponsor commits itself to a long-term horizon for building a power plant, bridge, or public-transport system. Bankers, conforming with practice, generally wish to limit their involvement to a payback period covering sixteen to twenty years. Contractors and builders bind themselves for short periods linked to the guarantees they provide. Governments may decide to bind themselves for long-term horizons but often reserve the right to renegotiate commitments. Each project needs a coalition of supporting organizations with commitments that extend far into the future.

Lumpy, Dedicated, and Irreversible Assets

Transactions in project-based industries are infrequent but large. (The average project size in the IMEC sample was US$985 million, with variance ranging from a few hundred million dollars to US$3 billion.) Furthermore, infrastructure projects are usually indivisible investments, first during front-end strategic development, but especially during the construction phase. Indivisibility means that projects cannot be broken into parts to reduce exposure. Since the option to build in stages is often closed, sponsors must commit large sums to build roads, dams, subways, or oil wells before they can generate revenues. Sponsors cannot usually test markets by building partial solutions simply because there is no market for them.

Engineering projects are also specific investments that are not usually redeployable. Mining equipment may be resold in secondary markets, but bridges, roads, tunnels, and power plants are sunk assets. Once built, these projects are extremely vulnerable to changes that may affect the flow of revenues needed to reimburse lenders. Sponsors and committed lenders are thus exposed to substantial downside risks.

High-Stakes Games

Projects are difficult ventures with very skewed reward structures and high probabilities of failure. They are unforgiving and often unrewarding investments. The price of entry—the up-front expenditure required to shape a project and have the opportunity to commit a further billion dollars in construction—is as much as 35 percent of the overall cost, depending on the project. The likelihood of an aborted effort during the development period is extremely high; the probability of having to write off heavy front-end expenditures in the shaping process is therefore real. Many sponsors have spent tens of millions, or sometimes hundreds of millions, of dollars on projects that are killed before construction.

The eventual total investment is close to US$1 billion on average. Once built, the project has little use beyond the original intended purpose. If it meets real needs, it might be useful for many years to come, but even so, such usefulness does not guarantee financial success. The original sponsors may still lose equity investments, and banks may never recover loans unless guarantees have been provided.

Potential returns can be good, but they are often truncated. Sponsors have full access to the downside but not to the upside. Should returns appear too high, there is a distinct possibility that some of the upside will be taken away. For instance, a sponsor making a return of 15 to 18 percent on equity capital will be asked many questions by government agencies or political authorities. A bountiful upside will likely be capped by public authorities in the short term and subjected to expropriation over the medium to long term.

The journey to the period of revenue generation takes ten years on average. During the ramp-up period, market estimates are tested and the true worth of the project appears; sponsors may find that it is much lower than expected. Bankers discover that covenants and payments will not be respected; new equity funds and rescheduling of payments may be needed. Restructuring of ownership and debt may be the only way to save prior investments.

Once a project is built and passes the initial market trials, its ability to generate revenues becomes clear. Yet little can be done strategically to alter its value potential. Sponsors or owners focus their imagination on operating efficiently, paying as little tax as possible and loading the project with the maximum level of debt.

The parties involved with the sponsors in promoting the project are often autonomous, independent organizations with their own strategic agendas. The failure of the project may not be a catastrophe for them. Moreover, executives managing projects within sponsoring organizations often have not worked extensively on LEPs, since such investments are not common for industrial firms.

Project Performance

The bad news about the projects studied by IMEC is that close to 40 percent of them performed very badly; by any account, many are failures. Instabilities created by exogenous and endogenous shocks set crises in motion; once perverse dynamics are triggered, unless institutional frameworks act as bulwarks, catastrophes develop.

Table I.2
The efficiency and effectiveness of projects in the IMEC sample (percentage)

Efficiency indicators	
meets cost targets	81.9
meets schedule targets	71.9
Effectiveness indicators	
meets most stated objectives	45.0
below target but satisfactory and without crises	18.3
restructured after experiencing crises	16.6
abandoned after high levels of development expenditure	6.6
taken over by public authority after sponsor's bankruptcy	10.0
abandoned white elephant	3.3

LEPs involve risks. Sponsors, bankers, and investors assess these risks and expect higher returns; in spite of this, they often get burned. In fact, LEPs often turn out to be bad investments. A majority of the projects that IMEC studied met sponsors' objectives fully or partially and were well evaluated by external and affected parties; a sizable proportion, however, faced substantial problems, difficulties, and crises. The economics press stresses that failures are imputable to ineffective planning; proposed remedies are usually better planning and stakeholder analysis. Our observation is that uncertainty is a basic fact of LEPs; their management can never be tidy.

In this book, project performance was measured by two sets of variables: (1) ratings by sponsors of the technical, economic, social, environmental, political, and developmental performance of projects; and (2) cost and schedule results. Table I.2 provides information about the efficiency and effectiveness of projects in the IMEC sample, which tended to be more efficient than effective.

Efficiency, an internally oriented method of evaluation, focuses on costs, schedules, and technical performance; the project-management field measures success mainly through these criteria. Most projects in the IMEC sample met schedule and functionality objectives but 18.1 percent displayed extensive cost overruns and 26.7 percent had long schedule overruns. In fact, many projects were efficient investments built at below expected cost. Whether a project meets cost targets depends on what targets are used; we used estimates made at the end of the front-end period.

Effectiveness is overall utility. A project may be a technical success but its sponsors go bankrupt or suffer large losses because markets did not materialize, or it may be built on time and below cost but fail to meet social, environmental, or developmental criteria because these issues were not embedded early in the design. Thus effectiveness is harder to reach than efficiency.

Project effectiveness is a composite measure, combining economic performance, technical functionality, social acceptability, environmental acceptability, political legitimacy, and economic development. Effective projects create value for all parties—sponsors, governments, and final users—and can generally survive their own inefficiencies (cost overruns, late completion, or early operational problems), but ineffective projects cannot compensate for their failures by efficient construction. In the IMEC sample, more than a third of the projects failed to reach acceptable effectiveness even though many met cost and schedule targets. Restructuring was necessary in about one-sixth of cases; many projects were abandoned early.

The indicator of performance used in the IMEC study measures effectiveness and was established in the following manner. Starting from the ratings of the various dimensions of performance made by sponsors, a principal component analysis was made. It showed that performance formed a single factor with an eigenvalue of 3.08, which explained 51.4 percent of the variance. Then, using the score of each project on this dominant factor, we formed clusters that were easily distinguishable. When we separated projects into successful (thirty-eight) and low-performance (twenty-two) groups, we were interested to note that all projects in the latter category were marred by public cancellation, abandonment, bankruptcy, major restructuring, or meltdown into social catastrophe.

Could a project become effective, by our measure, because of superior performance in only one or two dimensions? Could high scores on technical functionality or economic viability turn a socially unacceptable project into a high-performance one? The answer, from the IMEC data, is no. Sponsors' evaluations of performance dimensions were highly intercorrelated as is made clear by the presence of a dominant factor.

Project evaluation may evolve over time as conditions change. Initially, a project may be judged harshly by the media or the public, but if it has been well designed to meet real and socially valuable objectives, performance eventually rebounds. In spite of all the bad press, for instance, the benefits of the Eurotunnel are now beginning to appear. Failed projects also restart, especially when they were well designed to meet real needs but encountered difficulties because of unanticipated shocks. Dead white elephants and engulfing illusions are usually not restarted.

A reduced set of factors, which we will explore in this book, helps to influence project outcome. Projects become successful not because they have been optimally selected, but because sponsors and partners commit to sharing risks, shaping choices in turbulent environments, and embracing residual uncertainties. Both the state and the sponsors, as will be seen, can take actions that significantly increase the probability of success.

Organization of the Book

Four basic audiences will be interested in the findings presented here: practitioners in the field, managers who take part in large-scale projects on an off-and-on basis, professionals from the many fields involved in LEP management, and students of management and engineering.

A method was developed to ensure unity of view and coherence in IMEC. First, the research framework was developed by Roger Miller and Donald Lessard. Second, the data were gathered by teams led by Roger Miller and Pascale Michaud. Third, data analysis, both qualitative and quantitative, was performed by Roger Miller and Serghei Floricel. Fourth, the writing of chapters was allocated to teams of authors with field experience.

Chapter 1 presents a framework for understanding what influences project success or failure. The multitude of novelties observed by IMEC did not form disparate sets but generally fell into groups of findings that formed a coherent framework. Institutional arrangements for shaping and building projects are prime determinants of success. LEPs require competence to cope with risks and turbulence, and they become manageable through the design of strategic systems, the infusion of governability, the transformation of institutions, the design of financial arrangements, and the building of owner-contractor relationships.

In chapter 2, current and past transformations in the institutional arrangements for project shaping and building are analyzed. Arrangements based on large sponsors using formal planning were once the pinnacle of rationality in LEPs. The new governance arrangements are based on the use of alliances and interorganizational agreements for both sponsorship and execution of projects. This model has produced projects that perform well, but difficulties remain. Areas of innovation for fixing major deficiencies in governance arrangements are outlined in this chapter.

Chapter 3 focuses on risk mapping and strategizing. The major types of risks that projects face and the interactions of these risks are presented. Facing uncertainty is presented as a cascade process that starts with information search, design, and risk allocation, then moves rapidly into influence, legitimacy, agreements, and long-term coalitions. Embracing risk is the ultimate strategy of the sponsor who seeks returns.

Chapter 4 presents the management process by which sponsors rise to the challenge of LEPs. Projects fail not because they are complicated, but because they face dynamic complexity. Rising to the challenge of large projects calls for shaping them during a lengthy front-end period. The seeds of success or failure are planted early. Relationships among players can generate innovative solutions but may also lead to trajectories that become degenerative. Competent sponsors refuse to engage in trajectories that are likely to lead to failures.

The argument of chapter 5 is that high-performance projects use systems of strategies to match perceived risks. The following strategies are discussed: information search; flexibility and option creation; core coalition; external coalition and legitimacy; contract and institution; diversification (shock absorption); and risk transfers and shifts.

The topic of chapter 6 is the governability of projects in the face of turbulence. Governability is instilled in project structures by careful design of devices to ensure internal cohesion, long-term coalitions, reserves, flexibility, generativity, and diversification.

The impact of engineering projects on institutions is the focus of chapter 7. Because projects often face inadequate institutional structures that make their realization difficult, they require sponsors and regulators to formulate new rules, regulations, and norms. Projects are thus shapers of new institutional frameworks and breakers of old ones.

Chapter 8 looks at project financing, which concerns not so much the securing of funds as the establishment of structures of responsibilities, incentives, and ownership rights that make the release of capital possible. Bankers recommend the release of funds when a deal is well structured, partners are solid, and risks have been analyzed professionally.

Chapter 9 focuses on the changing relationships between sponsors and suppliers. Increasingly, project sponsors are abandoning arm's-length contracting to move toward partnership and long-term agreements with suppliers. The adoption of participatory relationships has led to spectacular results in some projects.

The concluding chapter 10 focuses on the planning paradox. Many management scholars claim that planning is ineffective. What we observed was not a reduction in planning expenditures but an increase. Managers obviously have a different view of planning. Strategic principles to deal with project dilemmas are sketched in this chapter.

1 Public Goods and Private Strategies: Making Sense of Project Performance

Roger Miller and Donald Lessard

Large engineering projects represent both a major economic activity and a poorly understood area of management. Although they are high-stakes undertakings, they can be managed. Their technical difficulties do not condemn them to failure; far more troublesome, however, are the difficulties arising from their complexity, irreversibility, and dynamic instability.

This chapter provides a framework for making sense of project performance. Sixty projects is too small a sample from which to draw statistically generalizable relationships, but with the addition of grounded theorizing, it is possible to make sense of how the factors that emerge from IMEC's research have an influence on performance.

Methodology

The methodology used to sketch a framework of the management of LEPs started with a high-level mapping of the phenomenon based on a variety of relevant studies and perspectives, especially those of Stinchcombe (1990); Hage (1980); Callon, Larédo, and Mustar (1995); Silverberg, Dosi, and Orsenigo (1988); and Hughes (1987). The key blocks of variables were institutional context, project-specific context, project architecture, managerial regulation, governance structure, project execution, financing, and project performance. This high-level frame was used, in turn, to guide data gathering.

The sample of projects was selected from the following population: LEPs undertaken from the early 1980s to the present in the fields of electric power, urban transportation, roads and tunnels, and oil production; and projects representing the main regions of the world. The sample comprised thirty-two power projects; sixteen projects in urban transportation, roads, and tunnels; four oil-production projects; and eight technology and other projects. Geographical representation was distributed as follows: seventeen projects in North America, twenty-one in Europe, ten in Latin America, and twelve in Asia.

Data were gathered following two distinct approaches. First, interviews were held with the key participants in each project and a narrative summarizing their responses was written. Second, project sponsors were asked to evaluate project performance and fill out a questionnaire to provide quantitative scores on items and variables.

Similarly, data analysis was performed in two simultaneous but highly complementary directions. First, the quantitative data were reduced to twenty dependent and independent variables through a lengthy process of introspection and factor analysis; second, a logistic-regression model was fitted to the reduced set of quantitative variables. The predictive validity of the logistic-regression model that emerged is evidenced by a chi-square of 43.45, with a significance level of .0205. The set of covariates that together predict 85 percent of project successes or failures, and that are all significant above the .01 level with 1 or 2 degrees of freedom, are turbulence arising from complexity (1); institutional arrangements (2); the presence of strong sponsors (1); and strategic scope as designed by sponsors (2).

Grounded theorizing was subsequently used to enrich the parsimonious logistic-regression model. By systematically comparing responses on issues such as risk, strategies, and institutions, this process helped to sharpen core concepts. The model that survived this analysis is thus based on grounded analysis and solid empirical evidence (Glaser and Strauss 1967).

Well-performing projects are the joint product of institutional arrangements and private strategies. When institutions are taken for granted, much of project performance is ascribed to strategic actions. The projects that we studied often required changes in institutional arrangements and/or had to adapt to changing institutions. This allowed us to see the interdependence between the public good and private strategies.

Complexity and Turbulence

Projects embody the knowledge and expertise that represent the best practices of the day for achieving low cost, versatility, and reliability. Technical knowledge has been accumulated on the design, building, and operation of technical systems such as electricity, urban transport, telecommunications, and oil (Hughes 1987). Engineers from sponsoring firms, suppliers, and contractors can tap codified knowledge to develop innovative solutions.

Concerns about accidents and quality of life impose stringent requirements. Systems must excel in reliability, fidelity, and safety. Failure is not tolerable because too much is at stake. Accidents resulting from inadequate air-traffic systems or problems due to faulty nuclear-power-plant designs are highly visible, costly, and socially unacceptable (Perrow 1984). Crises trigger public pressures for accountability and a search to reduce the likelihood of further failure. Reputations built over many decades can be lost overnight.

Projects entail external effects that raise issues of public legitimacy. Deleterious effects induce reactions, demands for redress, and often protracted political debates. Decisive actions often create fear and outright rejection when risks are perceived as dangers (Luhmann 1995). Projects often meet opposition from international pressure groups such as Greenpeace, International Rivers, and the World Wildlife Fund. Bankers respond by demanding environmental assessments and permits.

Selecting only technologically simple ventures is promoted as the obvious choice. Sponsors, it is argued, should favor smaller, technologically simpler, market-driven projects and shun large ones that involve social disturbances or innovations. Yet, retreating from complicated projects to look for "born winners" has obvious limitations: the supply of simple projects is finite, and many projects, such as bridges, oil platforms, dams, tunnels, and subways, do not fall into the category of small and uncomplicated investments. With a focus only on relatively simple projects, the returns from entrepreneurship will quickly be competed away, and many interesting possibilities will remain unexploited.

Technical difficulties, social disturbance, and size are not statistically linked to performance in IMEC's sample of projects and do not condemn projects to failure. Engineers have the requisite knowledge to solve difficult tasks. Large projects may be complicated, but they generate enough value to become worth tackling. For example, Verbund, an Austrian public utility, negotiated with the regional government of Vienna to develop the Freudenau dam on the Danube within the city limits of Vienna. In spite of widespread skepticism, the regional government of Vienna organized a referendum, and a strong positive response supported development of a dam that would produce power, control erosion of the Danube, facilitate navigation, and decontaminate old refinery sites. The referendum provided legitimacy. Expenditures made to shape and legitimize the power project represented one-third of total capital costs.

Projects experience difficulties, however, not so much because engineers cannot cope with technical complications or external effects, but because sponsors cannot rise to the managerial challenges of coping with unforeseen turbulence. Complexity and dynamic instabilities mean that the future of LEPs is difficult to predict. Risks burst out as projects are being shaped and built. The longer the development time, the higher the likelihood that the project will be affected by emergent events. Turbulence can originate from two sources: exogenous events, occurring outside of the control of management, and endogenous events, arising within project organizations. In the IMEC sample, turbulence was measured by the frequency of surprising exogenous and endogenous events that sponsors had experienced but not foreseen. Few projects sailed through without meeting turbulence: on average, projects met close to five unexpected events during shaping, construction, and ramp-up; some had up to twelve rocky events.

Exogenous turbulence stems from political, macroeconomic, and social events. The behavior of sovereign authorities and nature are frequent sources of unforeseen events. It may be argued that these turbulent events should be foreseen: in reality, managers do not always have full control either over the behavior of autonomous actors who act opportunistically or over nature. For example, Eletronorte's hydrological studies showed that the maximum flow on the Tocantins River in Brazil was rated at 60,000 cubic meters per second at peak time. All planning was based on this assumption. During the first year of construction, heavy rains showed that the flow of water could reach 70,000 cubic meters per second. From this point, research, design, and construction had to proceed simultaneously, leading to higher costs. Then, during construction, the discovery of large iron-ore reserves required that the dam be redesigned to make shipping possible.

Endogenous turbulence arises from breakdowns of partnerships or alliances, or from contractual disagreements. For example, the bankruptcy of Morrison Knudsen, a partner in the Northumberland Strait Crossing project, had to be faced by the leading sponsor. GTM International recruited a European firm skilled in complex bridges to replace Morrison Knudsen. Partners may also decide that their claims on value are higher than previously agreed. Parties know that opportunistic actions pay off; agreements, community of interests, and reputation are then pushed aside.

Turbulence, both exogenous and endogenous, is negatively linked to project performance. The tabulation of turbulence and performance yields a chi-square coefficient of 6.19, significant at the .031 level and with 1 degree of freedom. Three sets of factors to counter turbulence were identified in the logistic regression model.

Presence of Institutional Arrangements

The presence of coherent and well-developed institutional arrangements is, without a doubt, the most important determinant of project performance. (This topic will be covered in chapter 2.) Projects shaped in incomplete and shifting arrangements have a hard time taking off: they require deals and agreements that may not stand for long. In contrast, well-developed laws, regulations, and practices contribute significantly to enhancing project performance.

Sponsors do not operate in a vacuum but find a structure of practices, roles, and obligations that help to anchor a project. Institutional arrangements are sets of laws, regulations, and agreed to practices that form symbiotic relationships and provide effective ways of developing projects—or, to use Scott's (1994) definition, they are regulative, normative, and cognitive structures that form social frameworks and give meaning to behaviors. North (1990) and Giddens (1984) advocate for the action-enabling role of these arrangements, which form the public good that can benefit all parties. They help to make risk management and the infusion of governability possible by providing the structure for contracts, binding agreements, legal actions, and so forth.

The Njord oil platform was built in the North Sea in the late 1990s by Norsk Hydro. The development of oil projects in Norway is highly structured by a clear framework of laws and regulations to allocate exploration rights, build alliances between Norwegian and foreign firms, and set the criteria by which projects will be approved in the country's legislative assembly. The development of oil-and-gas projects in Norway is guided by three core laws: the Petroleum Act, the Environment Act, and the Joint Ventures Act. The Norsok agreement was recently negotiated between the Norwegian government and the oil industry to redefine tax structures and promote cost-reducing actions. Meeting all of these requirements contributes largely to project success. Sponsors can focus on creating economic value but know the precise rules of the game.

The nature of relationships among the stock of laws, rules, and regulations in various countries and the performance of projects was beyond the scope of our research. Such studies are better left to legal experts and the staff of international agencies such as the International Finance Corporation (IFC), the World Bank, and the Asia Development Bank. We preferred to focus on the influence that institutional arrangements have on shaping projects and providing them with support. Many LEPs, even in countries with generally well-developed and stable institutions, push the boundaries of these institutions and require development of new patterns of interactions and changes in institutional arrangements.

Anchoring Projects

The main function of institutional arrangements is to help anchor projects in their economic and political contexts and ensure that investments will be repaid and social utility be provided. Unless they are solidly anchored, projects will be at the mercy of shifting interests, caprices, and opportunistic moves. The concept of project anchoring outlines three generic conditions to buttress LEPs.

Stabilization of the long-term future to enable investments. Legal and regulatory frameworks, such as private monopoly regulation and concession frameworks, help to reduce risks by minimizing opportunities for clients, communities, or governments to attempt to capture revenues after the investment is sunk. The goal is to create the prospect of secure streams of funds in the long term to cope with the various uncertainties that can affect the project. To secure streams of revenues, the approach throughout most of the twentieth century has been to assign sponsorship and ownership to network operators. Recently, power-purchase agreements (PPAs), in which the regulator or the state forces a network to sign long-term supply contracts with independent producers, have been used as a tool for providing revenue flows. Concessions by the state to sponsors also provide a framework for future revenues but are less secure. Project practices such as purchase agreements, turnkey contracts, and project financing also reduce uncertainty by allocating risks among different types of participants.

Flexibility to face turbulence. During the front-end development of projects, when agreements are negotiated and commitments made, managers develop specific strategies to cope with foreseeable risks; they cannot, however, develop specific ways to cope with surprise events. Turbulence is likely to arise given the long time span required for development. Flexibility is provided by elements of institutional arrangements that enable projects to undergo rescheduling, restructuring, or bankruptcy. The flexibility provided by institutional arrangements helps many projects survive unforeseen events.

Enhancing the legitimacy of projects, participating organizations, and agreements. Many projects face opposition from interest groups. Laws, regulations, and practices that create well-structured assessment frameworks enable sponsors and interest groups to air their views through public hearings and even to oppose decisions through appeal procedures. Public-bidding frameworks structure the orderly selection of fitted sponsors and provide legitimacy. Practices such as inviting representatives of the public into planning and design meetings and proactively consulting conservationist groups and environmental regulators help to find credible solutions and reduce the likelihood of protest.

Frameworks for structuring voice, decision making, and public trade-offs make it possible to choose public transportation systems, erect power plants, and, in some countries, build nuclear facilities. To manage social-acceptability risks in siting of power plants in Japan, for instance, the Three Power Source Laws System was put in place by the Japanese Ministry of International Trade and Industry. This framework structures public consultations and hearings across the country; the population is consulted on choice of eventual sites for projects and their technical features. Successful sponsors will not start a project until its legitimacy is no longer challenged.

Shifts in Institutional Arrangements

Over the last two centuries, various arrangements for shaping and anchoring projects have been tried. During the nineteenth century, in both Europe and North America, projects were sponsored by entrepreneurs, at times in collaboration with governments. The entrepreneurial model came under fire as social costs rose, and it ultimately gave way to large public or regulated private networks for power, communications, and transportation.

The creation of large-scale systems was an attempt to overcome market failures by generating enough revenues to internalize most effects, coupled with regulations to avoid the inevitable abuses of market power that come with such size. The management style promoted by large networks is oriented toward long-term forecasts, formulation of detailed specifications, and centrally directed execution; a belief in formal analysis is the central pillar of this approach. A successful project is portrayed as the product of advanced planning by experts who carefully weigh alternatives and, having reached consensus on an optimal design, put their intent into action. Project failures are therefore seen largely as resulting from planning errors.

Although many studies showed that large projects did not always conform to the rational-system model, the ideal lived on; deviations merely reinforced the norm. What ultimately brought this model into question was the demand for competition, the inability of government corporations to borrow, and bankers' insistence on better risk allocation.

Governance arrangements, which emerged in the 1980s, challenged established practices by promoting the assumption of risks by private sponsors, the multiplication of collaborative agreements, and the sharing of risks among parties through contracts. Top-down rationality was replaced by collaborative rationality. Alliances among sponsoring partners and partnerships between sponsors and contractors helped to create value through innovation and reduce costs. Many institutional changes signaled a return to the entrepreneurial model, but there was no real enthusiasm for reverting to nineteenth-century approaches; the social and political environments had changed too dramatically to allow this to happen.

The diffusion of governance arrangements, as measured by the use of innovative practices such as project financing, build-operate-transfer (BOT), concessions, and risk seminars, varies by sector. Such arrangements are widely used in road, tunnel, urban-transport, and thermal-power projects, but are much less prevalent in hydroelectric, nuclear, and technology projects.

The projects that IMEC studied were initiated after the mid-1980s. Many projects are still built using rational-system arrangements; in spite of the diffusion of deregulation, many large network operators thrive on or are desired by governments. Although the pendulum has swung toward governance arrangements, IMEC's data indicate that projects built under these arrangements do not perform any better; they display a tendency to disintegrate because institutions are not yet fully aligned.

Whether projects are sponsored under governance or rational-system arrangements does affect their chances of success. Projects that use a rational-system approach experience fewer failures, while governance arrangements have not led to consistently superior performance; many projects built under the latter arrangements turned into failures as a result of market shortfalls, cost overruns, regulatory changes in midcourse, and confused ownership incentives. Yet, innovations such as collaboration between owners and contractors-suppliers and design-build contracting have led to substantial cost and time reductions.

Leadership by Sponsors

Sponsors are not equal in their competencies to shape projects. Shaping and anchoring LEPs, just like shaping and anchoring movies or operas, depends not only on the quality of the story (i.e., the project) but also on the talents of the players and the context in which they work.

Major projects are often associated with visionaries—people who stretch the boundaries of the possible because "it's there" (Hughes 1998; Shapira 1995). There is little question that the Grand Coulee Dam, the Empire State Building, the Panama Canal, and France's nuclear-energy system would not exist without heroic figures. The question is not why particular individuals or firms undertake a particular initiative, but why they are able to obtain competitive advantages from that initiative and sustain them across others. Taking this perspective, we see a very different picture.

Firms that are successful in undertaking LEPs appear to control the networks within which these projects are embedded, either technically or politically, or both. They may also dominate, through domain expertise, the development of specialized types of international projects, thus making it difficult for less experienced firms to compete.

The privatization rhetoric of recent years would suggest that the principal determinant of performance is whether or not sponsors are private. In the IMEC sample, however, it appears that competency in multiple projects is much more important than whether ownership is public or private. Both public and private owners can shape projects successfully; what is important is the ability to combine a balanced portfolio of projects yielding revenue streams, economies of scale and scope, and risk diversification. Three types of sponsors were observed:

network operators, international developers-concessionaires, and ad hoc alliances.

Network operators own geographical networks that exist because of economies of scale, scope, and network. Examples of network operators are Endesa, a private utility in Chile (now part of Endesa of Spain, an even larger network operator), which still owns about 60 percent of power production and distribution in the country, even though the system has been totally deregulated; and EDF, a publicly owned firm that has transformed electricity production in France from coal to nuclear.

Network operators are challenged by deregulation to unbundle activities, sign PPAs or concessions, or buy power from merchant plants. They are compelled by regulations to open their systems to entrepreneurs. Reconfigurations take place in certain countries and are resisted in others. Officials maintain that economies of scale, scope, and network truly exist.

International concessionaire-developers were often initially established by entrepreneurs or engineering contractors. They have emerged as major players in the last fifteen years as public policies unbundled network operators or fostered the entry of new firms. Operators of networks reacted vigorously by establishing subsidiaries that also sponsor projects worldwide. A process of consolidation has created new breeds of developers with specialized expertise and working on an international scale.

Concessionaire-developers may also be network operators within their own systems: they gain advantage through specialized domain expertise and international experience. Their competencies include scope, risk diversification, and knowledge. Although not in the same position as geographical network operators to "lock out" competitors, their experience, scope, and accumulated knowledge allow them to outperform new entrants. For instance, INTERGEN, a firm owned by Bechtel and Pacific Gas and Electricity, develops thermal-power plants in the United States and abroad. GTM Entrepose, a large French construction firm, also operates as an international concessionaire of toll bridges, roads, and tunnels. International concessionaire-developers sponsor many highly successful projects with domestic partners but are often caught up in insufficiently developed institutional structures. In the IMEC sample, a slight majority of such projects were successful.

Ad hoc alliances are formed mostly by entrepreneurs or engineering firms that wish to respond to bids or develop opportunities. These alliances are specific initiatives that may not be repeated elsewhere, as their main purposes are to win a contract, penetrate a market, and generate business. For instance, the M1–M15 project is an ad hoc alliance among Transroute, Strabag, and European banks for the construction of a toll highway between Vienna and Budapest. Similarly, the Tannayong Elevated Transport System in Bangkok is an alliance among Thai construction firms and German equipment suppliers.

The inescapable conclusion drawn from IMEC's observations is that ad hoc entrepreneurial sponsorship is highly risky. Large sponsors with either network control or domain expertise have advantages in the game of identifying projects that stretch the limits of the firm's capability, but, because of their complexity and risk, offer substantial benefits and high appropriability. Ad hoc alliances have not always performed well; bankers prefer the securitizing presence of large sponsors.

The Bundle of Skills for Project Sponsorship

Successful sponsors develop projects from the bundles of competencies learned through past projects. Creative entrepreneurial concepts, such as putting power plants on barges or redesigning communist-era industrial complexes by linking cities, factories, mines, and power plants, are bright but not sufficient. Deeper competencies are required to shape projects successfully.

The argument that competent sponsors succeed in shaping projects is both tautological and important. It is tautological in the sense that although it is possible to assess the competencies associated with successful projects, it is very difficult to identify those linked to failed ones. Nonetheless, competencies are truly important because sponsors differ in their ability to shape projects and get others to commit. Entrepreneurial sponsors often run out of resources as shaping progresses and pass the baton on to others. Here are the key competencies observed by IMEC.

Ownership competencies. The prime competency of any sponsor is the ability to think, select, and behave as a responsible owner who will have to operate the projects it builds. The obligation to make these trade-offs forces it to challenge cospecialized parties and contractors. The sponsor acts as a master contractor, paying for the project and living with the consequences of choices.

Evaluation competencies. Sponsors of successful projects have developed the ability to decide rapidly whether project ideas have option value. They quickly sort opportunities into categories and evaluate them based on prior experience and knowledge (Lampel 1998). For instance, effective sponsors will form international task forces in which project executives join with lawyers, consultants, and investment bankers. A few weeks of work leads to a decision on whether project ideas are worth the necessary shaping investments.

Projects are holistic systems in which technology, politics, ecology, and finance interact. Effective sponsors entertain no illusions about the possibility of short-circuiting decisions to arrive at fast commitments. In contrast, instead of rejecting unworthy project ideas rapidly, ineffective sponsors get tempted because they need contracts: they believe that projects can be reworked and winner's curse can be avoided. Rules for avoiding selection of bad projects are overlooked, or good projects are rejected. Such firms often find themselves having to kill projects after they and their partners have spent large sums (up to US$50 million). Worse, bad projects bid on simply to win contracts end up causing major operational losses.

Relational competencies. The ability to engage in credible discussions with clients, political authorities, bankers, multilateral agencies, and other parties separates successful from unsuccessful sponsors. Relational capabilities are especially pertinent when dealing with communities, regional governments, or affected parties. Many projects owe a large part of their success to communications officers who have maintained good, honest relations with mayors, unions, and public leaders.

Sponsorship of coalitions. Successful developers are able to build coalitions with government authorities, regulators, major investors, and communities. Sponsors need to be credible and reputable enough to enlist pension funds, development banks, or local partners, and to forge long-term alliances that will be able to watch over and support projects and save them from risks. Sponsorship coalitions accompany projects from birth to construction and ramp-up. They are particularly important at the ramp-up stage, when restructuring may be necessary.

In spite of the evolution toward globalization, LEPs continue to be domestic businesses. Sponsors of successful projects need deep local roots or ties enriched by legitimacy. Decisions concerning projects require knowledge about key influencers and decision makers. Some countries limit projects to national sponsors, while others search for foreign investors; linkages with local partners, regulators, and governments are even more important when the sponsor is a foreign firm.

Survivability. Successful sponsors have staying power based on strong assets and a diversified portfolio of projects. The revenues stemming from many projects make it possible to survive the cash bind of a particular project; independent sponsors and investors may sink. A diversified portfolio of projects is also an indicator of experience. Streams of revenue make it possible to fund adequate development of front-end choices and react flexibly in times of crisis. Furthermore, such sponsors generally have the ability to call on a network of partners and coalition members to help a project survive.

The shaping of projects is a costly business. Only competent sponsors know the extent of the requirement for funds: 3 to 5 percent of the total cost of standard projects, and up to 35 percent for complex opportunities. Many executives view such expenses as frivolous and focus on soft or nonbusiness-related issues such as compensation, negotiation, legal advice, and community involvement.

Effective sponsors also have the capability to bring projects to thresholds beyond which value creation is high. Incurring expenses to bring about a change in laws that allow pension funds to invest and preparing a referendum to provide a project with legitimacy are seen as hurdles not impossibilities beyond the scope of management.

The Quality of Strategic Systems

The shaping of projects by sponsors and complementary parties will result in decisions over time that lead to some control. High-quality management builds systems of strategies with scope to face foreseeable risks. The decision journey that brings projects to the point at which they generate revenues to pay for prior investments can be broken into three major periods: search, sprint, and ramp-up. Each period is composed of many episodes in which the strategic system is shaped (see table 1.1). Decision-making iterations are numerous, from a few in simple projects to close to a dozen in complex ones. Each period is long, arduous, and bumpy; progress involves many reconfigurations.

The search (front-end shaping) period is oriented toward building momentum and commitment. The sprint period begins once full momentum has been achieved and leads to the heavy capital investment through which sponsors, affected parties, or the state commit fully. The value of speed is that revenues will arrive faster. Turbulence at this stage is usually lower as major issues have been resolved.

Table 1.1
The decision journey: Search, sprint, and ramp-up

Dimensions	Searching and shaping	Sprinting	Ramping up to reality
Management process	Shaping a project configuration Iterative and recursive episodes	Building the physical artifact Adaptation to conditions Project management	Operations, marketing, and financing become central concerns Restructuring if necessary
Turbulence	High challenges and deadlocks High emergent uncertainties	Lower and often concentrated on affected parties	High when market projections fail and opportunistic behavior occurs
Strategic focus	Value creation through long-term commitments and agreements	Cost reduction, innovation, and speed	Rent capture or swift restructuring if necessary
Options/degrees of freedom	Many degrees of freedom Reconfigure, renegotiate Proceed by episode	Build fast Innovate real-time	Limited options except restructuring
Dominant players	Leading sponsor with partners, bankers, regulators, and the state	Leading sponsor with EPC partners, contractors, and regulators	Leading sponsor if successful project; bankers and the state if unsuccessful project

The ramp-up period tests expectations about markets, technical functionality, and social acceptability. Prior to ramp-up, sponsors retain some degree of freedom to modify project configurations. After six months to two years of ramp-up, the project either performs satisfactorily, survives as a lame duck, or undergoes ownership and financial restructuring as revenues fail to materialize.

The quality of strategic systems emerges as choices are made. Managers learn to cope with uncertainty by assessing risks and making decisions that provide strategic scope, governability, institutional influence, financial structure, and innovative owner-contractor relationships. Here are the key elements.

Risk mapping and strategizing. Risks and their interactions emerge during front-end, construction, or ramp-up to shatter carefully laid plans. As many executives point out, the only certainty is that unforeseeable events will materialize. Uncertainty springs up as issues are brought to the fore, dormant tensions emerge, and interdependent links are triggered (see chapter 3).

Contrary to practices described in the project-management literature, which views risks as a concern to be dealt with mostly through Monte Carlo simulations once projects have been scoped, we have observed that risk mapping is viewed as an important ex ante strategic concern by project sponsors. Risk is the possibility that future events will have downside impacts on projects. Figure 1.1 illustrates how emergent risks arose in a project that was developed by a network operator and about to start construction. The sudden inability to borrow internationally (financial risk) triggered the need to form a joint venture with industrial users, which required new regulations to ensure property rights (institutional risk). After many years of negotiations, laws were enacted and the new owners were able to reduce the construction cost substantially by collaborating with contractors. Industrial partners who agreed to purchase power lowered both market and financial risks.

Sponsors unbundle risks and view them in multidimensional perspectives, as originating in markets, technology, financing, supply, project management, institutions, social deadlocks, and governments. Strategies are developed to cope with each unbundled risk, and integrative higher-level strategies are forged to form coherent responses.

To develop risk-coping strategies, managers use decision analysis and, more often, multidisciplinary strategic thinking. Decision-analysis methodologies that have emerged over the last fifty years

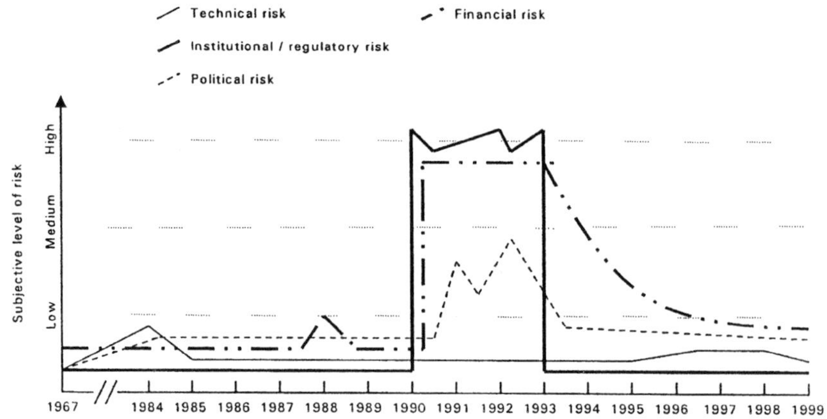

1967: Concession awarded
1984: Exploratory technical studies
1987: Economic and technical viability of project tested
1988: Basic design finished
Detailed design started
1989: Construction bidding for civil works
Contract awarded
1991: Development of new strategy: search for industrial partners
1992: Preliminary protocol between joint-venture (JV) partners
1993: Enactment of decree permitting joint ventures with industrial partners
Memorandum of understanding signed between JV partners
1994: Formal JV contract
1995: Concession transferred to the JV
Cost of civil works reduced from $350 million to $240 million
Construction restarted
1996: Equipment purchased on barter trade e.g. turbines
1999: Target completion date

Figure 1.1
The reality of uncertainty

include probabilistic trees, Monte Carlo simulations, industrial dynamics, multiattribute assessments, and so forth. These techniques are highly useful once a project has taken a structured form and the estimation of probabilities is possible. In the front end of projects, however, indeterminacy and ignorance reign.

Strategic thinking about risks is a reflective, experience-based, and knowledge-based exercise in prudence, which is defined as the intelligent and reasoned articulation of means to reach ends, not as hesitant action. Sponsors participate in numerous decision conferences over the many episodes of a project to discuss risks, devise strategies, test them intellectually, and converge over time on a set of strategies that they hope will help the project face turbulence. Risks that can be identified through statistical analysis can be dealt with through insurance, hedging, or contracts. Indeterminacy arising from unpredictable exogenous events, nonlinear interactions, and opportunistic behaviors calls for imaginative strategies.

Shaping projects. Sponsors do not sit idle, waiting for probabilities to materialize; they judge risks, invent ways to cope, and work hard to shape outcomes. (This topic will be covered in chapter 4.) Strategizing about risks may start with management science but rapidly requires managers to become experts in organizational science, diplomacy, law, and public affairs. Strong uncertainties and indeterminacy are thus reduced by the development of control strategies such as alliances and coalitions. Managers use repertoires of responses based on prior experience, current strategic models, and advice from cospecialized partners.

Projects are shaped during their front end over a number of evolving episodes, which last six to seven years on average. Few are the projects in which major and optimal choices are made in a single episode. Instead, sponsors start with a configuration hypothesis, attempt to shape it with strategic devices, meet countering forces, reassess their options, and eventually achieve temporary closure. With some issues resolved, they turn to others. Successive shaping episodes bring a project to full momentum and closure in an agreed-upon configuration. Simon (1976) referred to this as the shift from substantive to procedural rationality. Substantive rationality focuses on selecting the optimal option, while procedural rationality recognizes the unfolding of time, the presence of strong uncertainty, and the need for collaboration. Managers thus counter strong uncertainties and indeterminacy with a form of rationality that loosens the deterministic and reductionist straitjacket of hyperrational planning and grapples with nonlinear causalities, path dependence, synergistic effects, and endogenous structuring processes.

Building strategic systems with scope. Using project narratives and sponsors' responses, IMEC built an index of strategic scope that is significantly related to project performance. (This topic will be covered in chapter 5.) Strategic scope means the extent to which project sponsors implement ranges of distinct devices in the following areas: research and analysis; coalition of competent partners; incentives to face risks and innovation; influence and negotiation; preemptive commitments; project design; transfer of contractual risks; institutional influence; and modularity. The comprehensiveness of the strategic system built specifically to achieve control adds significantly to the odds of project performance. Highly successful projects display broad strategic scope, while those that fail are characterized by narrow repertoires of devices.

To develop strategies, managers rely on prior knowledge, templates, and the advice of specialized firms. Most industrial sponsors, for instance, are ill equipped to handle large engineering projects, as executives involved in prior projects have moved on. Experience is often lacking and corporate memory about LEPs is shallow. In contrast, network operators and international concessionaire-developers that handle two, three, or more projects at a time have rich corporate memories.

Building scope in strategic systems is costly—or it may appear so with hindsight. Complex projects require ranges of strategies whose costs represent up to a third of overall capital costs. Managers develop them thinking that the expected marginal value of each device exceeds marginal costs, thus contributing to value creation and anchoring.

Instilling governability in project organization. Sponsors develop reasoned strategic systems to face risks that can be anticipated. To deal with turbulent events that cannot be anticipated, however, they attempt to instill governability, which we define as the capacity for a project organization to react coherently to turbulent events that cannot be anticipated because it has skills, reserve, and self-organization (see chapter 6).

Turbulence brings surprises that introduce discontinuities, shatter agreements, and trigger processes that often lead projects to failure. Governability is the ability of project organizations to counter with processes of steering, response, and coalition. Instilling governability is a reasoned bet on the capabilities, skills, and resources of the project network. Projects that are infused with governability characteristics will, it is expected, resist shocks, restructure, and eventually rebound. In contrast, projects with low governability potential fall into disarray, bankruptcy, and even abandonment.

Building governability is second-order strategic thinking in which sponsors judge relationships and agreements for their ability to trigger appropriate responses. Relationships and agreements between sponsors, on the one hand, and among clients, banks and institutional investors, affected parties, and the state, on the other, are assessed, judged, and shaped accordingly. The art of designing governability focuses on providing each relationship with the capability to bind parties, trigger joint action, provide reserves, enhance flexibility, and create modularity.

In the IMEC project, a governability index was built by assessing each relationship and the devices employed to determine their contribution to bonding, coalition building, reserves, flexibility, governability, and modularity. Among projects that faced turbulence, the governability index was positively and significantly associated with performance. For projects facing low turbulence, higher governability was not linked to superior performance.

Modifying institutions. LEPs often hit the limits of existing laws, rules, and regulations. If institutions were exhaustive and complete, project shaping would be a matter of signing contracts and agreements and conforming to rules. Prevailing frameworks, however, are never complete (see chapter 7).

Most projects in the IMEC sample that were developed under emerging governance arrangements required changes in laws, rules, and regulations. Many of these changes were fostered by governments, international agencies, sponsors, or bankers to modernize institutional arrangements.

Modifying rules and regulations is not a determinant of performance, but it is often a necessary condition for developing projects. One-third of projects in the overall IMEC sample required development, improvement, or enactment of new legal frameworks for BOTs, concessions, project financing, permitting assessment, investments by pension funds, and so on. Changes were required in property rights, land rights, competition rules, and ministerial responsibilities.

Tremendous amounts of effort, financial resources, and time are required to understand institutions, assess legislative risks, and exert influence to shape laws, rules, and regulations. Institution management and influence are thus important competencies in the sponsor's toolbox. Many sponsors—especially international developers, Japanese *sosha,* and subsidiaries of network operators—thrive on projects that demand the transformation of institutions. In fact, they shun standard projects in developed countries in favor of projects in countries where institution shaping can be achieved through breaker projects because they believe that greater rent can be created and appropriated under conditions of effervescent institutions. Once institutional practices stabilize or freeze, the prospects of high returns decrease.

Matching risks and financial structure. The financing of LEPs involves not only the traditional goal of obtaining the cheapest funds possible but also strategic goals such as direct allocation of risks, structuring of ownership so as to trigger responses in case of turbulence, and organization of governance to make renegotiations possible at minimum transaction costs (see chapter 8). The direct allocation of risks is central in securing financing. Splitting the overall risk into constituent components and allocating segments to the parties who are best able to bear them and have incentives to do so is the ideal. Construction risk, for instance, is allocated to a design-build contractor, and political risks to a government or multilateral institution. Direct and complete allocation may not always be feasible, however, as risks are difficult to predict and contract.

The architecture of financial devices such as debt, equity, recourse, and guarantees not only may provide a direct way to allocate risks, but may also help to build a governance capability to adapt to future events. The indirect allocation of risk through the financial architecture relies partly on contracts but mostly on ownership and reputation incentives. Setting the stage for future renegotiations is made necessary by the incompleteness of contracts and by changes in circumstances that make the initial risk allocation inappropriate. Ownership rights, contingent contracts, and rendezvous clauses can lead to efficient renegotiations that save a project from bankruptcy.

Partnering alliances for engineering, procurement, and construction. Many sponsors want to profit from competitive conditions in national and international construction markets and thus build projects the traditional way. Experts design, engineers do detail work, and work packages are put out for bids. Substantial gains in costs, schedules, and project delivery, however, can be made by the adoption of generative owner-contractor relationships (see chapter 9).

In the traditional approach, owners and suppliers use arm's-length contracts. Suppliers are awarded contracts, through a competitive bidding process, to provide prespecified goods and services at predetermined prices. A cutoff point in projects' lives separates owners and contractors. Prior to this point, suppliers have little opportunity to influence design so as not to corrupt the competitive bidding process. After that cutoff point, the owner has limited ability to influence and, at best, gets what was specified.

The introduction of partnering relationships substantially improves the performance of project execution. Real partnering is not limited to team building but also focuses on incentives to innovate. Contracts are designed in such a way that suppliers participate interactively with owners in the design of engineering and the planning of construction. Furthermore, incentives make it economically interesting for suppliers to present their innovative ideas during design and even during construction. Relational contracting is usually achieved through frame agreements, long-term contractual relations, and collaborations between owners and suppliers.

Project performance is significantly linked to the degree of penetration of novel practices in engineering, procurement, and construction (EPC). Successful projects often use functional specifications, participatory engineering, design-build contracts, frame agreements, and other devices. Yet, none of these practices alone can explain superior performance. Innovative sponsors use sets of novel engineering practices that, together, can radically reduce costs and shorten schedules.

Project Trajectories

The hypothesis that there is convergence toward a best path in the sponsorship and execution of projects does not stand up to the facts observed by IMEC. Sponsors with varying sets of competencies and the shaping of projects of varying difficulties and within different institutional arrangements will follow different trajectories. Eight project trajectories were identified in the IMEC sample, each leading to good or mediocre performance. A trajectory is a sequence of moves by the sponsor and its partners to shape a project through many episodes and respond to turbulence, shocks, or challenges. Shaping efforts over time will roll the concept configuration forward, correct positive-feedback loops, and help a project move along the track desired by the sponsor. In contrast, sponsors may not be able to prevent and correct positive-feedback loops. Many strategic actions may be right, but the inability to cope with a single unexpected event or opportunistic behavior can create degenerative processes. Success requires most issues to be solved adequately.

Projects developed by competent network operators or concessionaire-developers in well-formed or modernizable institutional arrangements and with quality strategic systems have a high probability of success, whatever their technical complications. In contrast, projects shaped by sponsors with overly optimistic assumptions to gain business, in incomplete and shifting institutional arrangements and involving difficult tasks, have a much lower probability of success.

Why do sponsors enter paths that lead to success or failure? The choice of a trajectory is determined by the interactions of three factors: the degree of development of institutional structures, the technical and social complication of the tasks, and the managerial competencies of the sponsors. The importance of institutional arrangements is such that they largely determine who the sponsors will be. For this reason, we will present trajectories pursued by network operators, concessionaire-developers, and ad hoc alliances.

Projects Sponsored by Network Operators

These projects have a good probability of success; their sponsors usually have the resources and creditworthiness to carry the market, institutional, and completion risks. With a coherent and stable institutional structure, projects can be developed at the appropriate scale.

Network operators have the expertise to shape projects, integrate them into their systems, and develop capabilities to interact with the community; in other words, technical, economic, social, and political issues can be integrated in a coherent manner. Financing is done through bond issues: guarantees are provided either by the government or by balance sheets. Unless the country is badly rated, network operators backed by a government can get low-cost financing.

The negative sides of sponsorship by network operators stem from the dominance of technical experts and the prevalence of organizational failures. Managers are often technical specialists who view projects as engineering challenges, fail to engage in relational interactions with communities, regulators, or suppliers, and build in technical features that add to costs. Organizational failures include adversarial relations, refusal to collaborate with suppliers, preference for known solutions, and breakdown of projects into multiple work packages, which prevents the use of cost-reducing solutions.

Projects sponsored by network operators tend to be successful, as were nineteen out of twenty-five of these projects in the IMEC sample. Three trajectories in projects sponsored by large network operators were identified: development at all costs, traditionally shaped winners, and partners in technology.

Development at all costs. Six projects in the IMEC sample were designed as engineering solutions to meet growing demand in developing countries. These projects, sponsored by public utilities, were planned to be orderly and rational, but crises, and eventually postponements, emerged. Meeting demand rapidly, honoring contractual obligations, and respecting development plans were all good reasons for forging ahead without concerns about social integration. Because institutional structures did not force consideration of external effects and legitimacy, issues such as social acceptability, respect for the environment, and social disturbance were brushed aside: engineering problems became overpowering.

The probability of the success of projects following this trajectory turned out to be low, although most projects were eventually redesigned and restarted. Later, teams that included engineers, social workers, and communications experts were used and systemic perspectives were adopted. The costs of making these projects socially acceptable could easily have been internalized in the first trial, because the opportunities they pursued were intrinsically rich. Most projects eventually rebounded.

Electrosul, a Brazilian utility, for example, announced that it was going to build a series of dams totaling 23,000 MW on the Uruguay River in southern Brazil. A few months after the ITA project to produce 1,450 MW was announced, all engineers engaged in geological and hydrological studies had to be pulled out due to an armed rebellion. This part of Brazil had been populated by Italian immigrants. As the population had grown, each farm had been divided into prized family lots. Under the leadership of the local bishop, the residents formed a resistance organization and knocked out Electrosul. Reflecting on the nightmare, Electrosul's new president decided that he could buy engineering expertise outside, but that social skills to interact with affected parties and political leaders were strategic. Extended negotiations were undertaken; mayors and local leaders became strong supporters of the revised ITA project.

Traditional sponsorship and execution. Fourteen projects were shaped by networks that operated under rational-system arrangements. Large sponsors, whether public or regulated private firms, undertook to make long-term forecasts, meet environmental regulations scrupulously, borrow on financial markets by providing guarantees, and honestly attempt to meet project opponents' objections in advance. The execution of the projects also followed traditional patterns: internal design, detailed work packages, bidding, and owner control. Network sponsors tried to engage in productive relationships with regulator constituents and suppliers. Quite often, the goal was to outperform entrepreneurs and developers.

The traditional mode leads to both high and low performance, but a large majority of projects in the IMEC sample were successful. High-performance projects are characterized by good risk analysis, adaptation to socioenvironmental needs, and an ability to face challenges by lenders, regulators, and consultants. Low-performance projects are conducted in a context of urgency with narrow technical planning and limited risk analysis.

Technology-driven projects. Five projects in the IMEC sample focused on the development of complex technology-based solutions such as nuclear-power plants and air-traffic-control systems. These projects were led by strong sponsors aiming to develop needed and highly complex technical solutions. Suppliers were very competent, with the specialized expertise that the strong sponsors needed.

A majority of these projects were successful. The development of long-term collaborative relationships among owners and contractors and coherent institutional arrangements stressing the leadership role of the sponsors were determining factors. Two projects were failures because rigid contracting was used: sponsors insisted on using detailed specifications instead of relying on suppliers' abilities to develop highly innovative technical solutions.

Whatever the trajectory, the competencies required of large network operators who sponsor projects are creditworthiness, technical knowledge, and social capabilities. Successful network operators put in place decision systems to ensure that technical, social, regulatory, and political aspects are embodied in selection processes. They also build a small core strategic team, interact with suppliers and contractors to innovate, and build social expertise. Engineering staff is often reduced, but social scientists and communications experts are called in.

Projects Sponsored by International Concessionaire-Developers

These projects usually take place in governance arrangements that favor foreign investment, deregulation, partnerships, and participatory engineering. Sponsorship by domain specialists has many advantages. Leaders engage in risk allocation, build coalitions to help restructure projects when turbulence arises, and have learned that much can be achieved by engaging in discussions with regulators and government officials. The building of generative relationships with cospecialized firms such as investment banks and contractors is seen as useful for developing innovative solutions, confronting viewpoints, and tapping otherwise dormant knowledge. Sharing the fruits of innovative ideas with these partners is seen as a wise move.

Sponsorship of projects under governance arrangements, however, is difficult because of the present incompleteness of institutional structures and the associated opportunistic behaviors of governments. Loopholes exist in laws, regulations, and responsibilities. Governments cause the downfall of projects by failing to honor agreements, creating legislative and regulatory risks, and shifting public infrastructure risks to private firms. Sponsors also put a great deal of faith in rigid PPAs and concessions. Such projects often have been characterized by undue optimism and assumptions about the superiority of private-sector management.

As governance arrangements are diffused around the world, project concesssionaire-developers have pursued three distinct trajectories: scrutiny-based projects, institutional breakers, and engulfing illusions.

Scrutiny-based projects. Such projects use standard technologies to meet real needs in institutional arrangements that are well developed. As a result of their attractiveness, these projects are rapidly transformed into commoditized solutions: the rent they can generate is competed away and sponsors cannot support high levels of front-end expenditures. Financial returns may be high for early sponsors, but as competitive entries arise, yields fall.

Investment bankers, rating agencies, and regulators scrutinize these projects in detail. Rating agencies evaluate the sponsor's abilities to face risks. Bankers accept only the projects that meet the stringent criteria of nonrecourse project financing. Project ratings are often necessary for the public issue of bonds.

Scrutiny-based projects tend to be uncomplicated: few negative external effects and little environmental opposition are involved. The sponsor builds strong partnerships of owners, and the institutional structures within which they are built are well developed. Examples of such projects include thermal-power plants with PPAs, short toll roads near large cities, and bridges that relieve traffic congestion.

The Ocean State power project in Rhode Island was initiated in the early 1990s by J. Makowsky, an independent power entrepreneur who was aware of the evolution of economic regulations in the power sector and saw the opportunity to use Canadian natural gas. At the time, Federal Energy Regulatory Commission (FERC), the American federal regulator, wanted to encourage nonnetwork developers, so utilities were led to act as buyers of power from independent producers.

Rejecting Vermont and selecting Rhode Island instead because of its proximity to markets, Makowsky built an alliance comprising Trans-Canada Pipeline Co., Eastern Utility, New England Electrical System, and Boston Edison. He then enlisted General Electric to use the project as a proving ground for new gas turbines. Front-end costs were kept at around 3 percent of total investment. In spite of these favorable conditions, the front-end development period took four years and construction two and a half years. The project won awards for technical and environmental performance.

Most scrutiny-based projects are successful, yet sponsors do not confine themselves to such projects. Why? The supply is limited and opportunities dwindle rapidly.

Shaped institution breakers. Projects in this trajectory involve complicated technical tasks in incomplete institutional arrangements that need to be modified. Project configurations need to be adjusted many times to meet the shifting expectations of bankers, regional groups, and clients. Sponsors, however, are committed to shaping these projects well: they invest the resources necessary to ensure their survival—and even their restructuring.

Shaping efforts focus first on correcting the shortcomings of the institutional framework. For this, sponsors seek the collaboration of governments, legal advisers, and international agencies. New laws need to be enacted to protect property rights, foster social acceptability, and promote environmental standards. In other words, such projects challenge the existing legal and regulatory structures.

Shaping costs were high for projects that broke existing institutions, ranging from 15 to 35 percent of total capital investment. Concessionaire-developers invest resources to build sponsoring coalitions and make projects socially acceptable. The process of shaping is long, turbulent, and costly; sponsors need to be able to keep their eye on the project's value in the face of difficulties. A majority of these projects in the IMEC sample were successful.

In the mid-1980s, the push for modernization in Turkey focused on the Ankara subway project. A first phase was tendered by the Turkish government in 1987; a Canadian–Turkish consortium, led by Lavalin and Gama-Guris, won the contract. The project had been planned as a BOT to involve private-sector players. In 1991, the reality sank in that the BOT law of 1985 was in conflict with other pieces of legislation: BOTs were not considered to be commercial contracts and could not include foreign partners. Lavalin and Gama-Guris persisted, rearranging the venture as a traditional turnkey project. In 1991, banks also refused to support guarantees under the BOT scheme. The Turkish treasury eventually agreed to provide guarantees and accept funding by conventional export and commercial credits. This project is a good example of the difficulty in using idealistic approaches such as BOT or project financing.

Engulfing illusions. Engulfing illusions are often sponsored by engineering firms that wish to become international concessionaire-developers. Hungry alliances look for business opportunities but sometimes in governance arrangements that are effervescent and shifting. Sponsors miscalculate the degrees of engineering complications involved and make optimistic assumptions about market risks and social acceptability. Multiple interdependencies among sponsors, governments, and pressure groups are involved.

Sponsors are eager to take on urban infrastructure risks. Heroic assumptions, promoted by public and private players concerning technical conditions, geology-hydrology, and markets are naively accepted; assumptions are proved wrong and catastrophes ensue. When crises emerge, governments play opportunistic games, triggering processes of degradation; incomplete institutional frameworks are unable to act as a bulwark. Problems are pushed toward private sponsors. As one government legal adviser put it, "The sovereign is never a partner." In the IMEC sample, sponsors and bankers who engaged in such projects ended up losing a large part of their investment, even though the projects still had high social utility.

Engulfing illusions often end in costly retreats or white elephants. Costly retreats are projects for which extensive front-end expenditures are made but they are abandoned; such projects are desirable and innovative, but are eventually rejected because agreements cannot be reached. As participants are brought in to build legitimacy, their demands require nonviable solutions. Killing the project is the reasonable choice. Costly retreats reveal the main predicament of sponsorship: without front-end expenditures, opportunities do not exist. Without clear criteria to decide upon opportunities, sponsors may be dragged into costly retreats.

White elephants are desirable but difficult projects for which sponsors failed to build long-lasting coalitions and agreements with regulators, government authorities, and clients. Key decisions were left uncovered because the sponsors had preferences for particular options. Furthermore, they did not allocate all of the effort needed to secure solid commitments from parties whose contributions are important. These projects survive but are poorly shaped, and sponsors and banks lose large investments.

Orlyval, a privately developed link between Orly airport and Paris, was heralded as a novel type of project, combining private initiative and superior technical solutions. It was sponsored by MATRA, an aerospace firm that had developed VAL, an automatic light-train system. Market studies suggested a daily passenger flow of around 13,000. STP, the public regulator, stressed that the logical solution was to extend subway lines but yielded to overwhelming pressure to accept a private-sector project. As the line was being built, however, the regulator granted permits to competing alternatives. Market studies were proved wrong and bankruptcy was rapidly declared. The project was eventually operated by RATP, the Paris subway: volume is currently about 9,000 passengers per day. MATRA and bankers applied learned lessons when they later embarked on the Toulouse subway system using the same VAL technology. A very solid coalition of regional players was built to resist challenges and crises. The project was an outright success but was later expropriated as new political leaders expressed the opinion that it was too profitable.

The competencies required for project shaping under governance arrangements center, first, on the leading sponsor's ability to attract partners because of its credibility and reputation; and second, on their joint financial capacity to bear the cost of front-end strategic decisions. Successful sponsors also engage in positive relationships with governments because of their knowledge of public policies. They rapidly identify the value potential of projects that are worth shaping and reject others; they understand that projects are not selected in grand rational meetings but are shaped, negotiated, and redesigned over many episodes of risk analysis and strategy making, and that front-end shaping costs can be high, as projects must pass many tests. Accepting a bad project is viewed as worse than rejecting a good opportunity.

Projects Sponsored by Ad Hoc Alliances

A dozen projects in the IMEC sample were sponsored by individuals, entrepreneurs, or firms that formed ad hoc alliances. The advantages of entrepreneurial sponsorship are many. First, many projects, even socially valuable ones, would never get completed without heroic entrepreneurs overcoming the inadequacies of institutional arrangements and substituting their strengths for institutional weaknesses. Second, entrepreneurs capture novel practices abroad, diffuse ideas, and shape daring projects. Third, entrepreneurs pursue opportunities that large sponsors would reject, such as power from coal piles or garbage dumps, and they accept impossible deadlines.

The negative sides of entrepreneurial sponsorship are that socially suboptimal solutions are often pursued and deals are made without the benefit of public debate. Sponsors tend to reduce front-end shaping expenditures to the minimum and thus fail to build coalitions and governability structures to face future shocks. As a consequence, projects often end up in failure. Two trajectories were identified here: entrepreneurial pioneers and urgency-based projects.

Entrepreneurial pioneers. Such projects consist of fitting standard solutions to viable opportunities in countries where demand is growing but the institutional arrangements are woefully underdeveloped. Eight projects in the IMEC sample fell into this category but only four were successful. International and domestic firms that have advanced knowledge of the evolution of institutional structures seek these kinds of projects. Sponsors take high risks by supporting most front-end costs and even construction costs to move in rapidly. Solutions are developed rapidly to fit urgent needs. Entrepreneurs understand the dynamics of shaping and influencing institutional structures.

The danger is that weak institutional frameworks often allow unscrutinized and inefficient choices to be made. Institutions based on the rule of law and sector regulations are not well developed, and project anchoring is thus difficult. Political power is fractured into many simultaneously competing public agencies and concentrated at the political level. Pioneers have difficulty getting approval and must deal with ambiguity. They adopt innovations, such as concessions, turnkey contracts, and design-build-operate contracts, to appease bankers and international agencies.

The Bangkok Elevated Rail System was sponsored by a consortium of international firms led by Tannayong, a Thai construction firm. Bangkok, the capital of Thailand and the country's major port, had expanded so much that the already inadequate transport system had been completely overwhelmed. At peak traffic periods, cars and buses sat for hours on gridlocked and polluted streets. Once Tannayong's bid to build a mass-transit system was selected by the Bangkok Transportation Authority, a BOT concession was awarded and approved by the ministry of the interior and the Thai cabinet. A special-purpose company was formed to operate the 13.5 km railroad for 30 years. Faced with refusals by government agencies to grant permits, Tannayong decided to forge ahead. Its approach was to commit extensively, spending US$700 million to build most of the project without the necessary permits. Only an experienced domestic firm with strong political knowledge could assume such risks. The project survived the Asian economic crises, and the system was scheduled to open at the end of 1999. A shift in ownership, however, took place: Crédit Suisse First Boston bought Tannayong's shares. After ramp-up, Tannayong will no longer be required to own a majority stake in equity, as stipulated in an agreement with the Bangokok Transportation Authority.

Urgency-based projects. These projects are designed to meet real and urgent needs. Sponsors, domestic or international, agree to select socially inappropriate solutions because of the pressure to deliver fast and the absence of challenges by regulatory authorities. All parties, including regulators, sponsors, and clients who sign purchase agreements, push for fast action. Early choices lock projects on paths that cannot be modified. Such projects are inadequately shaped because political actors or institutional structures do not require extensive debates.

Most urgency-based projects in the IMEC sample did not perform well. One project, for example, concerned the building of a thermal-power plant in a South Asian country. The client, a publicly owned utility, was asked by political decision makers to sign a PPA. To build fast, an international developer agreed to take on completion and operation risks by rapidly assembling components, erecting the plant in record time, and operating it at full capacity. The government assumed supply and currency risks by delivering fuel at guaranteed prices and using the U.S. dollar as the currency for offshore accounting. The client assumed all market risks. The solution selected was outside the least-cost path, which would have taken more time to build. The client, the developer, and the bankers were all aware that a high-cost solution was adopted and that shortcuts might become unacceptable.

The competencies to succeed in entrepreneurial projects are, first, persistent leadership and, second, political connections. Entrepreneurs make bold commitments, but they need to ensure that public decision makers will eventually support them. The entrepreneurial sponsors in the IMEC sample were fearless: they made bold moves and personal fortunes were at stake. To ensure that projects would eventually gain approval and permits, political connections were necessary.

In short, project performance is not a priori determined by the difficulties of engineering and social integration; sponsors and engineers rise to these challenges. Turbulence is the contextual variable that has the highest negative impact on performance: to be durable, projects must survive the nearly inevitable bursts of turbulence that they will encounter. While the public good is provided for by existing institutional arrangements for shaping and delivering projects, competent sponsors face risks and turbulence by designing strategies that provide scope, governability, flexible financial structure, and innovative owner-contractor relations.

2 Transformations in Arrangements for Shaping and Delivering Engineering Projects

Roger Miller and Serghei Floricel

The sponsorship and operation of LEPs raises a unique set of issues. Such projects require large capital investments and have long time horizons. The investment is often indivisible and irreversibly sunk in a location for a specific use. Private actors have a limited ability to capture the benefits of these projects, while governments can appropriate many of them through taxes. These characteristics require that projects find a balance between securing a flow of revenues in the long term and maintaining enough flexibility and capacity to restructure as conditions change. The trade-offs among offering incentives for private participation, protecting local affected populations, and advancing the public interest are acute.

Institutions form the public good, which orients sponsors in their strategic choice and makes it possible to anchor projects. Institutions vary in degree of completeness from country to country—economists call this the stock of institutions—but, more important, they also differ in their content and direction.

In the nineteenth century, most railroad lines and power networks were built by private entrepreneurs (Caron 1997; Ellis 1954; Lanthier 1986; Lévi-Leboyer and Morsel 1994; Salisbury 1967; Stover 1997). They built coalitions of participants who contributed different resources and represented a variety of interests: engineers, bankers, landowners, industrialists, and small investors. Toward the end of the century, entrepreneurial coalitions were replaced by large multifunctional organizations, which owned and operated extensive technical systems and grouped most of the resources required to plan, design, and finance projects: projects were then integrated via hierarchical coordination into large systems (Williamson 1975).

By the early 1900s, most large private networks had become regulated private monopolies or had been nationalized. In the 1930s, even in the United States where private regulated monopolies subsisted, the federal government tightened its regulatory oversight and established agencies such as the Tennessee Valley Authority and the Rural Electrification Authority to supplement private network operators. By the early 1980s, the effectiveness and efficiency of dominant large network operators were being questioned; such challenges eventually gave rise to calls for privatization.

The Emergence of Governance Arrangements

In the mid-1980s, partnerships of private entrepreneurs, engineering firms, and financial institutions became increasingly involved in the development and operation of LEPs such as power plants, airports, bridges, highways, and urban-transport systems. A new approach to sponsoring projects was taking shape.

Many countries enacted special laws and regulations to create frameworks appropriate for such undertakings, such as the Private Finance Initiative (PFI) in the United Kingdom, the BOT laws in the Philippines, Pakistan, and Turkey, and the concession framework in France. A similar role in unleashing private initiative was played with power-plant construction in the United States by the Public Utilities Regulatory Policies Act (PURPA) of 1978. Efforts to transform public to private sponsorship by multilateral agencies such as the International Monetary Fund (IMF), the World Bank, and the International Finance Corporation (IFC) continue to this day, although early enthusiasm appears to have diminished in the face of difficulties faced by many projects.

In the late twentieth century, new sets of arrangements, called governance, started to emerge, and in many countries they now compete with other approaches to sponsor projects. In these arrangements, whose final shape is not yet completed, networks of sponsors, banks, private investors, and engineering contractors develop projects and finance them on a nonrecourse basis, using devices such as concessions, BOT contracts, and PPAs. In the late 1980s, leaders were often smaller entrepreneurial firms, but specialized developers with strong balance sheets and specific competencies now play a dominant role. In the United States, firms such as Bechtel Power Corporation, General Electric, and Pacific Gas and Electric have formed project-development entities. With new regulatory frameworks in place, large

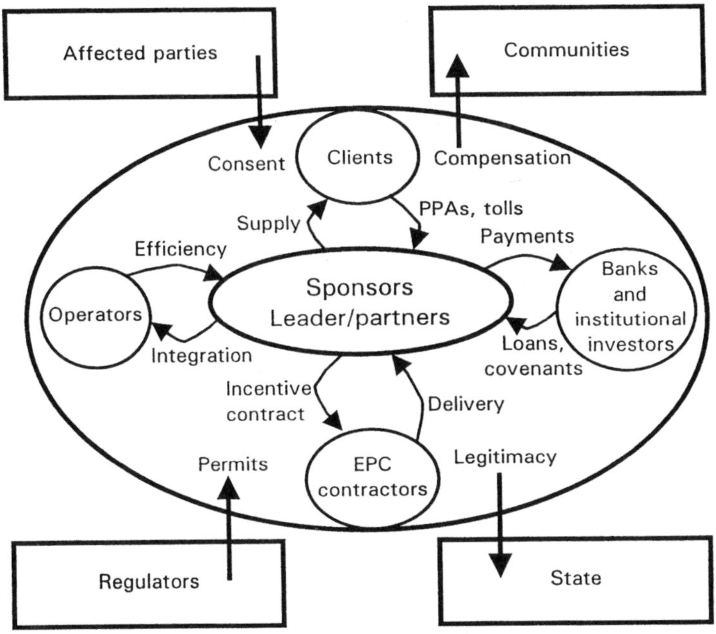

Figure 2.1
Relationships with potential to build governability

network operators also become promoters of projects through international subsidiaries, such as EDF International and Mission Energy.

Projects are sponsored by alliances that link four types of owners, on average: developers, EPC contractors, bankers and institutional investors, and operating firms. The sponsoring group (see figure 2.1) is itself embedded in a wider group of organizations representing affected parties, regulators, communities, and the state. Projects are thus molded in a wide interorganizational field.

Investment bankers act early as advisers. In some countries, where laws permit, they are also first-rank members of alliances that invest equity in projects. The international investment banking houses that play the roles of financial adviser and arranger are usually located in New York, Paris, London, or Tokyo.

Governments are present in the new arrangement as smart but generally smaller players, involved at three levels: development of concession frameworks, design and implementation of competition-enhancing regulatory frameworks, and forceful promotion of privatization policies by inducing state-owned companies to sign BOT contracts or PPAs. Concessionary frameworks, which were used extensively in the nineteenth century, began to reappear as BOT projects in the mid-1980s to attract private equity and debt capital. Two objectives are pursued with BOTs: (1) to transfer the responsibility of financing projects that was traditionally supported by the public sector to the private sector—hence transfering, partially or totally, the risks—and (2) to use innovative practices based on private-sector experience to improve effectiveness and efficiency in delivery. In other words, new regulatory frameworks are enacted by governments to foster competition and innovation. Regulations are designed to trigger entries, openness in the analysis of competing projects, and the unbundling of activities.

The allocation and sharing of risks is what distinguishes governance from nineteenth-century entrepreneurial approaches. Risks are now carried by alliances of parties best positioned to cope with them. Long-term contracts stabilize operating revenues and cost flows. Design and construction are contracted out to consortiums. Owners therefore divest themselves of many technical and construction risks by using design-build or turnkey contracts that contain incentives for early delivery and high performance. Contracts are based on functional specifications; hence, their preparation does not require significant engineering resources.

Clients that sign concessions or agreements become ultimate owners and absorb major risks. Eventually, privately sponsored projects revert to clients who signed concessions or BOT agreements. In the IMEC sample of projects, these clients were state-owned enterprises (34 percent), ministries of transport (24 percent), state transport authorities (20 percent), regional governments (14 percent), and private utilities (8 percent).

Financing of projects is characterized by reliance on both the balance sheets of sponsors and the intrinsic cash flows that each project is expected to generate. Lenders have limited recourse to the equity contribution of owners, often less than 5 percent of the capital investment, and are thus quasi-sponsors themselves. Investment bankers and scrutiny agencies are much more active in the new model because they emphasize project financing in their analysis of project viability.

Value is created by joint search and mutual problem solving among owners and cospecialized participants. Instead of relying mainly on expert designs and competitive bidding to create value, emphasis is put on generative relationships. Early in project shaping, sponsors look for complementary and cospecialized partners to share risks and returns.

Projects built under governance arrangements represented 40 percent of the IMEC sample; the majority are still built with the rational-system approach. Some projects displayed entrepreneurial characteristics. IMEC researchers therefore decided to study the historical evolution of arrangements used for project sponsorship and delivery. Over the last two centuries, three types of social arrangements were dominant at different times: entrepreneurial, rational-system planning, and governance (see table 2.1). Each arrangement arose as innovations were made to face difficulties and problems caused by failures of existing ways of sponsoring and building projects.

Institutional Arrangements: Ideal Types

Issues facing large-scale engineering projects have been solved in different ways over time. The solutions have been multidimensional configurations of mutually supporting elements such as laws, regulations, practices, and roles, which we term institutional arrangements. Because these types of arrangements form configurations, the concept of ideal types (Weber 1947) is particularly suitable for studying them (Doty, Glick, and Huber 1993). Ideal types highlight fundamental ideas, amplify traits to their limits, and provide a coherent configuration of requirements for action. Decision makers, deliberately or in a taken-for-granted manner, use the internal logic of ideal types when they respond to environmental stimuli (Burger 1976; Parsons 1947; Weber 1947).

To develop our three ideal types, we relied on grounded theorizing from the sixty IMEC field studies (Corbin and Strauss 1990; Glaser and Strauss 1967; Strauss 1987). Narratives were analyzed minutely using coded transcripts and constant comparison. We then turned to the historical literature to understand entrepreneurial arrangements. Each institutional arrangement is an accepted set of practices and a division of labor through which sponsors, bankers, governments, and builders play complementary roles in projects. There are several key components in institutional arrangements (Scott 1994).

Legal and regulatory frameworks. These set the rules of the game. Examples are laws defining regulation of private monopolies and the conditions and procedures for awarding concession rights. Laws,

Table 2.1
Characteristics of the three main types of institutional arrangements

	Entrepreneurial	Rational system	Governance
Institutions	Minimal regulation Exclusive rights or concession frameworks	Regulated monopoly (price or rate) Environmental regulation	BOT/concession Rules to foster competition and private ownership, environmental regulation
Economic context and trends	Space for expansion Cost-reducing and performance-enhancing innovations	Predictable cost reduction for output Room for system expansion	Urgent need for infrastructure (Third World) and room for new projects (West)
Technology	Emergent Local	Established dominant design Large-scale projects and systems	Stasis of core technology Information and environmental technologies
Main actors	Entrepreneurs Individual investors Investment banks	Network operators Regulators	Developers, entrepreneurs, EPC firms, banks, network operators, regulators
Risk allocation	Risks assumed by entrepreneurs	Risks internalized by large system	Risks allocated to participants
Project practices	Internal design Public stock issues Multiple construction contracts	Internal financing, planning, and design Multiple fixed-price contracts, bidding Detailed specifications	Partnerships-alliances Project financing Turnkey contracts Broad specifications
Ways to attain effectiveness and efficiency	Effectiveness: owner-performed design, control over construction Efficiency: competitive bidding	Effectiveness: rational centralized planning Efficiency: scale and network economies and competitive bidding	Effectiveness: diversity of competencies and risk allocation Efficiency: owner-contractor partnership
Organization forms	Small, dynamic	Hierarchical	Networks
Dominant ideology	Pragmatic	Modernism (rational planning, bureaucracy)	Deregulation, privatization, ecology

rules, and regulations make the anchoring of projects in a society possible.

Roles of players. Classes of industry participants have complementary roles, competencies, and dominant concerns. Each arrangement is characterized by specific allocation schemes for risk, responsibilities, property, and decision rights, as well as by mutual expectations and scenarios of interaction.

Practices. Typical practices include project planning and negotiation, ownership and financing arrangements, types of contracts, contractor-selection procedures, technical approaches, and organizational structures. Each set of practices is also characterized by schemes for the allocation of risk, decision responsibility, property rights, and expectations. These practices are found throughout the large-project field (Meyer and Rowan 1977) and play a major role in reducing uncertainty and facilitating the coordination of players.

Shared assumptions and communities of practice. Institutional arrangements are also defined by a basic set of assumptions about the means to attain effectiveness, efficiency, and legitimacy. Initially, novel ideas are applied hesitantly, but they are eventually shared in communities of practice formed of engineers, lawyers, bankers, and regulators involved in projects (DiMaggio and Powell 1991; Meyer and Rowan 1977; Swidler 1986).

Structures for solving collective-action problems. A minimally stable institutional framework is required to reduce the uncertainty faced by project participants and to allow investment to proceed (North 1990). Institutions such as laws, regulations, and contracts play a significant role in anchoring projects in the face of adverse events and in limiting arbitrary decisions.

Fabrics of institutions, practices, and ideas structure the attitudes and strategies of sponsors and parties involved: they form an outer circle within which projects can be embedded and anchored. Three types of institutional arrangements that have dominated at different times are reviewed.

Entrepreneurial Arrangements

Entrepreneurial arrangements began with the first railroad and electric-power projects. Most projects built in the United States up to 1830, such as the Erie Canal, the Pennsylvania System, and the Ohio Canals, were government sponsored. In most of Europe, the ideology of the Enlightenment held that governments were responsible for building roads and canals to facilitate trade. In France, the government financed, built, and operated a vast network of roads and bridges under the direction of the Corps des Ponts et Chaussées. A voluntaristic planning approach, aimed at creating new traffic flows rather than improving existing ones, was used (Caron 1997).

Entrepreneurs radically changed this perspective. In the 1830s and 1840s, railroad construction was sponsored by bankers and engineers. Early American railroads, such as the Boston and Worchester, Boston & Lowell, and Boston & Providence, were financed privately. In the United Kingdom, railroads began as local private attempts to reduce transportation costs. A major source of financing for projects was public subscriptions of corporate stock (Salisbury 1967).

Transcontinental railways in North America, such as Union Pacific and Canadian Pacific, were built by entrepreneurs. Railroads benefited, however, from land grants and government loans worth between US$16,000 and $48,000 per mile, depending on the terrain (Stover 1997). The government of Canada contributed CA$25 million in cash and 25 million acres of land and completed sections worth CA$38 million to help the private sector build a transcontinental railroad. In France, the concept of a government-owned railroad network was set aside in 1845 in favor of concessions. Sponsorship of railroads came primarily from investment banking houses (Caron 1997).

Although power projects began about fifty years later than railroads, their history followed a similar pattern. Several rival companies laid distribution lines on the same street. The advent of large-scale generating equipment and the development of alternating current technology soon made it increasingly clear that significant economies could be obtained by having a single system serve a territory larger than a single city (Hughes 1987).

The approach used by entrepreneurs to sponsor and build projects was characterized by both extensive partnerships and detailed contracts. Partnerships of industrial and financial entrepreneurs (often individuals rather than firms) promoted projects. For instance, Shawinigan Water and Power put together a group of industrial firms to use the power it produced and established Shawinigan Engineering to serve all of them (Hogue, Bolduc, and Larouche 1979). In the same vein, Montreal Trust assembled Trans-Alberta Power, Montreal Engineering and Co., and several suppliers to build power plants (Innis 1970). For execution, entrepreneurs developed the practice of having company engineers design the project and awarding contracts through competitive bidding, based on detailed specifications and estimates.

The demise of entrepreneurial arrangements was caused primarily by repeated market failures, including ruinous competition, duplication of investments, monopolistic abuses, corruption in the handling of subsidies, and financial speculation. Furthermore, entrepreneurial projects often did not capture all possible scale and network economies, and their reliability and safety were often neglected.

Rational Systems

Rational systems emerged with the development of regulated monopolies and the rise of modern management. The coordination required for railroad operation contributed significantly to the creation of the first large rational organizations, subdivided along functional lines (Chandler and Salisbury 1965). Management innovations, in turn, enabled the operation of even larger technical systems. Combined with technological innovations that opened the perspective for significant scale and network economies, rational management justified the construction of large railroad, power, transport, and telecommunications systems.

Contiguous railroad lines joined forces against competitors and formed interconnected systems. Similarly, the amalgamation of vertically linked power systems improved the reliability of service and reduced the cost of electricity. In the late 1920s, the sixteen largest holding companies controlled 75 percent of power generation in the United States. The Public Utility Holding Company Act (PUHCA) of 1935 introduced regulation of holding companies by the Securities and Exchange Commission. The sector was also regulated by the Federal Power Commission.

In other parts of the world, electrification was initiated by entrepreneurs, but subsequent consolidation eventually led to networks of more or less regulated regional monopolies. In many countries, the process continued as far as nationalization of private utilities and the formation of government-owned firms. In 1926, the British "national unity" government imposed coordination of all private electricity suppliers by the Central Electricity Board's national grid; in 1947, the Labour government decided to nationalize the entire power sector. In France, private firms that had been instrumental in the consolidation of distribution companies were nationalized in 1946. After a protracted ideological campaign against private monopolies, the postwar government nationalized virtually all private electrical assets and merged them into Electricité de France (Lévi-Leboyer and Morsel 1994; Morsel 1992).

System integrity became an overriding concern for network operators, as it was one of the main regulatory requirements. The development of projects was based on long-term (ten years and more) forecasting of system needs and proactive planning of required additions. This planning logic fitted well with the regulated-monopoly context, which gave the operator control over many system variables. In fact, system-oriented rational planning was explicitly enforced by regulators. For instance, in the United States, regulatory agencies of the states, or such federal agencies as the Rural Utility Service or the Department of Energy when they provided financial support for projects, requested demand analysis for the entire system and integrated resource plans. Project planning included simulations to determine the optimal size and fuel type for new plants, taking into consideration evolution of demand and the location of the other plants in the system.

The sponsorship and building of projects in the rational-system arrangement was led by large public or private network operators: they initiated projects, planned most tasks, and assumed most (upside and downside) risks. The engineering department designed power plants, which, in many cases, were built by an internal construction department; they were then operated by the power-generation department. Construction was financed from internal funds or by corporate issue of stocks and bonds. After they were built, the utilities filed a request with state regulators for the inclusion of new capital investments in their rate base to recover their own investment and make a profit. Revenues generated by portfolios of projects were used to sponsor projects to meet increasing demand.

Governments and regulators tended to enforce rational procedures. Functional specialization, uniform policies, and standard contracts prevailed. Given this solid anchoring, the main concern was the legitimacy of operators and the need to preserve the regulatory framework. National-scale utilities and railroads paid attention to issues of national interest and regional development, fostering an "obligation-to-serve-everyone" mentality. Large operators tried to project an image of probity and integrity. Bidding procedures were open and followed well-publicized criteria: utilities believed that they created value by selecting contractors and suppliers through intense competitive bidding.

The legitimacy of rational-systems arrangements began to be questioned in the 1970s, as new projects faced fierce opposition from ratepayers and interest groups. A crisis resulted from a combination of factors: cost overruns of construction projects, especially nuclear-power plants; a reduction in demand due to conservation measures and price hikes; increased environmental and risk activism; and adversarial stances initially taken by utilities.

The managerial culture of rational planning, forged in the era of technological optimism, had difficulty adapting to changes. Accustomed to dealing with technical systems, managers found that new environmental-protection devices required many skills and much patience. At the same time, emerging IPPs were putting a premium on environmental excellence and small-scale projects.

Governance Arrangements

At the end of the 1970s, rational-system arrangements were still dominant. Demand for competition and the inability of governments to borrow, however, led to a gradual shift from rational systems to sponsorship of projects by alliances.

The practices that characterize governance arrangements follow logically from the publicly shared desire to allow small business entities with limited assets and internal resources to assemble large-scale projects. At the heart of many practices also lies the contractual allocation of risks and incentives to various project participants. Nonrecourse financing methods rely almost exclusively on the prospective cash flow from the project, and lenders have recourse only to the owners' equity contribution, which often represents less than 5 percent of the total capital investment. Long-term contracts concluded, for instance, to supply power and purchase fuel are used to stabilize the flows of operating revenues and costs.

Project design and construction are often contracted out as a block to a firm or consortium under a fixed-price turnkey arrangement. The contracts are based on summary (or functional) specifications, and their preparation does not require significant engineering resources. Monitoring of work is often replaced with contractual incentives, such as bonuses for early delivery and high performance. Turnkey contractors are often equity investors in the project, which gives them additional incentive to do a quality job. Through these contractual structures, project owners attempt to divest themselves of many technical and construction risks. Contractors, in turn, rely on simple, standard technological solutions, already tested in commercial operation. The only exception is environmental issues, for which regulators impose stringent standards. Under governance arrangements, the concerns of project developers have shifted from the integrity of the system to contractual terms and deadlines.

Why the Transformation?

How can the current transformation from rational-system to governance arrangements, and the past transformation from entrepreneurial to rational-system arrangements, be explained? From an economic perspective, both transformations can be seen as contingent adaptations to changed circumstances. Normative models of industry structure, regulation, and incentives (Joskow and Schmalensee 1983; Laffont and Tirole 1993) are proposed as targets. The conditions required to produce and reinforce competitive structures are sets of rules and regulations that produce constraints, reduce uncertainty, and solve collective-action problems (North 1990). In contrast, social scientists point out that economic activity does not occur in a vacuum dominated by calculus, but is influenced by political considerations (Bergara, Henisz, and Spiller 1998; Katzenstein 1985), relational networks (Burt 1992; Granovetter 1985; Powell, Koput, and Smith-Doerr 1996), cultural assumptions and value systems (Swidler 1986; Weber 1930), and legitimate action models (DiMaggio and Powell 1983; Meyer and Rowan 1977).

Comparative historical analysis of economic systems is the preferred methodology of the schools that attempt to combine economic with political and technological concepts (see Lazonick 1992). Social-change theorists argue that "we must look at [large structures] comparatively over substantial blocks of space and time in order to see whence we have come, where we are going and what real alternatives to our present condition exist" (Tilly 1984: 10). Evolutionary economists (Dosi 1982; Hodgson 1993; Nelson and Winter 1982), the French regulation school (Boyer and Saillard 1995), and the governance approach (Hollingsworth and Boyer 1997; Jessop 1997) study how networks, communities, associations, the state, and political groups create conditions for the smooth functioning of markets and other economic institutions to promote innovation and the accumulation of wealth.

The transformation is best explained by a process of change, involving four periods: awareness-raising, innovation, realignment, and consolidation. The first two stages are dominated by innovations and ideological thinking, while evolutionary adaptation takes place gradually in the latter two periods, as reality creeps in.

Awareness Raising Due to Recurring Failures

Projects built under rational-system planning increasingly resulted in cost overruns, low profitability, and poor operational characteristics such as safety and security. The cost overruns and safety problems that American nuclear (and some nonnuclear) power plants experienced in the 1970s and 1980s focused the public's attention on the lack of accountability and the arrogance of regulated utilities.

The "technological stasis" (Hirsh 1989) reached by power-generation technology was such that, after steadily declining throughout the first half of the twentieth century, both the real and nominal costs of power for consumers bottomed out at the end of 1960s and began to rise. The oil crisis of 1973–74 not only added to the direct cost of producing power in some plants but triggered high inflation, which led to cost overruns in many new power-plant projects. These cost increases were passed on to the public through hikes in the price of electricity, which led to wide discontent.

The foreign-debt crisis of 1982 affected the ability of large state-owned network operators in the Third World to finance their projects. Many infrastructure projects under way stalled, and planned projects had to be abandoned. The suddenness of the crisis was conveyed to IMEC researchers by the minister responsible, at the time, for financing the huge Tucurui hydroelectric dam in Brazil: "When I woke up one day, the world had changed. Brazil could no longer borrow in the international financial markets."

Similarly, the transformation from entrepreneurial to rational-system arrangements started with awareness-raising issues. In the 1850s, in the United States, farmers and communities, especially in the prairie states, began attracting railroads to their region. After tracks were built, however, farmers, many of whom had invested their savings, accused the railroads of raising prices in communities served by only one line, and their welcoming attitude turned into fierce opposition (Buck 1913). Private railroad projects with government funding, including construction of transcontinental railroads and reconstruction of the railroads in the Confederate states after the Civil War, were plagued by corruption scandals and financial machinations. Later, waves of consolidations were widely perceived as attempts to limit competition and increase prices (Stover 1997).

The electricity industry experienced similar difficulties. Duplication of lines was expensive; service was not stable and safety poor. For instance, in 1903, a tramcar accident killed schoolchildren, producing a public outcry that eventually led to the amalgamation of over 500 small gas, electric, and transportation companies to form the Public Service Co., a regulated utility that served most of the state of New Jersey.

From a theoretical point of view, one might argue that awareness-raising issues altered previous arrangements and prepared the path for change (Argyris and Schon 1978; Bennis and Sheppard 1956; Lewin 1958; Schein 1969). Diffuse discontent produced direct responses, which initiated the shift toward governance arrangements; U.S. regulators "disallowed" imprudently incurred project costs from inclusion in the utility rate base. Many American states introduced legislation compelling regulated utilities to obtain a "certificate of need" from regulatory commissions prior to starting construction of a new power plant.

Innovations Leading to New Institutions

The innovation stage is ushered in by a surge in novel practices for sponsoring projects. In the face of discontent and failures, coherent alternatives to existing arrangements are proposed and begin to take form. For instance, to counter difficulties in rational-system arrangements, innovations were proposed that eventually formed governance arrangements.

Concessions and BOT contracts. Caught in the midst of financial crises, Turkey was unable to finalize needed projects. Turgut Ozal, then the prime minister, is widely credited for coining the BOT concept, which became the "organizing vision" (Swanson and Ramiller 1997) for the upcoming transformation. In a BOT scheme, a private consortium develops, finances, and builds a project under a concession-like agreement with the government. A number of risks that had previously been borne by governments or regulated utilities were assigned to private parties, including obtaining financing, completing, and operating the project.

Many governments saw a way to develop infrastructure projects in BOTs without increasing borrowing. Yet, they often conflicted with existing legislation. To reduce legal and regulatory uncertainties, special laws enabling BOT projects were enacted. Nevertheless, judicial battles delayed the implementation of many of these projects for long periods.

In developed countries, concession frameworks were established as early as 1969: France had the Paris-Poitiers turnpike and the United Kingdom had the Dartford Crossing project. The British government formalized the conditions under which such projects were to be awarded in a scheme called the Private Finance Initiative (PFI). Many other developed countries followed the British example, including Canada, Australia, and the United States.

Deregulation to meet demand for competition. The demand for competition to counter monopoly situations triggered shifts in regulation. In the American power industry, competitive entries were fostered by the passage of PURPA (Public Utilities Regulatory Policies Act), designed to diversify energy sources and increase the efficiency of power generation. A class of nonutility power generators called "qualifying facilities" was created, with cogenerators or power plants using biomass, waste, and renewable resources as the primary energy source. Qualifying facilities could not be more than 50 percent owned by a network operator and it was guaranteed that the latter would purchase all of their power output at a price based on the incremental "avoided cost" of electricity production.

By 1992, more than 63 percent of all generating-capacity additions came from nonutility sponsors (*Power* 1994). Most of them relied on long-term PPAs and were financed with nonrecourse loans and public issues. For the design and execution of plants, developers concluded sole-responsibility, fixed-price contracts, also known as turnkey contracts (*Power Engineering* 1990). Pricing based on "avoided costs" led, in many instances, to an oversupply of generating capacity.

The strong response to PURPA demonstrated that competition was possible. The act's success prompted another step in the deregulation and unbundling of the American power industry—the Energy Policy Act (EPACT) of 1992. A new class, called exempt wholesale generators, was created to spur a wholesale electricity market by mandating utilities to open access to their transmission lines. Meanwhile, the British government had begun its deregulation drive (Hunt and Shuttleworth 1996).

Evolution of technologies. The enhancement of economies of scale and scope caused by technology dwindled. The production of large turbine generators, the development of alternating-current technology, and the invention of transformers had enabled the growth of large systems, but a plateau was eventually reached (Hirsh 1989). Technological optimism, which had characterized large systems, was replaced by technological pessimism and the rise of ecological movements.

At the same time, the development of information technologies, which enabled the unbundling of generation, transmission, and distribution, and the creation of electronic power exchanges favored both nonutility power projects and wholesale markets. Yet, progress in information technologies also spurs the development of large, real-time intelligent networks that are favorable to established network operators.

Precipitating crises. The inability of many large public network operators to build projects rapidly to meet urgent demand created calls for radical change. Organizational failures were such that new power plants could not be built quickly enough; therefore, foreign investors were sought to build rapidly. Crises and the diffusion of the idea of privatization in the 1980s led the governments of many countries to shift away from public ownership.

Owner-contractor relationships. Partnering practices were developed to reduce the problems associated with the claims and lawsuits entailed by adversarial owner-contractor relations. New relationships have led to substantial cost and time reductions in engineering, procurement, and construction. Projects built under collaborative relationships often reduced capital costs by 25 to 30 percent and construction time by 10 percent. For instance, Norwegian and British oil firms operating in the North Sea were faced with the economic impossibility of developing low-yield oil deposits applying practices learned over the previous thirty years and were forced to change their ways. Standards were abandoned and joint problem solving with suppliers was used to reduce costs radically.

Almost a century earlier, innovations had focused on creating regulated monopolies to gain economies of scale and scope. A wave of railroad consolidations, until about seven major companies remained by the mid-1890s, had triggered fears. In the public sector, to prevent public takeovers as a result of the growing public fear of monopolies, industry leaders borrowed the "regulated monopoly" model that had emerged as a solution to the problems in the railroad industry. As early as 1898, through Samuel Insull, the industry voluntarily proposed a system of private monopolies with state regulation. In 1907, the industry-sponsored Commission of Public Ownership published a report echoing Insull's call (Rudolph and Ridley 1986). The same year, three American states established utility regulatory commissions (Energy Information Administration 1996). By 1921, all states except Delaware had such commissions. In the process, uniform accounting procedures and other regulation-enabling practices were perfected.

Realignment

The realignment stage of institutional arrangements starts when innovative organizing visions—such as BOTs, concessions, and project financing—reach impasses as theory and ideology meet reality. For instance, spectacular failures experienced in the 1990s by concessions for roads, tunnels, and power plants led to doubts on the part of bankers, governments, and developers about concessions and project financing.

Governments initially viewed BOTs, concessions, and project financing as ways to transfer risks to private parties in exchange for the prospect of high returns. Sponsors could not realistically assume all market risks, however, and governments were not able to divest themselves of such risks, either.

Project financing presupposes that the only guarantee for debt repayment is expected cash flow from the project. As a result, projects lack the shock-absorption potential provided by a strong balance sheet when corporate financing is used. Learning from previous project failures, bankers increasingly require creditworthy sponsors ready to offer corporate guarantees for debt repayment. Entrepreneurial sponsors with weak balance sheets find it difficult, if not impossible, to promote large projects. They are replaced by large network operators, engineering firms, and equipment suppliers that create subsidiaries dedicated to project development. Such companies as National Power International (United Kingdom) and Enron (United States), which have developed worldwide portfolios of large private projects, point toward new forms of sponsorship.

Complex webs of contracts, however, have not prevented project failures. Contracting requires a sophisticated understanding of risk allocation, which not all entrepreneurs and organizations have. Contracts cannot protect projects from an arbitrary government decision to back away from previous commitments as shifts in public opinion take sponsors "hostage." The interdependent, rigid, and slackless contractual structures on which many projects are based under governance arrangements create tight couplings that tend to amplify shocks and bring otherwise viable projects to bankruptcy.

In developing countries, the selection of projects by government officials has been replaced, in many instances, with selection by international sponsors and banks. Hard-nosed selection has probably led to underinvestment. Project financing requires significant effort devoted to analysis, negotiation, and coalition formation, thus increasing barriers to project selection. The World Bank has observed that private financing of infrastructure projects is progressing slowly in the Third World, where few true BOT projects are implemented. Bankers usually reject projects built ahead of demand and accept urgent projects that may be suboptimal from the point of view of the country's technical and social systems. In addition, the legitimacy of PPAs is often contested by the public because of high prices.

The shift toward governance arrangements has not yet reached stabilization; it is still in the process of realignment as opposing forces compete. For instance, network operators maintain that economies of scale and scope justify their existence. The proponents of BOTs, concessions, and deregulation argue for independent sponsorship. It will take many more years to correct imbalances, control opportunism, and articulate state participation to make governance arrangements dominant.

In contrast, rational-system arrangements reached the stabilization stage in the early twentieth century, and they stayed stable for nearly seventy years. After the principle of regulated monopolies was established, American utilities, regulators, and equipment manufacturers elaborated many complementary practices, such as uniform accounting and reporting, rate hearings, and proactive planning, and they embarked on a steady pursuit of technological innovation that increased scale economies and captured network economies. By the late 1960s, in almost all countries, railroads and electrical utilities, operators of highway networks, and other project operators were predominantly private regulated monopolies or state-owned entities serving large geographical areas.

Hesitations and Concerns about Governance Arrangements

The multiplication of innovations in the sponsorship and execution of LEPs led to the emergence of governance arrangements. Concessionaires, independent developers, and subsidiaries of network operators became project sponsors. Entrepreneurs convinced government officials that building roads, power plants, and public-transport systems with the old rational-system approach was inefficient. Many projects built using the governance approach, however, failed to live up to expectations; new projects did not always deliver the superior performance that they were expected to produce. IMEC's results indicate that high- and low-performance projects are found in both rational-system and governance arrangements. Many concerns are expressed about the latter.

Skepticism about concession BOTs. Public-policy makers stress that the prospects of high returns to private investors justify the shifting of public risks to private sponsors. Few sponsors and bankers are now willing, however, to participate in concessions in which private parties assume investment risks but are at the mercy of legislative changes. Shifts in regulations, for instance, have caused havoc in the Eurotunnel project. Because many concessions have brought large losses to private investors, bankers now hesitate to lend. Bankers and sponsors want concessions to be secured through public guarantees such as shadow tolls, volume commitments, and cross revenues from existing installations. Governments are thus expected to become more involved.

A renewed preference for strong balance-sheet financing. In the most ideal form of project financing, a project stands on its own, is rated as an acceptable risk, and can be funded without sponsor or government guarantees. Sponsors invest equity and bankers issue loans or investment houses sell bonds that are covered by foreseeable returns. The reality of project financing is quite different: most projects involve guarantees, subsidies, and adjusted rates. Bankers increasingly look at creditworthiness of sponsors and prefer those with a balance sheet composed of a portfolio of projects. Entrepreneurial sponsors find it difficult to promote projects because of their weak balance sheets.

The unsustainability of long-term contracts. Utilities that signed PPAs as clients find that the security of supply these agreements once provided has turned into an obligation to pay above current market prices. Many of the contracts concluded in the 1980s were priced well above the wholesale-power-market prices of the 1990s. Rather than continue to pay such high prices, many utilities purchased plants back from their owners and shut them down. Faced with the impossibility of renegotiating such contracts, governments impose taxes and utilities contemplate the possibility of not honoring contracts. Some utilities now express the desire to rely on merchant plants with no pur-

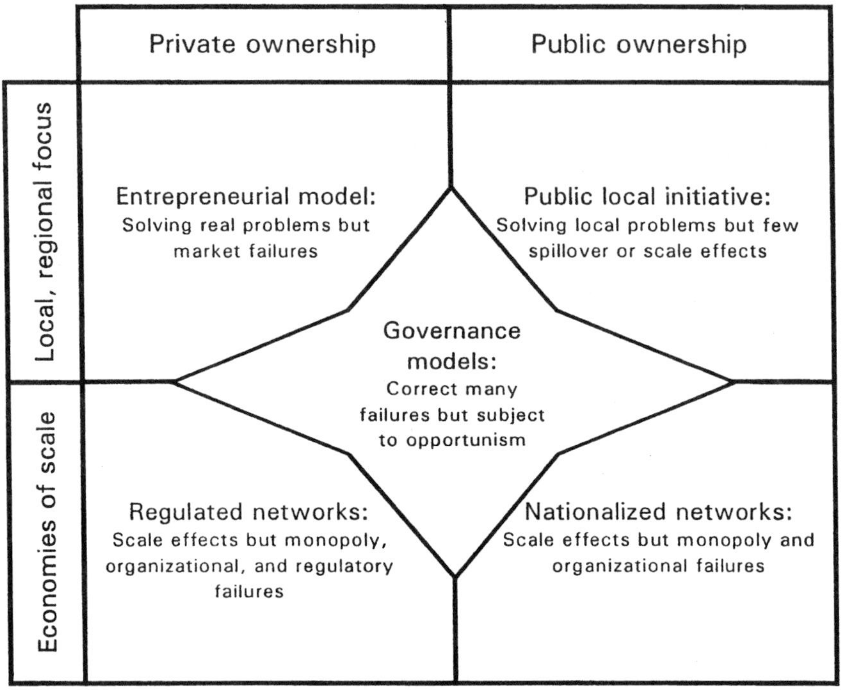

Figure 2.2
Models for the sponsorship and execution of LEPs

chase agreements. In developing countries, government-owned utilities were often forced to sign PPAs to implement privatization policies; they now want to renegotiate such contracts and engage in legal battles.

The Difficult Search for an Optimal Model

Do governance arrangements represent a fundamentally better way of shaping and delivering LEPs? IMEC's research does not give an unambiguous answer to this question. Each arrangement has its advantages and shortcomings. The best answer is that LEPs involve characteristics that make it difficult to design institutional arrangements that will remain optimal in the long term. The governance model is an attempt to navigate among four types of issues, each with advantages and failures (see figure 2.2).

Over the last two centuries, many approaches to shaping and building LEPs were tried, but each approach has generated failures of some kind. The entrepreneurial approach built projects to solve real regional or local needs but tended to generate market failures: projects were too small, areas with no markets were skipped, technical choices lacked scale, and so forth. At the beginning of the twentieth century, as technology made scale possible, the rational approach to sponsorship was developed. Network operators built projects that were highly effective but entailed failures linked to monopoly situations, cooptation of regulators, and organized top-heaviness. Publicly owned network operators could also develop projects at the right level of scale; the French nuclear-power sector is a good example. Network operators, however, whether public or private, tend to generate organizational failures such as rigidities, inability to respond, low productivity, and political obedience.

At the start of the twenty-first century, governance arrangements are being promoted by firms and governments. Many criticisms are now directed at this approach for failing to take real public needs into consideration and for heightening rather than reducing risks. The main weakness of governance arrangements is their vulnerability to opportunism: contracts cannot protect projects from arbitrary decisions by governments or from shifts in public opinion. Today's governance arrangements combine private sponsorship with institutional frameworks that take competition, social consent, and public–private partnerships into consideration. Yet, they are not optimal.

Obviously, no optimal solution exists. Each type of institutional arrangement induces some form of failure that has to be corrected. Governance arrangements aim to remedy the failures of rational systems, but they themselves generate failures due to opportunistic behavior, state withdrawal, and possibly underinvestment. Table 2.2 lists the failures that limit entrepreneurial, rational-planning, and governance arrangements. The search for a balance of responsibilities and risks among governments and private participants will thus need to continue through realignment of governance arrangements. Here are the most obvious areas where improvements must be considered.

The long-term commitment of the state is often a key requirement for successful projects. Innovations need to be made by legislators to ensure that projects are well anchored and protected against legislative risks.

When built at the proper scale, LEPs serve multiple generations. Ensuring that projects take account of a long-term future, and not only the sixteen to twenty years in loan covenants, demands innovations.

Table 2.2
Failures within institutional arrangements

Entrepreneurial	Rational systems	Governance
Duplicated investment and destructive competition	Network operators are symbols of national pride, tools of vested interests	Vulnerability to government opportunism
Small projects fail to capture economies of scale	Bureaucratization: specialization and formalism lead to slow decisions and high overhead costs	Complexity of front-end negotiation processes, which increase transaction costs
Fragmented systems and markets not capturing network economies	Arrogance, inability to deal with ecological groups and local opposition	Rigidity of contractual structures
Tendency to form monopolies to increase prices	Tendency to build expensive and unneeded projects	Incapacity of contractual structures alone to protect from failure and opportunism
Underinvestment in underpopulated areas	Overreliance on internal planning and definition of projects precludes joint problem-solving and cost reduction with contractors and equipment suppliers	Predilection for simple and conservative solutions that reduce technical risks but produce technically suboptimal projects
Rate discrimination between places where there is competition and places where firms enjoy monopoly, as well as between large and small clients	Incapacity to focus on small or marginal projects	Underinvestment in projects due to increased selection hurdles
Financial speculation	The "capture" of regulators who are unable to impose efficient investment	High cost of capital for private projects using project financing
Issues of probity, corruption, accountability, and conflict of interest		

Public–private partnerships with the long view in mind will need to be developed.

A contingent perspective needs to be cultivated. Some projects should be built by entrepreneurial sponsors. Major opportunities need strong sponsors, however, which may be network operators with a monopoly, specialized developers with portfolios of projects around the world, or government firms.

Providing shock-absorption potential to irreversible investments is necessary to face turbulence. The need to provide some form of security is likely to call for the bundling rather than unbundling of many projects, the presence of shadow revenues, and the support of revenue guarantees. Large domain specialists and network operators bundle many projects into portfolios to protect against risks.

Changing conditions often threaten the survival of projects. There is a need to develop flexible contractual arrangements in the form of rendezvous clauses that establish a priori the terms and conditions under which agreements will be renegotiated. Bankers, sponsors, and governments all have an interest in developing innovative solutions in this area.

3 Mapping and Facing the Landscape of Risks

Donald Lessard and Roger Miller

Understanding risks and strategizing about ways to cope are the starting point of effective project shaping. Some risks can be anticipated; others are difficult to predict but emerge as turbulence sets in. This chapter describes best practices that emerge from the composite of successful projects in the IMEC sample as well as the lessons drawn from the failures.

Risks in Large Engineering Projects

There is no question that LEPs are risky. Different types of risks carry widely varying exposures. Examples of the risks encountered in the sixty projects examined by IMEC include the following: the technology functioned as planned but the alliance of sponsors failed; costs exceeded estimates because of changes in technology; the natural conditions encountered differed from those expected; demand did not materialize as projected because substitutes were allowed by the regulator; due to shifting agendas, stakeholders did not agree on modifications; rules of the game and environmental regulations were changed.

Many perspectives on risk taking exist, including those that focus on individual decision makers from a cognitive-behavioral perspective (Shapira and Berndt 1997; Tversky and Kahneman 1986) or a decision-theoretic one (MacCrimmon and Wehrung 1986); those that focus on the firm as a strategic actor (Bromiley 1988), as a social actor (Pfeffer 1978), or as an agent of shareholders in a (relatively) complete capital market (Brealey, Cooper, and Habib 1996); and those that view society as a representative decision maker-benevolent dictator or as a complex political structure (Stinchcombe 1990). The primary perspective here is a management one.

What Is Risk?

In the most general terms, risk is the possibility that events, the resulting impacts, the associated actions, and the dynamic interactions among the three may turn out differently than anticipated. There is a great deal of debate over whether risk is an objective characteristic or reflects the subjective perceptions that drive decision making. A key concept in the psychological literature on risk taking is that individuals anchor their perceptions of risk relative to some level of aspiration (Shapira and Berndt 1997; Tversky and Kahneman 1986).

Distinctions are often made between risk and uncertainty: risk is typically viewed as something that can be described in statistical terms, and uncertainty characterizes situations in which potential outcomes are not fully understood. Yet another distinction is often drawn between situations that involve the potential for variations in gains and losses and those that involve only the risk of losses. Financial economists further distinguish between risks that are diversifiable at a national or global level and those that are not.

Here, risks and uncertainty combine with indeterminacy to create ambiguous decision-making contexts. The usual approach is to view risks as the Gaussian distribution of outcomes. Managers, however, not only are interested in the variability of returns but they pay attention to the drivers of risks that are likely to affect future project performance. From a managerial perspective, uncertainty is ignorance of the true states of nature and the causal structures of decision issues. Weak uncertainty holds when managers have enough information to structure problems, estimate distribution, and build decision models. Strong uncertainty characterizes situations in which there is such an absence of knowledge and information that decision-making issues are ambiguous. Indeterminacy means that future outcomes are not only difficult to assess but depend on exogenous events or endogenous processes that can lead to multiple possible futures. Indeterminacy is thus a risk that can be partly solved by strategic actions.

A Taxonomy of Risks in Large Engineering Projects

Risks differ according to types of projects. Figure 3.1 positions the various types of projects according to the intensity of technical, market, and social-institutional difficulties that they pose to sponsors.

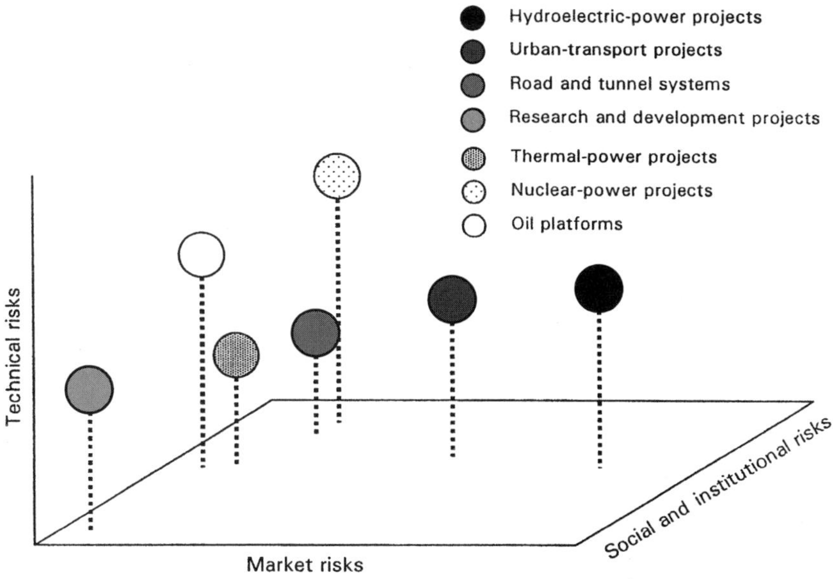

Figure 3.1
Illustration of risks associated with projects

Oil platforms are technically difficult, but they typically face few institutional risks because they are built far from public attention and are socially desired because of the high revenues that they bring to communities and countries. Since the output is sold in integrated world markets, the primary market risk is that of volatile prices rather than the quantities that can be sold.

Thermal-power projects tend to be less technically difficult. Market risks can be reduced if PPAs compel clients such as private utilities or public networks to make regular payments. Merchant thermal-power plants, however, do not have the security provided by PPAs and long-term contracts: they sell on a spot basis to clients, using a transport firm to wheel the power. Thermal-power plants can be designed to be socially acceptable if they provide central heating to cities or come with regional-development packages.

Hydroelectric-power projects tend to be moderately difficult on the engineering side but very difficult as far as social integration is concerned. They cause external effects and social disturbances that make them easy targets for protest and challenge, though some offer complementary benefits for navigation, erosion, or water management. Benefits can combine with compensations to make them socially acceptable. The market risks of dams are moderate, as they require the presence of large buyers with extensive needs.

Nuclear-power projects pose high technical risks but still higher social and institutional risks. Market risks tend to be lower because sponsors are usually network operators that can forecast and have a need for power. Only a few countries and network operators have dealt with social and institutional risks in such a way that nuclear-power plants can be built.

Road and tunnel systems present surprisingly high levels of risk. Roads are not usually technically difficult, but digging tunnels always presents geophysical and geological risks. Rock formations can hide surprises. Social-integration difficulties are high, especially if user fees are applied: social movements may tend to contest. The market difficulties of roads, bridges, and tunnels are very high when they are built under concessionary schemes by private sponsors who must face public pressures and judgments.

Urban-transport projects must meet real needs for segments of the population and thus pose average market, social, and institutional risks. They still pose technical risks, however, as they regularly involve underground geological work.

Research-and-development projects present scientific challenges but face fewer social acceptability and market difficulties. The technology projects that were part of the IMEC study could be broken down into parts, had a willing client, and were socially valuable. The technical challenges they posed, however, often led to overruns and delays, especially in software projects.

The multidimensional view of risk unbundles outcomes and drivers into many components. The premise is that each of the parties involved in a project can face and address risks. In the IMEC study, managers were asked to identify and rank the risks they faced in the early front-end period of each project. Market-related risks dominated (41.7 percent), followed by technical risks (37.8 percent), and institutional-sovereign risks (20.5 percent). Figure 3.2 gives the frequency of citations of the risks that managers ranked first, second, and third in the early parts of projects. Each of these risks will be discussed in three groups: market-related, completion, and institutional.

Market-Related Risks

Market risks. Market forecasts for roads, transport systems, and power projects are based on assumptions about the structure of demand.

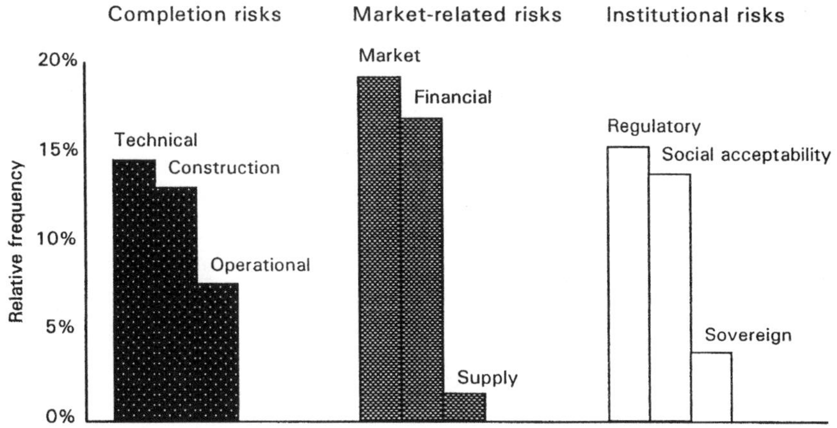

Figure 3.2
Relative ranking of risks faced by projects

Multiple scenarios and outlooks are considered. Yet, in many of the projects IMEC studied, projections turned out to be widely off the mark, despite the fact that bankers often used consultants to check projections. In some cases, errors resulted from shortfalls in overall economic growth; in others, because the structure of specific demand turned out to be different than anticipated. For instance, the Dulles Greenway, the first privately financed highway in Virginia since 1816, is a fourteen-mile extension of the Dulles toll road built in 1984; operations began in 1995. Since its opening, traffic flows have averaged 10,000 to 12,000 units per day, instead of the forecast 30,000 to 40,000. Because it was built as a concession by a partnership linking construction firms and local business partners, the sponsors have been forced to ask their bankers to reschedule debts.

The ability to forecast demand varies with the type and specific attributes of each project. The output of oil projects is a fungible commodity sold in highly integrated world markets. In contrast, many projects face only a specific set of customers: some have many options and others have few. The prospective users of public transport in emerging economies, for example, have limited options, while users of highways, tunnels, bridges, airports, and ports often have alternatives that make forecasting difficult.

Financial risks refer first to the potential difficulties that any project faces in attracting lenders and investors given its potential returns and risks. They also entail the inability to restructure financial arrangements in the event of unexpected changes in cash flows.

Financial risks are often defined broadly and confused with technical and economic risks. If a project fails because initial studies show insufficient returns to attract financing, the failure is not the result of financial risk, but merely an indication that the project's economics did not add up. If the project offers an adequate prospective return, however, but is unable to go forward because of the parties' inability to work out acceptable risk-sharing arrangements, this is the result of financial risk.

The classic example is the case of a project that suffers major setbacks, reducing its value below the expected value of the associated debt financing and subsequently requiring new injections of equity capital to go forward. Even if the present value of going forward is positive, equity holders will not make the investment because some or all of the value it creates will accrue to the holders of the overhanging debt. Negotiating a write-down of the debt claims, however, is often problematic, and value may be destroyed because of such conflicts.

Supply risks are similar to market risks—both involve price and access uncertainties. Supply can be secured through contracts, open purchases, or ownership. In our sample of projects, supply risks were not seen as very important. Typically, they are greatest when the economics of a particular project are premised on supply of a key input on terms that are more favorable than those obtainable in markets at large. The Equate petrochemical project in Kuwait, for example, is premised on favorable access to the feedstock. Should alternative uses for the feedstock be developed, the supplier would have an incentive to raise the price to the detriment of Equate. Thermal-power generators that compete with hydroelectric projects face a price risk of supply, which is typically passed on to distributors or users. Such agreements are often broken or renegotiated, however, if the contract prices move too far out of the "shadow" of the market. Hydroelectric projects, in contrast, face a supply risk based on precipitation levels.

Completion Risks

Technical risks. Projects face a variety of technical risks that reflect their engineering difficulties and novelty. Some of these risks are inherent in the designs or technologies employed. The Northumberland Strait Crossing project, for example, was premised on the ability to build the major spans offsite, transport them by barge to the bridge site, and hoist them into place with massive self-jacking cranes—something that had never been done on this scale and certainly not in an estuary with high currents.

In some cases, the technology is known but interactions with natural conditions may be encountered, causing risks. Tunneling projects are notorious: geological formations shift and render boring technologies inadequate. Technical risks are exacerbated by the fact that many aspects are locked in and cannot easily be reversed. If a suspension bridge is found to have sympathetic harmonic vibrations, it is hard to "retune" it after the fact.

Construction risks. These are the difficulties that sponsors, prime contractors, and contractors may face in the building of the projects. Sponsors rely on the skills of contractors to perform difficult tasks. Building a thermal-power plant is a well-known task, but builders take enormous risks when they commit to deliver an oil platform, an underwater power cable, a tunnel, and so forth. Many of the projects that IMEC studied involved some high construction risk because both sponsors and contractors assumed, in creative fashion, that solutions would somehow be found in due course to meet contract obligations. To gain business, sponsors bid aggressively based on assumptions about geological, hydrological, geophysical, and other conditions. Once they have won the contract, reality strikes back and "winner's curse" may set in.

Operational risks refer to the possibility that the equipment will not function adequately. These risks can be reduced substantially by investment in building high-quality systems from the start and by the selection of an operator with an economic interest in enhancing revenues and controlling costs.

Institutional Risks

Regulatory risks. Even when the rules defining the boundaries of projects and the relationships with customers, suppliers, competitors, and other stockholders are clear, projects still face a wide array of institutional risks. When rules are ill defined, these risks are even greater.

Projects depend on laws and regulations that govern the appropriability of returns, property rights, and contracts. Some countries are governed within constitutional frameworks and the rule of law, while others are led by powerful political parties or clans. Politicians and bureaucrats often seek compensation for granting permits or concessions. Building large projects in these contexts is a difficult task.

Institutional risks are typically seen as greatest in countries with emerging economies where laws and regulations are undifferentiated and in a state of flux. These risks are even greater when foreign investors have neither experience nor bargaining power. Although some are associated with macroeconomic or political events, many are of an institutional nature. Regulatory risks associated with delays and difficulties in obtaining approvals for environmental, sectorial, or social permits are among the most common; government agencies are in a position to delay or effectively endanger projects simply by refusing to grant the necessary permits. Professionals working in these agencies are often more committed to their technical domains or to public-accountability requirements than to the needs of specific projects.

Sector rules on pricing, entry, unbundling, and other elements are undergoing major changes in many countries. The traditional regulatory framework, which relied on price and profit control, is moving toward competitive regimes that encourage entry. Under the old regulations or regimes, firms were at risk on allowed rates of return, whereas under the new regimes they are likely to find that high-cost facilities are "stranded" with low value. Public demand for competition is pushing legislators to break up integrated systems.

Social-acceptability risks refer to the likelihood that sponsors will meet opposition from local groups, economic-development agencies, and influential pressure groups. The reality of external effects and the possibility of capturing parts of the rent trigger actions that make social-deadlock risks very important. During the course of negotiations or after a project is built, affected parties may raise their claims on the rent; they learn that tough, organized action pays off and proceed accordingly.

Sovereign risks involve the likelihood that a government will decide to renegotiate contracts, concessions, or property rights. Changes in rules, property rights, and so forth, triggered by general economic or political shifts, become sovereign risks.

Most projects contain clauses allowing the sovereign or its agent to reclaim ownership with compensation. When the upside turns in favor of investors, the authority that has granted a concession may decide to reverse its decision and reclaim ownership. At the other extreme, sovereign risk results from regime changes that are hostile to private investments, such as those in Cuba and, to a lesser degree, in Chile. They may also result from procompetition policy changes, such as those that occurred in Chile in the 1970s and in Mexico in the early 1990s, when tariffs were dropped. Projects whose economics had been premised on protection were suddenly wiped out.

Concessions that place most risks and rewards in private hands are often asymmetric in that losses are privately borne but gains may be appropriated through rule changes. Investments are most secure when they are made within general regimes of overlapping investment, tax, and competition regulations. Controlling the behavior of governments or inducing them to become real partners in projects is not an easy task. In fact, bringing security to projects by developing new roles for governments is probably the most difficult risk to master.

The Asian financial crisis has brought home the impact of macroeconomic collapse and the ensuing changes in exchange rates, interest rates, prices, and demand. The Hopewell Bangkok transit project, already mired in institutional and stakeholder risks, has been postponed indefinitely. The Bakun hydroelectric complex in Malaysia, which faced technical, economic, and institutional risks, is also off the table. Many projects already under construction, and even some in operation, have been thrown into disarray, especially in cases where revenues are largely determined but borrowings were undertaken in foreign currencies.

Dynamic Interactions of Risks

Over time, choices that appeared sound all of a sudden become ungovernable. Not only is uncertainty a palpable tension but turbulent events burst out and interact. Figure 3.3 illustrates that risks emerge from the decision to initiate a project and form a range that challenges sponsors to a formidable journey.

Many risks are viewed by sponsors and managers as linked to the life cycle of the project. Regulatory risks, for instance, diminish soon after permits are obtained. Technical risks drop as engineering experiments are performed, elements of design are defined, and construction is completed. Errors are identified and corrected as the system begins operation. Even the number of failures resulting from hidden causes follows the well-known bathtub-like curve, with most defects surfacing in the initial and ending periods of project operation. Financial risk, the possibility that the project does not find a lender or that requested interest rates are too high and loan covenants too rigid, is also a hurdle risk. Once the financial deal is closed, sponsors normally

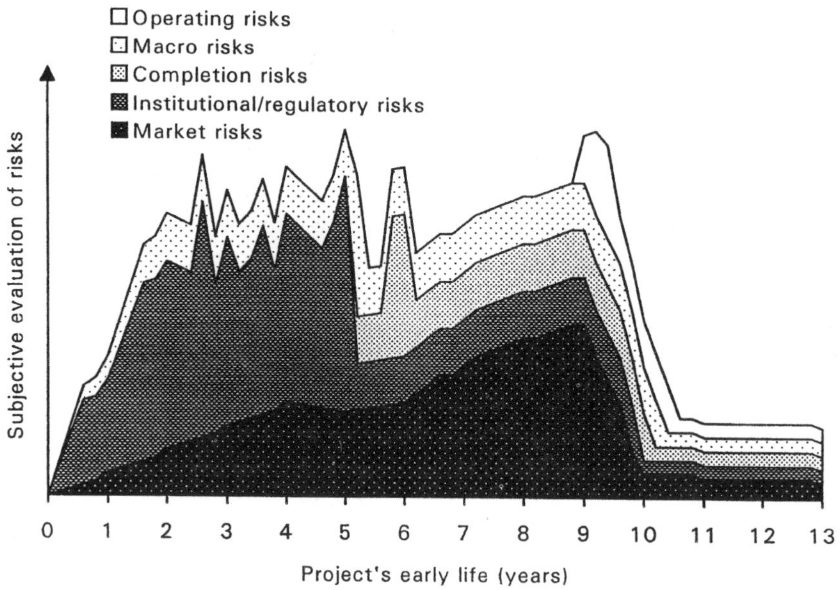

Figure 3.3
Dynamic evolution of risks

put the issue behind them and concentrate on project implementation. Should conditions turn favorable, refinancing the project may be an option. Risks linked to the project life cycle are *hurdle risks* because they appear to sponsors as obstacles that, once solved at the required stage, pose few subsequent problems.

Some risks, especially market-related ones, are partly independent of project life cycle. The demand for a project output, such as electricity or transportation, is determined by external factors, such as general economic activity, the growth or decline of a region, and market deregulation. For instance, in the 1980s, the southern American states witnessed growth in population and economic activity; to satisfy electricity demand, many power projects were initiated. The recession of the early 1990s, however, reduced forecasted demand growth and many projects were stalled. For some projects, though, market risk is not entirely unpredictable: bridges or toll roads have ramp-up periods during which users shift from their previous routes to new ones, then demand changes and reaches a plateau.

Sponsors sometimes get into difficulties because partners fail to deliver or engage in forms of appropriating upsides or avoiding responsibility for downsides. They may do so because the incentives built into the partnership are inappropriate or because they experience substantial losses on other projects.

The range of risks is itself embedded in a layer of global market risks that are outside the control of virtually all players. Should there be fluctuations in major currencies, world interest rates, or key commodity prices, projects may be thrown into jeopardy. Countries are thus embedded in yet another layer of institutional risks associated with the world financial, economic, and political order.

Approaches to Risk Management

Difficulties in managing LEPs stem largely from the fact that most of what we know about risks has been inherited from either Wall Street or Las Vegas. At the casino, the odds are public knowledge: success is strictly a matter of beating them. In financial markets, price fluctuations are not probabilistic, but indices make for investment decisions that are relatively easy to model and optimize. Barring large and unexpected crises, risk management in most financial markets is a straightforward, though sophisticated, craft.

It is useful to distinguish between two broad categories of approaches to risk management: *decisioneering*, which comes from management science and assumes that the future is probabilistic, and *managerial approaches*, which match risks with strategies but assume that the future is indeterminate or, at best, highly uncertain. In decisioneering approaches, analysts study payoffs and sets of options, and select the optimal course of action. The ways that effective sponsors manage risks, however, cannot be captured by the metaphors of gambler (decision theory), portfolio manager (financial market theory), or chess player (game theory).

Decisioneering is also concerned with the drivers that influence the distribution of output variables, such as profit, rates of return, utility, and so forth. In projecting outcomes, decision makers typically focus on projects' most likely or modal future (e.g., expected outcomes conditional on the most likely scenario). The practice is to adjust levels of risk, often discounting future cash flows—a rate that reflects a risk-free situation plus a premium for systematic risk (Brealey and Myers 1997). Clearly, this model is an oversimplification, especially when an investment entails abandonment options that create nonlinearities in the dependence of cash flows on events. The discounting rate can be lowered when international agencies or guarantees are involved. Conversely, it is raised when regulatory instability prevails.

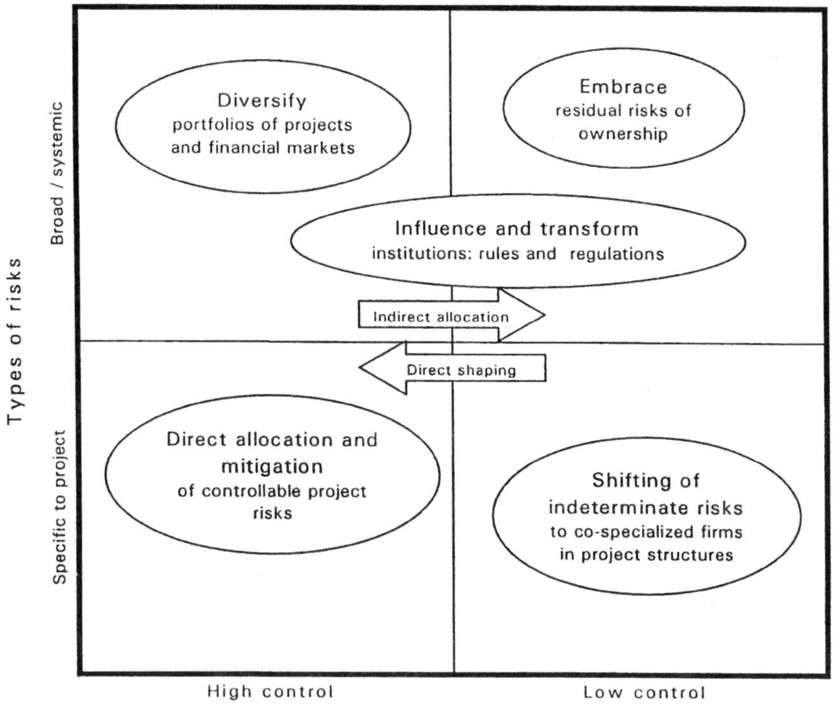

Figure 3.4
Managerial approaches to risk management

The managerial approach is most appropriate in conditions of indeterminate futures. Project sponsors do not adjust hurdle rates, but use repertoires of responses to match risks with strategies and allocate responsibilities to parties that have a comparative advantage in coping with risks. Sponsors do not sit idle, waiting for the probabilities to yield a "win" or a "loss," but strategize to influence outcomes.

The managerial approach has four main risk-management techniques: shape and mitigate; shift and allocate; influence and transform institutions; and diversify through portfolios. Figure 3.4 uses two axes: the extent to which risks are controllable and the extent to which they are specific to a project or systematically affect large numbers of actors. When risks are endogenous—that is, specific and controllable—the prescription is to shape or to mitigate by shaping. In contrast, when risks are specific but outside the control of any of the potential parties, shifting or allocating them by using contracts or financial markets is the appropriate solution. When risks are poorly defined and depend on affected parties, governments, or regulators, transforming them through influence is the way to gain control. When risks are broad, systemic, but controllable, the approach is to diversify exposure. In portfolios of projects, residual systematic, uncontrollable risks beyond strategic control have to be embraced.

The Layering Model: Strategizing to Face Risks

Strategizing in conditions of indeterminacy, strong uncertainty, and turbulence involves two simultaneous processes: a reasoned assignment of risks for imaginable futures and the infusion of governability into project structures to face presently unknowable risks. The reasoned assignment of knowable risks starts with a layering process in which risks are discovered, imagined, and assigned to a coping strategy. Some risks will be dealt with by using financial markets, others by institutional shaping, still others by project coalitions. Many can be assigned to partnership members according to these parties' knowledge, influence, and ability to shape, exploit, and bear them.

Some risks are unknowable in advance but demand appropriate actions when they manifest themselves. Sponsors can achieve some degree of control by eventual joint decisions with parties that have the information, knowledge, and resources to face risks. Aligning the incentives of these parties with the interests of the overall coalition or partnership helps to build indirect control. This way, risks do not have to be fully modeled in an integrated fashion; rather, they can be sliced off and assigned as black boxes. By building risk-management incentives into various aspects of projects, the layering process creates the potential for enactment of unknowable and unforeseeable solutions by alliances of partners and stakeholders in a particular context. Because of this emergent governability, it can be said that successful projects are made rather than selected.

Tracing risk management in projects in the IMEC sample, we identified six primary mechanisms used by managers for layering risks (see figure 3.5). Assessing and understanding risk is the first, and perhaps most complex, stage. The others are shifting risks to financial markets or contracts; diversifying or pooling risks; creating options to allow a greater range of responses in line with future outcomes; transforming or shaping particular risks whose drivers are, at least in part, the result of choices or behaviors by other social agents; and bearing and embracing residual risks. This layering process is repeated in many iterative episodes.

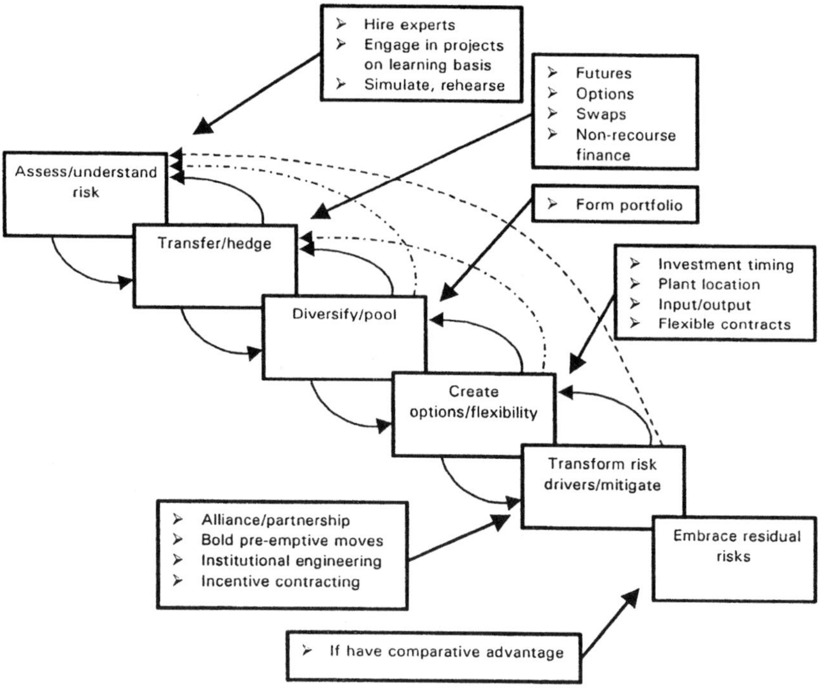

Figure 3.5
The layering model: strategizing to face risks

Strategizing about risks is almost always beneficial, but at some point diminishing returns set in and the costs of acquiring additional information or gaining control over risks fall short of their value. The design of responses to risks must be judged on a cost-benefit basis. Aligning performance incentives is critical when particular parties to the project have a significant degree of control over the economic value created by the project but do not have an incentive to maximize this overall value. If the risks are endogenous, then shaping incentives to modify the risk favorably is a relevant option. If the institutions or rules within which the project exists are the result of choices by some parties, then transforming or mitigating these risks is also relevant.

Comparative Advantage in Risk Taking

Potential participants to be selected for membership in a project structure should display a comparative advantage in taking the lead with a

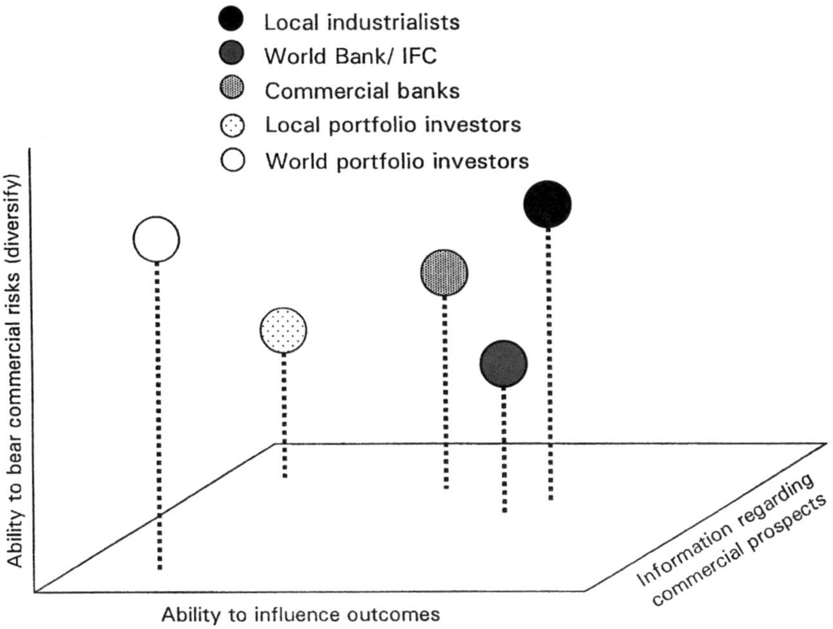

Figure 3.6
Relative advantage in bearing risks

particular risk. Comparative advantages are recognized in risk allocation in the context of project financing but are often ignored in other forms of financing. Relative superiority in risk bearing may arise for any one of three reasons: (1) some parties may have more information about particular risks and their impacts than others; (2) parties or stakeholders may have different degrees of influence over outcomes; or (3) investors may differ in their ability to diversify risks, largely as a result of the first or second reason. Figure 3.6 illustrates how potential partners differ in their ability to control and enjoy a comparative advantage. For instance, local partners can influence outcomes but have little ability to diversify risks and little knowledge about commercial prospects worldwide. World portfolio investors certainly diversify risks, but their ability to know about local commercial prospects or to influence outcomes is low.

The following example illustrates the search for partners with distinctive comparative advantages. The Chilean firm Endesa is planning to acquire an independent power-generating plant in Argentina. (This example is based on public information about Endesa's investment in

Argentina.) Endesa's strategic advantage in Argentina lies largely in its successful prior experience with privatization: it could be said that it knows more about the future of the Argentine power sector than do Argentines. Based on its experience as an operator, Endesa has a clear information and influence advantage when it comes to operating risk. In fact, this was the strategic rationale for the investment. Endesa may be at a double disadvantage on demand risk: first, Argentine projects may become too large a part of its overall portfolio; second, as a visible "foreign" firm, it may be singled out for "contract renegotiation" should terms prove onerous to Argentine consumers. Therefore, it will shift these risks both to more diversified international players and to Argentine players with greater legitimate voice within Argentina, such as local strategic investors and "common folk" or, better yet, "widows and orphans" via pension funds. Ultimately, an independent power-plant project in Argentina is a bet on the viability of the Argentine economic program.

Effective risk management involves many aspects, including determining whether potential benefits of the project are sufficient to offset risks; allocating risks so that incentives and capability to bear them improve project performance and reduce the probability of disasters; and building in sufficient governability to respond to the changes or shocks that inevitably occur. Projects that turn out well may have been well managed but they may also have been lucky. Conversely, projects that fail may have been mismanaged or they may have been simply unlucky.

Effectiveness in risk management can be measured only on outcomes. Ex ante, however, one can ask how management assessed risks and what steps were taken to manage and allocate them; ex post, whether projects turned out well or poorly, one can ask whether the source of variation was identified before the fact. The most interesting cases are those in which the project was unlucky on some important dimension. Did management then respond appropriately to shocks or changes as they occurred? Were relevant options built in and exercised on a timely basis?

In reviewing the sixty IMEC projects, a strong and statistically significant correspondence was noted between the types of risks that each project entailed and the way that these risks were managed. In most cases, project sponsors allocated risks in ways that would elicit information and actions from the stakeholders with the greatest knowledge and influence. Regarding risk assessment and incentive alignment, the mechanisms observed most frequently were the selection of projects that appear ex ante to promise reasonable revenue and the establishment of a decision framework that leads to analysis, research, and scrutiny, and thus forces information to surface. Projects are contested until a choice can be made after thorough challenges. In most cases, firms built sufficient robustness and responsiveness into the project arrangements to avoid financial catastrophes.

The risks of financial catastrophe are manageable to a degree through the embedding of shock-absorption potential such as shadow revenues, sponsor balance sheets, revenue guarantees, and government subsidies; the committing of high levels of equity by sponsors; and the development of loan-repayment profiles that match the logic of bankers with the reality of projects. With completion risks, we observed that there was early investment in information search while commitments were low and the options many; many sponsors avoided difficulties by refusing to lock in early and by postponing choices as long as the value of information remained high. Firms refused to commit to projects in bidding situations where information was inadequate. Sponsors relied on suppliers' knowledge to develop technical solutions and reduce costs.

With respect to market (demand and supply) risks, we observed similar mechanisms: investment in market research was made not only by using computer modeling of traffic flows, but also by behavioral marketing studies and focus groups. Concession agreements and purchase contracts also served to reduce risks for sponsors by shifting variations to clients: shadow volume, guaranteed volume, secured revenue levels, and so forth.

Many sponsors addressed social and institutional risks in a forthright fashion, recognizing that exerting influence is necessary. They also employed communications strategies to enter into relations with affected parties and their representatives by providing them with factual and comparative data, negotiating trade-offs with them, and offering cultural or regional compensation packages. A planned approach may end up being very costly, representing as much as 15 percent to even 30 percent of the total project cost.

Sponsors found that regulatory risks are difficult to manage directly. A number of innovative avenues were used: establishment by a legitimate authority of formal procedures to structure decision making, delimit information, and eventually provide legitimacy by decision or referendum; development of environmental or social plans, guided by international standards such as International Standard Organization–14000; establishment of coordination offices located at the most senior level of government to expedite the issuance of permits by environment, agriculture, transport, energy, and other agencies.

The key finding from observing how project sponsors wrestled with the risk inherent in projects, as well as with those arising from possible conflicts among the various cospecialized partners or stakeholders, is that the lead sponsors have developed a strong repertoire of strategies for coping with risk. The ability to frame risks and strategies represents a core competence for them. This competence spans the five types of layering responses we observed: (1) obtaining and framing information; (2) designing a process with a long "front end" before technical, financial, and institutional details are locked in, followed by rapid execution of the physical project; (3) building coalitions that bring together varying information and skills and are structured to create strong incentives for performance and mitigate conflicts of interest; (4) the allocating of risk to parties best able to bear it; and (5) transforming institutional environmental risks through the creation of long-term coalitions that incorporate powerful influences on laws and rules.

4 Project Shaping as a Competitive Advantage

Roger Miller and Xavier Olleros

Not all LEPs turn out to be disasters. In fact, a majority of projects perform adequately and some attain high levels of effectiveness. Furthermore, innovations such as design-build contracts that more closely align the various participants' payoff potential and risk exposure with their influence over outcomes have led to substantial cost and time reductions. Projects built according to these novel practices result not only in efficiency gains, often reducing capital costs by 20 to 30 percent and time by 10 percent, but also at times in breakthrough ways of providing the desired services.

The main argument developed in this chapter is that successful projects are not selected but shaped. Rather than evaluating projects at the outset based on projections of the full sets of benefits and costs over their lifetime, successful sponsors start with project ideas that have the possibility of becoming viable. They then embark on shaping efforts that are most likely to unleash this value during a long front-end process. The seeds of success or failure are thus planted and nurtured as choices are made. More often than not, successful projects start as promising approaches that are shaped and reshaped over many episodes by persistent sponsors. Successful firms, however, cut their losses quickly when they recognize that a project has little possibility of becoming viable.

The Managerial Challenge of Large Engineering Projects

LEPs are certainly difficult technical tasks, but they are primarily managerial challenges. Complications can be solved by engineering calculus, computations, and detailed planning. Complexity, however, because of its dynamic and unpredictable nature, has to be met by versatile managerial approaches. The challenge of LEPs requires more than financial engineering, incentive contracting, or alliance formation, even though each of these is important. Three types of management approaches may be used to rise to the challenge of LEPs: rational planning, adaptiveness, and shaping, but the latter is most appropriate.

Hyperrationality

The field of management has produced a number of theories that, though useful, are clearly not able to account for success and failure in shaping LEPs. Hyperrationality leads to long-term planning perspectives and assumes that the future can be forecast. These theories are often part of the problem, as they propose recipes and "silver bullet" solutions that may not fit. Here are two.

LEPs are gambles. Projects are certainly risky but they are not gambles (Keeney, Lathrop, and Sicherman 1986). Gambles are games in which strategists study states of nature, select a move with a high payoff, make a bet, and wait for the probabilities to materialize. Gambles are a matter of calculation and comparative data analyses: groups of executives brainstorm to identify options, probabilities, and possible consequences. Decision trees are built, and the selected solution is the one that promises the highest expected utility. Other examples of project-selection models are internal rates of return, numeric scoring models, and weighted-factor scoring models.

The gambling metaphor is not applicable to the front-end parts of real-life projects. First, it is simply impossible to predict the future of projects over the ten to fifteen-year period of shaping, building, ramping up, and early operation—not to mention the entire life of the project. Second, decision making is not an intellectual exercise in which the set of relevant futures are laid out, but a facing of reality as issues arise, time passes, and affected parties react. Third, sponsors do not sit idle, waiting for the probabilities to yield a "win" or a "loss," but work hard to influence outcomes and turn the selected option into a success. They shepherd their initial choice in light of changing conditions and often they succeed against the odds.

LEPs are ventures that can be planned and specified in advance. Project-management theories start with a business case and assume that experts design a solution, define work packages, and select contractors using bidding processes. Uncertainty is viewed as manageable through investments in information and life-cycle strategies (Clelland

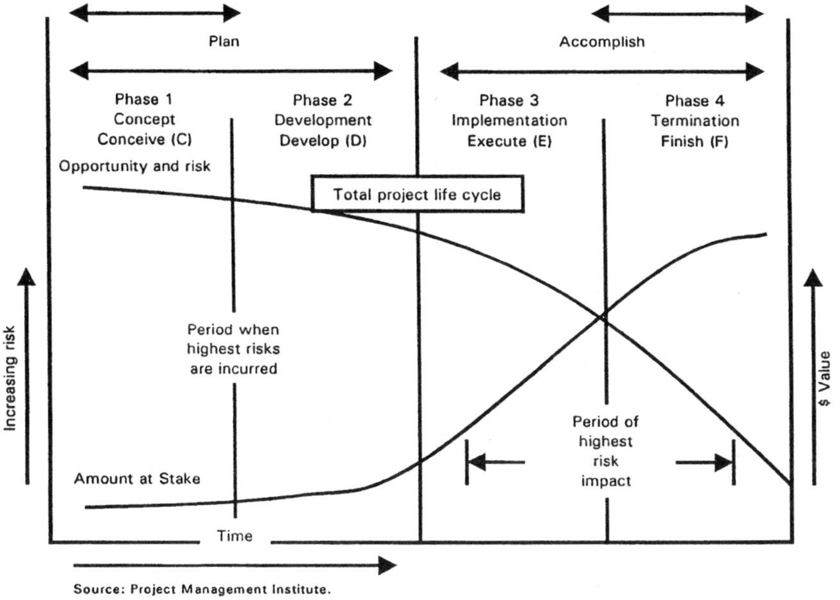

Figure 4.1
Risk reduction and commitments

and King 1988; Meredith and Mantel 1995). The future of projects is dictated not by circumstances but by management (Urban and Hauser 1980). Project-management theories assume that analytical tools can scope, reduce, and eventually minimize risks.

Careful analyses of trade-offs between costs and risks, it is claimed, can yield good approximations for the appropriate timing of investment in projects. Accelerating a project will increase development costs to the point that there is a danger of sinking it. Proceeding with prudence increases the danger of missing the opportunity that the project aims for. In the presence of uncertainty, commitments ought to be low and flexible until sufficient exploration allows a viable concept (Utterback 1994).

The central difficulty of hyperrational approaches is the core premise that the future is probabilistic. Planning decisions focus on selecting the optimal project. With the help of specialists, it is assumed, sufficient information can be gathered to identify and evaluate the costs and benefits of a range of options: risks are reduced during the front-end period while commitments rise (see figure 4.1). This approach is probably valid for simple projects, but it is not a valid representation of projects facing indeterminate futures. As sponsors make decisions, risks arise that call for actions. Eventually, key issues are resolved and risks fall.

Messiness and Improvisation

The front-end decision processes observed in the IMEC sample were messy, often chaotic. This messiness, as opposed to hyperrational approaches, has led many observers to argue that LEPs are unmanageable and that success is a matter of luck. Projects are described as games in which chance, force, or improvisation dominates. Project shaping is a thankless task, in which, at first glimpse, surfing appears to supplant analysis. Accepting imperfect solutions is the norm and alignment of goals is never complete. Here are a few indicators of this untidiness.

Projects are often launched by promoters who need to convince and charm potential participants. Truncated uncertainty and optimistic expectations become the basis for persuasion and communication. Judgments, not facts, dominate.

High levels of expenditures need to be allocated to soft issues such as opinion research, public affairs, participation, and debates that appear to many executives to be money spent on nonbusiness issues. In other words, substantial sums are spent with no corresponding concrete actions.

Politics and power are more important than analysis. Decisions are never final but are remade, recast, and reshaped until the project is feasible. Turning points recast even firm commitments.

Confrontation not only overtakes collaboration but often brings deadlocks. Crises punctuate orderly development and create a climate of disorder for those who believe that decisions ought to be made in a deliberate fashion.

Instead of collaborating, many players appear to be governed by strategic agendas. Both local and international opponents thrust projects into the media, target bilateral or multilateral agencies, and even initiate legal challenges. Gains from noncollaboration are tempting.

The untidiness of decision-making processes has brought many authors to develop a pessimistic view about the possibility of managing. LEPs are so greatly affected by unpredictable uncertainties that it is said to be misguided to put so much trust in analysis only. Firms play games, information is incomplete, and emergent events change the context. Here are some approaches that challenge the rational-planning perspective.

Heroic entrepreneurs have the social skills to convince others of their optimistic, and sometimes distorted, view of the future that they will be good sponsors (Shapira 1995), as they have the required vision, intent, and persistence (Prahalad and Hamel 1990). In fact, champions certainly have a strong influence on the evolution of projects, but individuals cannot single-handedly account for the success or failure of projects.

Flexibility and improvisation. A new paradigm of management stresses adaptiveness (Bettis and Hilt 1995; Illinitch, D'Aveni, and Lewin 1996; Sanchez 1997). The argument is that in the face of turbulence, strategies must incorporate flexibility—the ability to sense changes, conceptualize adequate responses, and reconfigure resources to execute swiftly. The need to compete in high-velocity environments calls for agility. Strategies for building flexibility include viewing investments as staged options, building modularity into investments, forging alliances, and developing low-cost probes (Brown and Eisenhardt 1997).

Flexibility is usually not possible in LEPs, however, because of their indivisibility and irreversibility. Without strong commitments, not much progress can be achieved. Projects can rarely be broken into modules but require heavy commitments through which sponsors, partners, and affected parties lock in on a choice, thereby giving away most of their degrees of freedom. Commitments, not flexibility, are required to communicate credibility to affected parties or government agencies.

Consensus and trust. These are often promoted as both prerequisites and solutions. In the absence of trust, planning and market mechanisms, it is claimed, may fail to bring about complex collective goods such as LEPs. Design of interactions builds a negotiated order (Wildavsky 1993). Participation and inclusion make it possible to arrive at a consensus on project configurations. Goodwill and extensive negotiations make the real world manageable.

The reality is that opportunistic games, unexpected events, and changing conditions often require renegotiation of agreements. Projects need to be embedded in robust networks of institutions while simultaneously facing conflicts. In managing relationships, the possibility of governance failures cannot be ignored (Jessop 1997).

Project Shaping and Steering

Both the glorification and the rejection of planning are inadequate. No sponsor would agree to reduce investment in planning, analysis, and simulation because the future is unpredictable or unknown. Planning may be portrayed as ineffectual (Mintzberg 1994), but, paradoxically, sponsors are spending increasing amounts of resources and time on this activity.

Few projects are preordained by selection processes that identify ex ante winners nor are they hopelessly messy. Projects are born as hypotheses, nurtured as concepts, sold to coalitions and opponents, and eventually formalized into viable commitable configurations. Shaping means the writing of a script in a succession of episodes spread over an average of six and a half years. (Commedia dell'arte, in which actors make up the script as they play structured sets of interactions and roles, is the best analogy.)

A variety of intertwined issues are resolved one by one by the leading sponsor, alone or in cooperation with partners or cospecialized firms. Because of the high levels of interdependencies and conflicts they entail, projects pose the problem of coordination—that is, the need to steer along a solution path that leads a project to be evaluated positively. (Solving all issues at once is possible only when decision making is dominated or simple.) Resolution of the ambiguities of needs and solutions is usually achieved through successive redefinition, bringing the project toward commitable closure. Many project concepts will have been killed early, midcourse, or at the end.

Strategic interventions have the highest leverage during the front-end period. Listening to the right people and adopting the right perspective appear to bear fruit. Talking to regulators, public-affairs specialists, lawyers, or bankers makes for a better understanding of issues. Sponsors have the intuition that the value of the project pie can be raised by adopting holistic perspectives that view problems beyond the immediate engineering task.

The Structure of Shaping Episodes

The shaping process combines deliberate actions with emergent responses to events. The structure of the shaping process presented here results from analyses, introspection, and the comparison of successful and unsuccessful IMEC projects. Projects are highly sensitive to

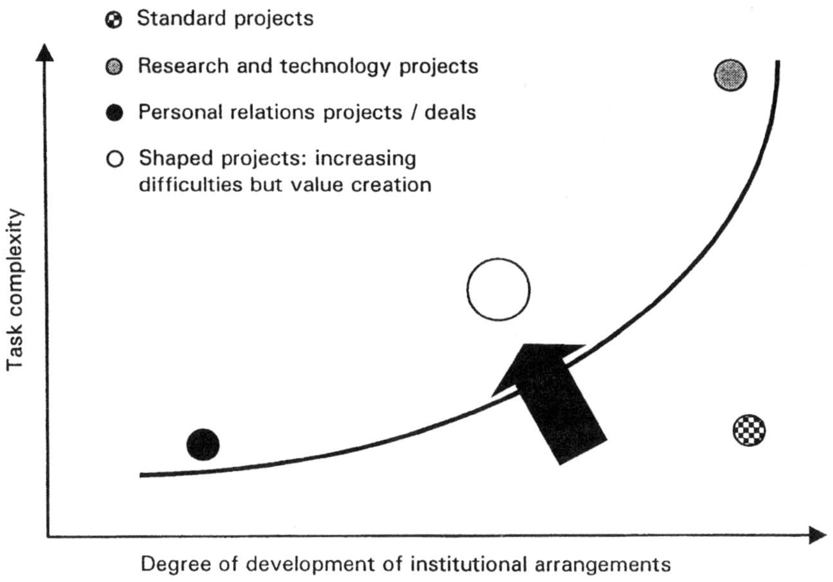

Figure 4.2
Creating value through difficult projects

turbulence, and managers introduce strategies to control it to some extent by creating feedback to correct chaotic situations and self-amplifying cycles. This, rather than selecting, is the essence of shaping.

The shaping of a project depends simultaneously on task complexity and the degree of development of institutional arrangements (see figure 4.2). Task complexity is more than technical difficulty or risk; it is a situation in which the outcomes being sought are known, but future problems are not fully specified and the parties most likely to solve them are not completely identified. It requires exploration and testing, and therefore rules out locking in a solution in advance. Furthermore, to the extent that it requires the collaboration of multiple parties without the ability to specify fully the role of each party, it requires organizational flexibility and relational contracting that result in the inclusion of the right parties with appropriate incentives.

The degree of development of institutional arrangements depends on core legislative, administrative, and judicial processes that make project anchoring possible. A large part of the shaping problem is to create coalitions that substitute for inappropriate institutions and eventually help to create new institutionalizable patterns. This typically involves "buying in" some stakeholders and "buying off" others.

In some cases, the roles of stakeholders can be specified in advance. In many cases, though, it is not clear how to accommodate various interests, so the leading sponsor must exploit the front-end period to identify a mutual-gains trajectory.

At first glance, it might appear that successful sponsors are those that select projects with lower degrees of complexity. This ignores the fact, however, that opportunities are often greater when the difficulty factor is higher (see figure 4.2). If the project's value proposition requires solutions that are hard to put together, the potential payoffs are less likely to be competed away. Thus, competent sponsors will focus on shaping difficult projects that have some possibility of high payoffs, where the challenge extends to the process of organizing the various interests. Using a mountain-climbing metaphor, competent sponsors do not rush to climb the tallest mountains or only the mountains that they are best equipped to climb. Rather, they seek to select, equip, and train a climbing party that should be capable of meeting the challenges that will unfold as the project is developed, even though these cannot be fully specified in advance.

In fact, the game consists of identifying projects that stretch the limits of the firm's capability but that, because of their complexity and risk, offer substantial benefits to clients that cannot be achieved with simpler, less risky undertakings. These benefits have high appropriability, since few other firms will have the capabilities to exploit them. If we trace the development of leaders and the projects that they sponsor over time, we see that they have regularly "pushed the envelope" to identify projects on the frontier of their capability but not yet commoditized. At the same time, as more firms gain the ability to undertake such projects, they slip from the frontier and become subject to greater competition. Firms push the envelope in the following ways.

Reproducing, in an institutionally unstable or emerging economy, a project concept that has been proven in an advanced economy. An example is the Hub project, a large-scale 1,300 MW power plant in Pakistan, where difficulties were not so much technical as political and institutional. The sponsors were National Power International of the United Kingdom and Xenel Industries of Saudi Arabia.

Linking public and private benefits in cofinanced projects. An example is a dam in Mexico, which generates electrical power (presold to obtain financing), irrigation (prepurchased by a government agency to provide financing), and flood control (partial payment of capital costs in return for this "unappropriable benefit").

Adopting new technologies. Of course, technical changes will create new frontiers of complexity-value, but they will also reduce the difficulty of old ones. For example, the advent of cellular telephony broke a natural monopoly and this opened many opportunities for new projects.

Pushing the envelope is a game in the true sense, with a continuing competition among potential sponsors and efforts by clients to reduce the sponsors' advantage. Nevertheless, as with most economic games, it is not zero sum: efforts by both parties to create advantage appear to spill over and create mutual advantage. High-value projects, as figure 4.2 shows, differ from personal-relations projects, which rely on deals to build technologically simple artifacts; from innovative projects, which are complex technical tasks in well-established institutional frameworks; and from standard projects, which are highly commoditized and set in well-developed institutional frameworks.

Shaping projects requires a competent leader with a team of partners and complementary cospecialized firms. The importance of selecting, equipping, and training the "climbing party" is clear from the IMEC cases. Conditional on the degree of task complexity and institutional development, we found that a project's probability of success depended on the extent to which it was characterized by a front-end process with sufficient time and resources to shape the project and its context. A project is never foreordained, but early choices point early toward success or failure.

Hypotheses about Issue Resolution

Projects emerge in successive shaping episodes that start with the sponsor-leader forming a hypothesis about the progress that can be achieved on the issues that need to be resolved and the efforts that are required to develop strategies to bring resolution to issues. The leading sponsor and its partner start with a broad hypothesis about what nested issues need to be addressed and what resources are necessary to achieve progress toward closure. Projects are made economically viable, technically functional, and socially acceptable by progressing on solutions to deal with the following issues.

Negotiating a project concept or proposition that truly creates value and can be progressively refined in the overarching issue. Holding discussions and negotiations within a coalition of partners gathered by the leader to ensure a strong sponsorship entity is the key strategic device.

Reaching a satisfactory balance between ownership rights and commitment to bear risks allows progress in concept definition. Frequent risk seminars and decision conferences are used by a persistent leader to shape the value proposition.

Developing stability for the future of the project, to ensure that investments will be repaid and protect against opportunistic behaviors, conditions financing. Strategic devices are numerous and contingent upon the project: regulatory decisions, long-term contracts, assumption of market risks, and so forth.

Gaining and ensuring legitimacy is achieved through consent from affected parties and approval by governments. Strategic devices include explicit recognition of rights, negotiation of compensation, public assessment and voice framework, and proactive strategies with communities. Strategies to gain legitimacy with governments include policy debates, formal concessions, BOT contracts, and conforming to regulations and permitting conditions.

Achieving shock-absorption capabilities to handle crises by responding and restructuring projects requires second-order strategizing. The infusion of governability in project structure is achieved through design devices that provide for funding, cohesion, reserves, flexibility, generativity, and modularity. The architecture of the financial structure to allocate risks also helps to ensure governability through devices such as penalties, rendezvous clauses, and ownership rights and duties.

Ensuring capital-cost reduction while increasing technical functionality requires the setting of generative relationships between owners and contractors. Strategic devices include early integration of pertinent parties, the provision of incentives to reveal innovations, and the sharing of benefits in the implementation of creative solutions. Design-build-operate contracts requiring trade-offs and frame agreements are also useful devices.

Dynamic Interplays in Shaping Episodes

Projects are shaped in episodes to transform the initial hypothesis, make progress on issues, and solidify initial coalitions of players to achieve temporary and eventually final commitment. Each episode opens new options and closes old ones until sponsors and partners achieve final lock-in, thus binding their commitments and losing most of their degrees of freedom. Shaping episodes start with momentum

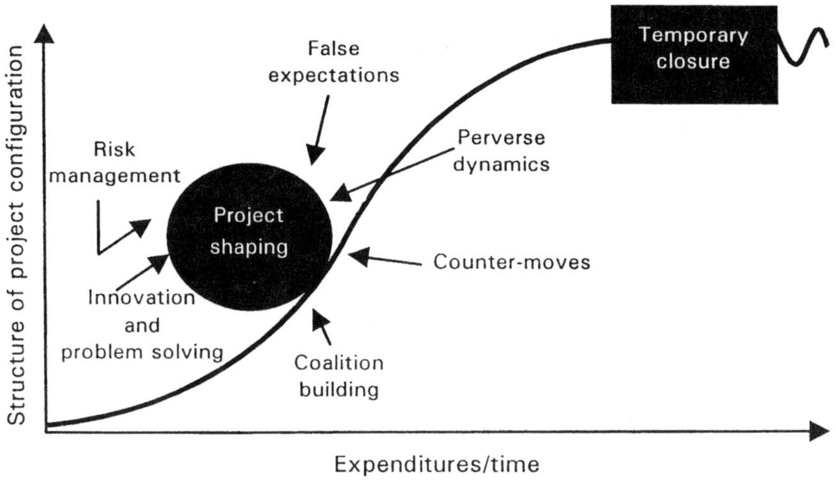

Figure 4.3
Shaping efforts to build momentum

building, continue with countering opposing forces, and end with closure. Figure 4.3 pictures the shaping effort as going up a hill through coalition building, problem solving, and risk management in the face of counterdynamics such as cynicism, false expectations, and feedback effects.

Momentum building. Momentum is built by imagining solutions to face risks directly or indirectly, promote legitimacy, and design a project configuration such that partners, affected parties, and governments believe what is proposed. Outside parties commit to credible projects sold to them optimistically by reputed sponsors.

Coalitions are built through mutual accommodation in which the parties exchange and agree to reciprocal nonzero-sum games. Shaping efforts aim to resolve indeterminate situations through bold commitments and leveraging of pertinent factors to arrive at agreements that are optimistic but not delusional. Eventually, imperfectly coordinated but stabilized understandings move toward focal points at which temporary agreements become enforceable.

In situations of incomplete antagonism—when desire to collaborate is mixed with the intention to oppose—parties learn opponents' values, communicate promises, and make veiled or overt threats to arrive eventually at meetings of minds. Situations of incomplete antagonism are solved often by self-binding moves in which sponsors display voluntary nonconfrontational attitudes: sponsors hope in this fashion to have their commitments understood and appreciated by opponents (Schelling 1963).

Strong, competent sponsors with prior experience, credibility, and slack resources have advantages in facing issues. The countering forces that will come into play over time can easily sidetrack weak sponsors into wrong choices or simply lead inexperienced ones to kill a good project hypothesis.

Countering forces. Forces such as doubts, cynical actions, and fear limit the effectiveness of shaping efforts and may even plant seeds of later failure. Sponsors sometimes believe their own overly optimistic assumptions. Weak analyses, incomplete market research, and the search for contracts lead to the selection of erroneous paths. Early lock-in thus closes off reconsideration of project configurations and downplays future options.

Excessive realism, in contrast, leads to skepticism and the eventual rejection of good opportunities. What is basically a good project is painted negatively by some and rejected by others. Leaders lacking in shaping experience and credibility cannot communicate believable expectations. Unfavorable judgments about events, exposures, and design choices drive away parties whose contributions are critical. Doubts, negative stories, and emergent problems set in motion self-fulfilling prophecies.

Sponsors often yield to the temptations of unreasonable commitments. Clients, bidding frameworks, or business relationships demand that project solutions be developed fast. Sponsors accept risks, hoping that the downside will never materialize, but winner's curse often sets in.

Leaders and sponsors can become blind to particular risks and develop no mitigation strategies. Blindness generally comes from the inability to form coalitions that include partners with the relevant viewpoint. Parties that have committed to behave in specified ways fail to assume their responsibilities.

Strategic games between agencies and sponsors take many forms: refusal to grant permits, delimitation of project conditions by regulators, changes of rules during project construction, the risk of legislative changes against which no action is possible, and absence of support when crises arise. Perverse dynamics can take hold when inefficiencies and feedback are not countered by further strategic efforts. Projects survive only when leaders and sponsors have the resources, willingness, and competencies to respond to destructive forces.

Closure. Each shaping episode ends with a process of closure that opens new options, suggests abandoning the whole project, or calls for temporary agreement on a project configuration or final lock-in. Closure is a shared agreement among the leaders, sponsors, and key players that the original hypothesis about progress on solving issues is confirmed. When final closure is made, proceeding to engineering, procurement, and construction is the next step.

Closure takes many forms as sponsors progress through multiple episodes: memorandum of understanding, business case, negotiated agreement, formal public commitment, sets of formal contracts, and so forth. The dangers associated with closure are that choices can be made too early, too late, too rigidly, or too flexibly. Missing the boat—rejecting a good opportunity—is just as real a possibility as selecting a bad option or pursuing the wrong project. Premature closure locks a project into a rigid configuration, narrow sets of agreements, or irreversible choices that limit degrees of freedom for the future. Generative closure, in contrast, is the selection of a temporary project configuration that opens a new hypothesis, triggers new options, and retains degrees of freedom for later actions.

Crossing Hurdles over Many Shaping Episodes

Projects are rarely decided on in one shaping episode. Instead, sponsors search their way through a sequence of decision-making periods. Figure 4.4 and table 4.1 illustrate the early front-end shaping efforts for a bridge project that was examined in greater detail than the other sixty projects in the IMEC sample. Five episodes characterize the progressive reduction from initial hypothesis to formal contracts. Many projects, however, do not go through all of these episodes because lock-in occurs early or sponsors kill them.

Initiation and exploration. The initiation period is usually short (six months to a year) and closes when a credible party conveys to others that the idea has relevance and should be sponsored. The credible party states openly that it is ready to allocate funds and lead debates on the ways and means of shaping the idea and financing the artifact. In the IMEC sample, project ideas were initiated by network operators (32 percent), entrepreneurial firms (20 percent), political leaders (20 percent), technical entrepreneurs (12 percent), and owners of rights (8 percent).

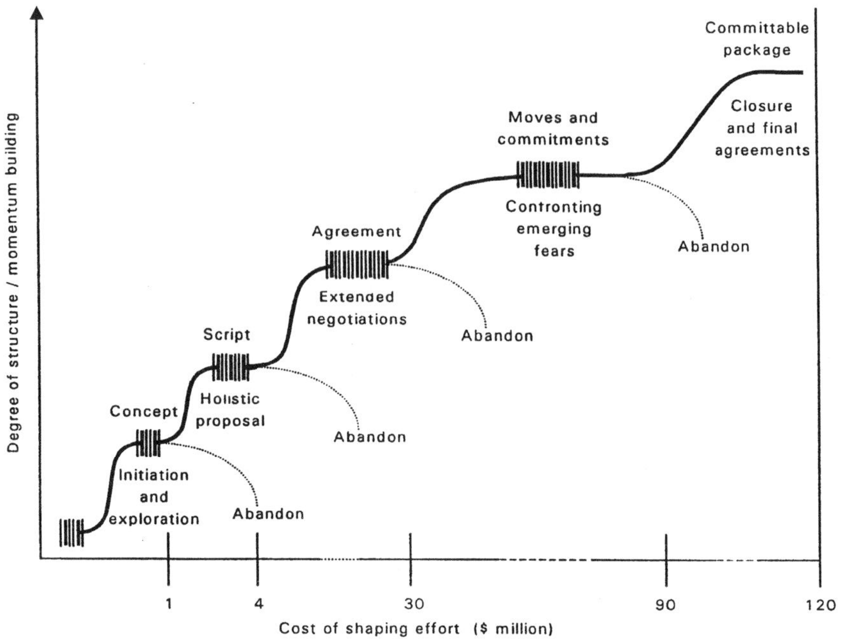

Figure 4.4
Crossing hurdles over many episodes

Resources of a few million dollars are assigned for exploration of a project concept. To test the initial hypothesis, feasibility can be studied in a planned manner, as in large utilities, or in a rough venture approach, as by entrepreneurial groups. Exploratory searches are conducted internally or in collaboration with external parties; at this time, solutions and perceived risks are sketched out. In the IMEC sample, the dominant modes of exploration were a team in symbiosis with external consultants (16 percent), open idea competition (20 percent), strategic-planning groups (30 percent), and entrepreneur design (28 percent).

Conceptual closure is achieved after a year or two, when independent studies confirm the viability of the concept. The output is a series of documents sketching out ideas covering a variety of topics but with an emphasis on technical issues. The most common form is a position paper presented to legitimate authorities, such as ministers or boards of directors.

Development of holistic proposals. The leading sponsor starts with "horseback" assumptions on most dimensions of the project, as

Table 4.1
Episodes of successive shaping efforts

Episode	Coalition building	Dominant risk	Configuration and conceptual closure	Leadership sponsorship
Initiation and exploration	Narrow coalition led by a champion	Is there a sponsor able to carry risks and finance development effort? Is project holistically feasible: economically, politically, socially, technically?	Sketchy definition of initial hypothesis: multidimensional concept, memorandum of understanding	Entrepreneur, developer, or government group promotes initial hypothesis
Development of holistic proposal	Initial coalition plus developers ready to sponsor project	Do early estimates still leave the project holistically feasible?	Proposal containing "horseback" estimates	Leadership shared between client and developers or bidders
Extended negotiation	Core coalition includes leader, developers, bankers, and government agencies	Working details to ensure viability, identify risks, assign responsibilities, and provide guarantees	Volume of contracts detailing all dimensions of project configurations	Leadership shared between client and chosen developer
Confronting emerging fears	Sponsorship coalition extends to gain consent from social and environmental groups	Is the feasible project able to carry real social-environmental costs that arise?	Viable concepts expanded to include social benefits, compensation, environmental plan, and symbolic aspects	Leadership is the sponsorship coalition with affected parties as autonomous decision makers
Closure on a committable package	Sponsorship coalition may include government agencies	Formal agreements lock projects into decisions allowing execution	Complex project documents detailing formal agreement	Leadership is passed to developers/owners interacting with engineering contractor and suppliers

sketched out in the previous episode, to develop a holistic proposal: financial and technical parameters, social acceptability, environmental challenges, and regulatory decisions and permits. Innovative ideas can be articulated on how to bring costs down, raise revenues, and gain consent. The central issue is to maintain a perspective that avoids blindness to risks.

Early on, sponsors and partners outline a proposed system of governance, a division of responsibilities, the competencies required, and the necessary commitments. The sponsor then builds a fully developed script addressing pertinent risks and providing concrete solutions. The holistic proposal is then presented either as a bid to a client or as a business case to investors. Preparing a proposal when the client-owner is a government can be expensive, representing an average of US$15 million for a bridge or subway. Bidding costs are so high that many sponsors can no longer afford to play.

Extended negotiations. Assuming that the holistic proposal has been selected, the leader and its partners work through the assumptions concerning risks, revenues, costs, guarantees, engineering design, and other factors. Assumptions often need to be reworked. Many relationships were sketched, but they now have to be made operational.

Numerous issues skipped in the bidding process are discovered that require solutions through negotiation and problem resolution. Such issues may include definition of property rights to protect sponsors; development of guarantees to protect clients from completion risks faced by sponsors; negotiation of terms of guarantees and covenants to protect banks and investors; determination of the public contribution in the case of projects where toll revenues are insufficient; determination of pricing structures and conditions of the concession; and identification of rules, regulations, and laws that will have to be modified to provide security to the project.

When a government is the client, negotiations of agreements have to meet additional criteria of transparency, probity, and accountability. Negotiations usually extend over many years because different departments have distinct requirements and expectations. Many winners of competitions, with beautiful holistic proposals, are dismayed when they have to restart negotiations after winning a bid and spend US$15 to 20 million just to work out issues that they thought were resolved.

Confronting emerging fears. During negotiations, social and environmental issues have been studied but not faced. As information is made public, however, external effects and pressure groups are triggered.

Issues rise high on the political agenda. In a large number of projects, extensive delays occur at this stage.

Facing social and environmental fears is an expensive affair. Sponsors have to bind themselves through negotiations and actions to gain consent. Promises to engage in future actions are insufficient. Concrete moves and commitments to meet expectations and solve social and environmental issues have to be made.

If parties are unable to forge agreements, they must wait for court or government decisions. The presence of public social- and environmental-assessment frameworks is extremely important here in helping to solve dilemmas. Delays are the inevitable consequence of such formal assessments, but the public framework builds legitimacy and forces parties either to make trade-offs or to kill the project.

Closure on a committable package. Commitment on a final package takes place when all major issues have been resolved. In many projects, sponsors have spent a few hundred million dollars to gain consent, solve social and environmental issues, and build agreements. The slow front-end shaping period closes with agreements on a committable package, and the sprint to engineering, procurement, and construction may then begin.

Leadership may tend to be different in each episode. During the initiation period, entrepreneurs or political officials tend to be leaders until a credible client accepts the project as a viable idea. In developing proposals and negotiations, two leaders, the client and the sponsor-developer, interact. During construction, leadership is shared between the owner and contractors.

Practices followed by the leader during shaping may induce efficiency or inefficiency. Practices that contribute to efficient shaping range widely: early involvement of bankers and partners, early integration of suppliers, debates and a contention framework, joint decision making, and so forth. Practices that induce inefficiencies, on the other hand, usually involve narrow diversity of expertise, early lock-in, urgency, dominated decision making, disregard for opponents, and so forth. Yet, no single best practice will determine the success of a project.

Shaping as the Creation and Exercise of Options

The front-end process and its many episodes can be readily interpreted in terms of the real-options framework that is currently revolutionizing academic treatments of project evaluation. In fact, as is often the case with cutting-edge practice, sponsors have been successful at creating value through the creation and exercise of sequential options without explicitly framing the process in options terms. Academics have simply codified this practice in the form of a new conceptual framework. The fact that development of the framework follows rather than leads practice, however, does not imply that it is of little value. Rather, it helps to identify elements of practice that are truly important to success and provides a high-powered framework for adapting practice to new situations.

The real-options framework is based on the same logic as that of financial options as developed by Black and Scholes (1974). Dixit and Pindyck (1995) and Trigeorgis (1996) extend options theory to real options, while Laughton and Jacoby (1993) provide exact operational specification for options valuation in the case of energy and other natural-resource projects with "well-behaved" exogenous value drivers. Amram and Kulatilaka (1999) suggest pragmatic approaches to applying real-options logic in a broader set of cases. Kulatilaka and Lessard (1998) demonstrate how the real-options approach can be combined with a decision-tree framework.

The real-options approach recognizes that decisions determining project cash flows in conjunction with exogenous events are not all made at the outset but are made sequentially over episodes. The key insight of this approach is that uncertainty or volatility can increase the value of a project, as long as flexibility is preserved and resources are not irreversibly committed. As a result, the economic value of a project when it is still relatively unformed is often greater than the discounted present value of the expected future cash flows. Value is increased by creating options for subsequent sequential choices and exercising these options in a timely fashion. For example, a proposal for a project that loses money under most circumstances but makes a great deal of money in a few scenarios may be highly valuable, even if it loses money on average, if most of the investment can be delayed until the key outcomes are known. Thus, sponsors seek projects that have the potential for large payoffs under particular institutional and technical circumstances, and then they embark on learning paths and institutional trajectories that open up these possibilities.

Learning takes the form of a series of practice climbs that scope out the terrain at the same time as the team develops competencies. These new competencies, in turn, allow the climbing party to tackle mountains that they previously could not and also to spot new high-value peaks to climb. Each of the five episodes of project shaping described above can be reinterpreted in options terms. The initiation and exploration episode for instance, seeks to open and explore a project concept at relatively low cost. If this investment is successful, the option obtained is "exercised" by investing in an integrated project scheme that is used as a basis for negotiating a series of reciprocal commitments among the sponsor, providers of specialized services, key sources of finance, and key external stakeholders. These parties typically contribute cash to further development of the project, but they also use their reputation as hostage to developing the project potential in good faith.

Cumulative experience and reputation is the core capability of leading players in LEPs. If the project does not pan out for reasons beyond the control of the parties, their cost is limited to their cash investment. If it fails due to the opportunistic behavior of an individual party, though, that party also forfeits its reputation and its associated options to enter into future prospects. Ultimately, to go ahead with a project, the leading sponsor and its partners must commit the full resources required, but this is usually only after a period of many years.

A specific design configuration should be locked in only when the option of postponing the choice is no longer attractive, either because postponement is not feasible or because further negotiations and study are unlikely to reveal valuable new information. A project should be abandoned if the options it represents no longer have economic value in excess of the cost of keeping those options open.

One notorious example of premature lock-in was the choice of drilling technology for the English Channel Tunnel before soil conditions were fully known. To have kept this option open for a longer period would have required not only duplicate engineering expenditures but also a more relational set of arrangements among the various participants to provide the right incentives for the selection and execution of a particular technical task. Thus, the ability to create options depends not only on envisioning possible circumstances under which alternative approaches might be desirable but also on creating the relationships among sponsors, specialists, financiers, and stakeholders that will allow choices to be made at future points free from opportunistic behaviors by specific parties.

A contrasting case of keeping organizational options open is provided by the revived ITA project in Brazil; having abandoned the project in 1983, Electrosul restarted it in 1993. Faced with an increasing annual demand growth of almost 8 percent but unable to borrow, Electrosul sought external proposals. Four industrial firms, forming the CAPI consortium, took the project and reshaped it totally, funding all expenditures and studying many options. Financial lock-in occurred after construction started. Sponsors had spent almost US$1 billion on engineering work without having decided on final financing solutions.

There is no question that long front-end shaping processes are costly. But is this complexity, and the resulting high transaction, negotiation, and social costs, worth the benefits it brings? Governance costs have to be added to capital and operation costs if one is to understand project efficiency. High planning and negotiation costs are expenses needed to explore unknown terrain and adapt to changing environments. Complex governance structures are required when tasks cannot be specified in advance, especially in LEPs that are characterized by low appropriability and significant investments in specific assets that cannot be redeployed easily to other projects (Williamson 1991a, 1991b, 1992).

The IMEC findings indicate that projects that later display good performance usually had messy or stormy front-end processes and were often characterized by high shaping costs. In other words, later performance, while taking into consideration the inherent difficulties of projects, is better when the front-end decision is characterized by long duration, complex coalitions, numerous iterations, and strong leadership.

5 Strategic Systems and Templates

Serghei Floricel and Roger Miller

The economic success and social integration of a project depend not only on sponsors' abilities to overcome constraints, such as limited resources and regulations, but, to a large extent, on their capabilities to avoid future, not yet real, events. Hence, sponsors work to prevent risks, reduce the probability of their occurrence, and minimize their negative effects on the project.

Viewing risks as "dangers" requires the identification of specific future events, such as the enactment of a regulation or the failure of a contractor. As specific events are difficult to imagine, managers attempt to identify relevant classes of future events, which we term risk categories—market, regulatory, social acceptability, financial, and so on—all of which might cause difficulties to the project.

Risks anticipated ex ante during front-end shaping and events that later occur in the course of implementation and ramp-up are not necessarily the same. First of all, many of the anticipated negative events simply do not occur; worries prove to be unfounded. Second, totally unexpected events occur. These "surprises" result from lack of knowledge and information, including outright errors and oversights, or from the indeterminate nature of reality. The outcomes of dynamic, nonlinear processes are impossible to predict, even with the most complete knowledge of the present situation. Emergent processes, whether exogenous or endogenous, create turbulence. Figure 5.1 presents schematically the difference between anticipated risks and real events. Following Luhmann (1992), we term the distance between anticipated risks and sets of events that really occurred the *time discontinuity* experienced by managers. This distance reflects the perceived turbulence that affects projects.

Analysis of the projects in the IMEC sample made it clear that sponsors' strategizing focuses primarily on creating a strategic system of

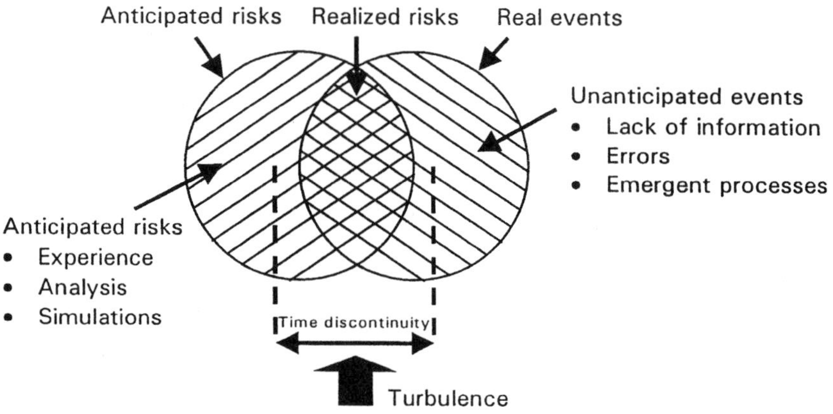

Figure 5.1
Anticipated risks and real events

devices to cope with anticipated risks. Turbulence—the possibility that completely unexpected events will threaten the project—is, at this stage, a secondary preoccupation. This issue will be dealt with in the next chapter.

This chapter focuses on the way managers build strategic systems with scope. Existing approaches tend to focus on execution risks rather than front-end ones. For instance, the Project Management Institute (1996) presents risk management as an activity that follows project definition and planning. IMEC research, on the contrary, observed that risk identification, imagining, and strategizing are the central activities of front-end shaping. Risk identification focuses on strategic issues, such as the possible inability to obtain adequate financing, the leveling off of the project's market, a significant increase in fuel costs, or widespread protests against the project. Strategizing looks for solutions to avoid or to mitigate these undesirable futures.

Risk strategizing follows the layering process described in chapter 3. First, managers engage collectively, in formal or informal ways, in prospective envisioning and imagining to identify as many of the potential risks faced by the project as possible: this is risk unbundling. Second, managers use templates to help understand how risks might be dealt with. Third, managers call on their own experience or consultants to design a series of devices to provide scope to the strategic system that they design to cope with anticipated risks. The devices that managers use are adapted to the nature they attribute to a given risk. The matching of risks with devices is always incomplete and subjected to cost-benefit analysis.

The strategizing process is highly empirical and grounded. First, while resulting from a prospective endeavor, a strategic system is not necessarily built through detached theorizing about the future by a group of experts. Rather, reality is tested through probes, experiments, and debates, and strategies are selected with the participation of many organizations and groups through negotiations or even disputes. Second, the resulting strategic system will not be a contingent adaptation to some abstract risks but a construction that is highly dependent on subjective perception, the flow of events, and the knowledge of coming changes.

The Unbundling of Project Risk

The identification of dangers—risk events—is the basis for the construction of a strategic system with scope. The role of risk unbundling is to focus sponsors' attention on certain aspects of the project and its relations to the environment, and to extend the conceptual focus into a future in which dangers may originate from many sources. Each identified risk or risk category is later addressed, for instance, by allocating responsibility to cospecialized participants, requiring commitments and covenants, and so forth. Identification and strategizing are done informally or formally in strategy sessions, negotiations, and risk seminars. Investment bankers and lawyers are often key actors in managing the decision conferences in which risks and strategies are openly discussed.

Chapter 3 presented the managerial unbundling of project risks into three categories—market-related, technical, and institutional—each of which was further broken down into many items. Figure 5.2 summarizes the categories of unbundled risks and suggests some relations among different categories.

Templates for Strategizing about Risks

In designing strategies to face risks, managers use their experience but also conceptual templates that are shared within the project community around the world. Templates are practical models that are widely promoted and can be used to inform strategic decisions. Conferences on infrastructure or on public–private partnerships are held regularly

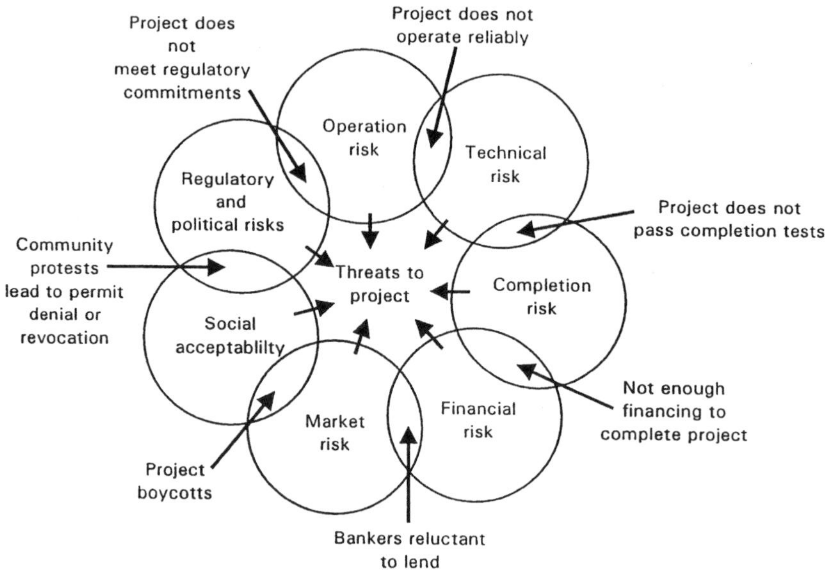

Figure 5.2
Categories of unbundled risks

around the world to promote templates such as BOTs, concessions, and project financing.

Templates are produced and promoted independently by consultants, academics, engineering firms, law firms, banks, governmental agencies, international financial agencies, and project owners; they are given life in conferences and publications. They circulate rather quickly through consulting interventions, industry seminars, books, and electronic media. Some templates are presented as best practices to underscore the "rational" motives for their creation, use, and diffusion. Others, however, are "rationalizing myths" (Meyer and Rowan 1977), because their adoption is based more on expectations and hype than on proven benefits (DiMaggio and Powell 1983; Tolbert and Zucker 1983). As Abrahamson (1996) pointed out, the initial excitement often leads to dysfunctional phenomena, such as the emergence of consulting firms that specialize in overpromoting certain templates.

Table 5.1 lists the twenty templates used by sponsors in the sixty IMEC projects; the templates were identified by a careful reading of narratives. Instead of offering specific solutions to particular risks faced by a project, templates sketch systems of solutions, which simultaneously address several risks by combining different strategies. The

Table 5.1
Templates used in IMEC projects

Financial	Nonrecourse project financing
	Public placement of bonds
	Credit grading by rating agencies
	Risk-analysis seminars
Ownership	Alliances of partners
	PPA-BOT-concession
	Repowering
	Entrepreneurial projects-IPPs
Contract	Turnkey contracting
	Round-table decisions
	Design-finance-build-contract
	Frame supply agreement
Organizational	Participatory engineering
	Continuous commissioning
	Partnering with contractors-suppliers
	Coengineering in design with suppliers
Legitimacy	Codefinition with regulator
	Public-private partnerships
	Mutual-gains approach
	State agreements

twenty templates in the table are grouped into areas of concern: finance, ownership, contracting, organizational, and legitimacy.

Despite the uncritical adoption and often faddish nature of some templates, they play a positive role in reducing managers' confusion and anxiety in the face of new circumstances by offering cognitively legitimated solutions. Sponsors find in them a shared vision and language that replace the challenges to coherence provided by rational-system arrangements. They give managers building blocks for developing the strategic system of each project. Here are descriptions of some of these templates.

Nonrecourse project financing appeared in the mid-1980s as a method for financing projects strictly on expected future revenues without the security provided by sponsors' assets or government guarantees. Traditionally, projects were financed by owners on their balance sheets—that is, by including the investment among the firm's assets and guarantees. Nonrecourse project financing became popular because entrepreneurial sponsors and developers needed capital, had few assets, and could lay off some of the risks to bankers for an interest premium. Lenders were invited to assess not the corporate balance sheet but the project as an equity to be funded exclusively on its merits. The main features of nonrecourse project financing are the establishment of a separate firm for the project, an important equity position provided by the sponsor, extensive contractual agreements linking sponsors and clients, and the project operating with a high ratio of debt to equity with lenders having only limited recourse in the event of default (Brealey, Cooper, and Habib 1996).

A good portion of the projects that IMEC studied were financed using variations of this template. Even established utilities attempted to use it to keep new projects off their balance sheets. What surprised IMEC researchers, however, was that few projects met the idealistic criteria of nonrecourse project financing because bankers felt uneasy and demanded guarantees, strong assets, and the bundling of multiple streams of income to provide security.

Build-operate-transfer arrangements. BOTs address the economic and legitimacy issues created by the private ownership of infrastructure projects. In the early 1980s, in the aftermath of the Third World debt crisis, many countries were faced with the impossibility of financing their infrastructure projects in the traditional way, by government borrowing, multilateral agencies, and export credit corporations. In the BOT model, governments award a concession to a private sponsor, which operates it for a number of years, sufficient to repay the debt and even make a profit. After the end of the period, the project reverts to the government. Based on this concession, the sponsor and its consortium can arrange financing, construction, and operations. The BOT template assigns private developers a number of risks: financing, completion, operating, and, in part, market. In rational-systems arrangements, all of these risks were normally borne by large sponsors and government agencies. Many of the projects IMEC studied used variations of the BOT model: the Ankara Metro and the Birecik hydroelectric dam in Turkey; the Hub thermal-power project in Pakistan; the Navotas project in the Philippines; the Hopewell project in Thailand; and the Bakun project in Malaysia.

This template was also applied in many developed countries. Road-transportation infrastructure in most countries was traditionally managed and financed by government agencies. Tight public spending policies, however, did not provide sufficient funds to cover growing needs. Banks and engineering contractors proposed various schemes to allow for the private financing of these projects.

Turnkey contracts. Such contracts address issues raised by the contractual relations between owners and contractors. In the traditional approach, owners design projects and divide them into many work packages that are awarded competitively. With the transition toward entrepreneurial sponsorship, completion risks had to be shifted to skilled parties: sole-responsibility fixed-cost contracts, also known as turnkey, became common.

In a turnkey contract, a single organization contracts with a sponsor for the design and construction of the project, usually for a fixed price and with a set delivery date. Heavy penalties and liquidated damages are stipulated. Almost all projects built using a concession BOT approach or PPAs have used turnkey contracts for execution. Network operators also began adopting this approach.

The prime contractor in a turnkey project may decide to use cooperative relationships with subsystems or module contractors and suppliers to achieve cost reductions. It may, however, prefer to use fixed-price sole responsibility in the traditional manner.

Repowering. Repowering means reusing the site or some of the equipment of an existing but outmoded plant by bringing in new systems: for example, old boilers are replaced with gas turbines and heat-exchange steam generators to produce a combined-cycle plant. It is a common template in Japan, eastern Europe, and North America, and has been heavily used by American utilities. Although repowering raises efficiency, sponsors use it mainly because it makes it easier to obtain environmental permits and "certificates of need." No new sites, transmission lines, or social agreements are necessary; furthermore, pollution is drastically reduced. Utilities use repowering to prevent IPPs from invading their turf.

Credit grading. This template, used by agencies or banks, can be very helpful to sponsors. The creditworthiness of a project is ultimately judged on the ability of expected cash flow to pay debts. In assessing projects, Standard and Poor, for instance, explicitly uses a two-dimensional typology proposed by Perrow (1984). The model assumes that projects can be evaluated on the degree of interaction between technical subsystems and the types of linkages. The degree of interaction between subsystems can range from linear to complex. Linkages can be loose or tight. Nuclear-power projects are complex and lightly linked, while telecommunications projects are complex and loosely linked. Risk assessment focuses on issues such as project assumptions, engineering and design, construction, operation and maintenance, and financial pro formas. Weaknesses in project information are indications that sponsors have not adequately addressed critical areas; they tend to raise concerns and lower ratings.

Mutual gains. In this template, the emphasis is on how sponsors can face affected parties with rights, voice, and power. Disregard of the capabilities of affected parties, whether their fears are judged to be founded or irrational, can and does lead to disaster. Once triggered into organizing themselves, affected parties can stop almost any project. Stonewalling, faking, and designing dubious counterattacks will backfire. The worst case is when the sponsor claims to represent the sovereign, which would find it humiliating to negotiate.

The mutual-gains template provides a framework for dealing with affected and angry parties (Susskind and Field 1996). First, the sponsor tries to frame the problem from the perspectives of those who are unwillingly affected, taking a few steps back from its own interests. Second, joint fact finding is encouraged to deliver believable information. Third, commitments are offered to compensate for both knowable and unknowable effects. When the unexpected occurs, the sponsor must accept responsibility, admit its error, and share power. Only by acting trustworthily and building long-term relationships will the sponsor induce affected parties to consent.

Templates evolve, are enriched, and eventually are abandoned. Applications in projects reveal problems and refinements are then proposed. For instance, turnkey contracts were criticized because they allowed little control over project quality by the owner. Burns & McDonnell, an engineering firm, devised a new type of turnkey contract that allowed the owners to request changes, as long as a balance was maintained between additional costs and savings, and included an original mechanism for resolving disputes.

Project financing has also evolved from the ten- to eighteen-year bank loans and the 4:1 debt ratio that were typical of initial applications. Later projects sought ratings from credit agencies and issued bonds on public markets by registering with the Securities and Exchange Commission. Guarantees are sometimes sought to buttress payments. Moreover, financial managers have discovered that contractual securitizing often cannot save a project. Analyses get tighter and few projects survive screening processes: each year, only one out of every eight projects succeeds in obtaining financing.

Some templates become archetypes around which new laws are built. For instance, the BOT model became the basis for the Private Finance Initiative in the United Kingdom. In Pakistan, the experience gained in the Hub project led to the establishment of one of the most comprehensive pieces of BOT legislation in the world.

Designing Strategic Systems with Scope

A risk can be thought of as the result of a process that sponsors cannot entirely predict or control because they ignore the underlying causal structure. The future is difficult to assess, because it depends on factors over which sponsors have little control, evolution can only be imperfectly monitored, or processes are complex and nonlinear. Strategizing to face risks under these conditions is particularly important at the front end.

The layering process of strategizing described in chapter 3 will be used by sponsors to build a strategic system to cope with risks. Sponsors will try to avoid certain risks, reduce uncertainty by investing in understanding risks, share risks with others, and shift risk to others. They will further attempt to achieve control by endogenization, increasing flexibility, building provisions, and diversifying.

The matching of unbundled risks and devices as imagined from templates, experience, and the specifics of each project is the sponsor's responsibility. Through reasoned approaches, sponsors match—as best they can—templates, devices, and risks to form a strategic system with enough scope to cope with most risks that can be anticipated.

The devices used by sponsors to provide some degree of risk-facing capability are numerous. Table 5.2 lists the twenty-seven devices used by sponsors in the IMEC study. The devices fall into the following categories: information search, network and coalition building, design and configuration, structuring incentives and contracts, and influence and bold actions.

Information Search

Devices in this category include studies, expert evaluations, debates, scenarios, risk seminars, and strategy teams. Studies take many forms, including documentary research, surveys, engineering studies, and simulations. Building scenarios or simulation models with a Monte Carlo risk generator is a frequently used device. Each method has different values as a function of the nature of the problem and the types of anticipated risks.

Well-performed tests are among the most reliable tools for solving technical and interorganizational problems. Relying on historical data

Table 5.2
Devices used in building strategic systems

Information search	Research and studies Expert judgments Debates, scenarios, risk seminars Multidisciplinary strategy teams
Network building and cooptation	Early involvement of financiers, operators, and others Public-private partnerships Alliance of owners sharing equity Partnerships with suppliers-contractors Coalitions with affected parties
Structures of incentives, and contracts	Risks-decision rights allocation Type and number of contracts Incentives-penalties Frame agreements Methods of contractor selection
Project-design configuration	Select geographical location-site Complementary investments and linkages Contract flexibility, ability to restructure Flexible-modular technical solutions Flexible contracts-contractual options
Influence and bold actions	Educate regulator, rating agencies, and others Side payments: compensation, add-ons Preemptive action, signals Climate of optimism Windows of opportunity Signal probity (e.g., bidding) Seek and improve on legal requirements Change laws and regulations

to extrapolate may be useful in stable environments but has limits in a turbulent environment, as information quickly becomes obsolete. Nondestructive tests, such as floating proposals or ideas in negotiations, may reveal much about the strength of commitment and the credibility of players.

The most successful devices tap proactively into as many different perspectives on the project as possible, both inside and outside the sponsoring company, and build scenarios of the future. Devices include seeking, as early as possible, the opinions of opponents, governments, bankers, regulators, and local communities through face-to-face meetings. Visiting suppliers and similar projects, issuing calls for idea competitions, hiring suppliers as consultants, and starting negotiations with suppliers are also useful devices. Opening discussions with bankers early opens paths to innovative funding solutions.

Explicit information and tacit knowledge are used to build scenarios in decision conferences or risk seminars. Scenarios are designed by collecting subjective judgments, imagining likely future events, and arriving at some agreement on likely trajectories. They are not plans but rich alternative futures that have been conceptualized enough to be discussed and shared across executives or firms.

The involvement of cospecialized players is particularly important in early front-end analyses. GTM-Entrepose, a large French EPC firm, has developed a network of experienced partners in law firms, investment banks, and financial intermediaries that it can call upon to assess project opportunities. Teams of approximately ten senior managers, working for a two-week period, can decide, with a degree of informed knowledge, whether a project opportunity is worth the expensive shaping efforts necessary to create value.

Public Service Electric and Gas Co., a New Jersey utility, set up a multidisciplinary strategy team from the engineering, finance, environmental, and public-relations sectors to uncover the risks facing its Bergen repowering project. The strategy team recommended, as suggested by public relations, to talk to regulators to uncover their concerns. This approach substantially reduced regulatory risks; in fact, the regulator proved to be interested in innovative approaches. Another developer literally "spent hours on peoples' porches" to understand their concerns.

Knowing more about the underlying processes that create risks does not mean that uncertainties are adequately addressed; thorough studies may even give a false sense of security. A biased focus may give the illusion that all risks have been studied because so much energy was expended on a few. A manager who participated in a failed project spoke about risks with IMEC researchers:

> Concerns about the risks associated with the project were rationalized away. There was a recognition early on about the risk entailed by the ability to commit power from the plant. Through studies and analysis, people convinced themselves that risks did not really exist. We recognized risks but did not address them.

Network Building and Cooptation

Devices for using this tactic include alliances, public–private partnerships, early integration, and frame agreements. Cooptation strategies allow the project sponsors to secure a basic set of core competencies to increase control over the critical areas of the project, and to gain access to financing or political influence. Other basic cooptation devices include hiring, expert contracting with competent firms, and initiating long-term coalitions.

IMEC research shows that successful sponsors favor early development coalitions with partners of varying expertise: developers, EPC firms, investment banks, local firms that understand the environment, and government agencies. These complementary participants bring not only knowledge and experience but also reputation, influence, and financial resources. For instance, the coalition for the Hub power-plant project built in Pakistan was led by a Saudi firm that understood the local environment and the particularities of doing business in an Islamic environment. The project also included a large European power-plant operator, the World Bank, Japan's EXIM Bank, and other banks.

Many of the projects that IMEC studied were not internally financed but used external sources such as banks, bond markets, or international financial institutions. Sponsors often hire investment bankers to assist in identifying sources of funds, structuring the financial package, helping in relations with rating agencies, and promoting bond issues to potential investors. Some partners with "deep pockets" are coopted as equity investors to offer security to lenders. For instance, US Generating Co., which was at the time jointly owned by Bechtel and Pacific Gas and Electric, brought GE Capital in as a 40 percent equity partner in three projects that it developed in the early 1990s.

Firms that lack the required technical, project-management, and operating competencies bring in consultants or hire experts. Engineering consultants assist in project definition, feasibility analysis, detailed engineering, preparation of specifications in the selection of contractors, and other activities. Banks use independent engineers to perform due-diligence reviews of designs and cost estimates, propose and negotiate changes, monitor construction, and so forth. Sponsors seek partners who have complementary engineering, technical, and operational experience. In innovative projects, engineering firms and equipment suppliers are invited to join in the ownership.

To mitigate social-acceptability and political risks, stakeholders such as regulators, community, and environmentalist groups are also included early. In some cases, the government is even brought in as an equity partner. Cooptation of parties that retain autonomous agendas, however, is always incomplete. The purpose is to bring outside parties to express their points of view inside the coalition and exert influence. If this is badly done, however, intransigent reactions may emerge from those who feel that cooptation has led to buyoff.

Structures of Incentives and Contracts

These devices use incentives and contracts to build project organization and allocate decision rights as well as risks. Examples are assignment of authority and allocation of responsibilities, incentives, and risks; hierarchical, quasi-hierarchical, and contractual links; project organizational forms; and financial structure. Using structural devices, sponsors can increase control and allocate risks, limit negative consequences, and diversify.

The allocation of risks and responsibilities between different participants is a recurring theme in the project-management literature (Chapman and Ward 1994; Floricel and Lampel 1998). The goal is to allocate responsibility for dealing with a certain risk to the participant deemed to have the most adequate combination of skills, resources, control, information, and risk-bearing capacity. Incentives are designed to trigger appropriate behavior. For instance, if a contractor is awarded a contract with a fixed cost and a certain delivery date, but must pay liquidated damages in case of nonperformance, the completion risk for the agreed scope of the contract is allocated to the contractor. This solution creates new risks, however, stemming from the loss of direct control by the owner.

The number and types of contracts into which the project execution is divided are also structural devices. By awarding a large number of contracts, owners maintain a higher degree of control than by awarding the entire project design and construction to only one firm or consortium. Methods of contractor selection are also important. An open bidding process usually seeks to squeeze price reductions out of contractors. In contrast, an invitation to bid addressed to selected expert firms and direct negotiations with a sole source, perhaps within a frame agreement spanning several projects, are ways to create relationships in which owners and contractors will work together to develop innovative solutions.

Contractual risk-allocation devices can be very subtle. For instance, formulas can be designed in which the additional costs resulting from operating a power plant at a suboptimal level are passed on to the utility that signed a PPA and is responsible for dispatch, including the capacity at which the plant is used. Hence, a part of the operating cost is passed to the client, which has both control of and an interest in using the plant economically and reaps systemic gains from dispatching decisions.

Organizational devices also reduce the likelihood of risks by creating conditions for effective monitoring and problem resolution. Among the most important forms identified by IMEC's research are roundtables and decision conferences that bring together managers from the client, owner, and contractor organizations. For instance, in the Njord project, an oil platform in the Norwegian continental shelf, Norsk Hydro used decision conferences with contractors and suppliers to address issues proactively and solve them in innovative ways. This led to a 40 percent reduction in capital required for the project. Frame agreements were built after this positive experience.

Contractual devices can be designed to avoid rigidities. Contracts are made flexible by introducing special clauses and can be used to alter the timing and sequencing of activities to achieve reduced risk. Faced with the prospect of a delay in regulatory approval, for instance, the managers of a project may decide to continue with material delivery but to delay all but the most essential construction activities, as the contract allows.

Project Design and Configuration

This aspect includes devices such as siting, complementary investments, technical choices, and add-ons. Project attributes, such as size, capacity, and basic technological solutions, can be used to reduce the likelihood of adverse events and to increase flexibility or control. For instance, to obtain permits for a new power plant, a developer may target depressed areas in need of job creation and avoid locations close to natural parks, sensitive ecosystems, and areas in which environmental pollution exceeds federally mandated limits. Japanese industrial firms own old steel-plant or factory sites that are valuable for locating power plants.

Instead of the customary arrangements of buildings and equipment according to technical rationality, the Nanko project in Osaka Bay was also designed as a recreational park named Phoenix Alley, with palm trees and fishponds. After consultation with local authorities, Kansai Power decided to organize school visits, which became extremely popular. Redesigning the site reduced permitting risk and turned what could have been an ugly site into a socially valuable part of the Osaka Bay region. In fact, the site was on land reclaimed from the ocean.

Design strategies can also include flexible technical solutions. General design, however, may be hard to fit into the needs of a specific project. Perhaps the most extreme example of design to minimize risk is to put power plants on barges, as has been done in countries such as Guatemala, the Philippines, and the Dominican Republic. The architectural–engineering firm hired to design the airport in Oslo was asked to produce a design that would not be specific to any given location but feasible in the greater Oslo area. Debates involving politicians, the community, the military, and the general public raged for twenty years. The country's parliament, which was ultimately to decide, changed its preferred alternative several times.

Influence and Bold Actions

Influence devices range widely and may include communication strategies, side payments, education of regulators, signaling probity, and so forth. Such strategic tools have in common the fact that they are based on the actions of project sponsors: convincing and influencing stakeholders, exchanging favors, making symbolic gestures that enhance the legitimacy of the project, taking preemptive actions to change the environment, and making signal commitments to rivals or friends. Publicizing parallel action tracks is also used to communicate independence.

Proactive, persuasive, or political influence can avert many challenges. For instance, the Northumberland Strait Crossing project established a project office in the community and held town-hall meetings. Opposition weakened, and the region became an ally of the project. Similarly, MEG International in Montreal educated environmental regulators and the population, both of whom were concerned with environmental performance and the visual aspect of the chosen technical solutions for the Gazmont project. Consultants made presentations to regulators and the public to show that no fog would result in winter days; opposition then waned.

Marshaling political coalitions is a prerequisite in many projects. The Freudenau Dam on the Danube in Vienna was approved by a referendum after extensive joint efforts by Verbund, the sponsor, and the city of Vienna. In contrast, the sponsors of the Lambach project forged ahead without a proper coalition and were forced to stop. They had allied themselves with the bourgeois part of the city but forgot the working-class section called Stadl-Paura. When they recognized their mistake, they hired a professor from the University of Linzt, who held town meetings and worked out an agreement that eventually made the Lambach project feasible. Similarly, Destec Energy marshaled a wide coalition of coal-miners' unions and local chambers of commerce to sell its gasification project.

In exchange strategies, project participants and stakeholders usually commit not to use leverage against the project in exchange for benefits offered by sponsors. Some of these benefits take the form of compensation packages for affected parties. To appease the concerns of the homeowners located near the future site of a power plant, a sponsor created a property buyoff program through which the properties of dissatisfied owners were purchased. Other benefits include "gifts" offered to nearby communities, ranging from museums to theme parks and science centers. The same exchanges occur during negotiations with environmental permitting authorities. Project owners "voluntarily" reduce the emissions limits for their plants to help regulators.

Bold moves aim at taking advantage of windows of opportunity that emerge as projects evolve. Examples are signaling a strong commitment in spite of opposition; creating a climate of optimism, bordering on overconfidence; and marshaling political resources. Relying on his personal charisma, a young entrepreneur was able to convince the Canadian government to bend the rules of an oil and gas-drilling program to drill for gas in a large garbage dump.

Effective sponsors know that success depends on being able to demonstrate and uphold the conviction that the project has "all the elements in place," especially when support swings into adversarial attitudes as prospects of profitability diminish. Bold actions also consist of creating a regulatory precedent or seeking changes to laws. Often, especially in developing countries, LEPs hit the limits of institutions in areas such as land, ownership, and capital markets.

A reputation for being modern, law-abiding, or concerned is another way to reduce risks by gaining support. Project legitimization can be obtained by using procedures that signal probity. An effective legitimacy-enhancing strategy is to tell the truth and do better than legal requirements.

Finally, managers have at their disposal a wide variety of devices to build strategic systems and protect projects from dangers posed by

Table 5.3
Scope of strategic system and project performance

Project performance	Scope of strategic system: Low	Medium	High	Total	Percentage
Low	11	8	3	22	36.7
High	8	12	18	38	63.3
Total	19	20	21	60	
Percentage	31.7	33.3	35.0		100.0
Chi-square			Degree of freedom		Significance
Pearson	8.3		2		.01567

risks. All of these devices have costs. Some of them are out-of-pocket expenditures, such as those required for exchange strategies, design add-ons, or compensation. Other costs are intangible, such as rigidities and conflicts between client and contractors that limit the ability to respond to turbulence.

Project Performance and the Scope of Strategic Systems

Designing a strategic system with scope is costly but makes value creation possible by providing security to projects. There is obviously a point at which the costs of devices to cope with risks no longer contribute to value creation. Project sponsors know subjectively the marginal value of contributions of devices. What appears to outsiders to be an excessive expenditure may be justifiable when seen from the subjective viewpoint of sponsors.

Strategic systems—the set of distinct devices used to face risks—are usually effective when they have scope. In fact, one of the great exhilarating moments in the IMEC program was the testing of the link between the scope of strategic systems and project performance. By analyzing the content of the narratives written for each IMEC project, we created a list of twenty-seven of the most-used strategic devices (see table 5.2). Then, using the same project narratives, we identified which devices were actually used in each of the sixty projects. We then built an index of the scope of the strategic system for each project.

A statistical analysis showed that the index of the scope of strategic systems was significantly associated with project performance, defined as effectiveness in the introduction to this book. Table 5.3 presents the tabulation of strategic scope against project performance.

Strategic scope was defined according to three levels: high (more than seventeen devices), medium (seventeen to ten devices), and low (less than ten devices). The average number of devices used was 14.1, with a standard deviation of 5.58. The chi-square coefficient between strategic scope and project performance is 8.3 and is significant at .01567 with two degrees of freedom.

Scope, measured by counting devices, has obvious limitations as an indicator of strategic systems. First, devices are considered to be of equal impact, while in reality some may have more importance than others. Second, projects with high potential for value creation will allow sponsors the leisure of affording many devices to ensure success. Third, sponsors with high levels of resources will multiply devices and create positive-feedback loops. Further research is certainly recommended on the strategic impact of devices and their links to project performance.

Once a set of devices forming a strategic system with scope has been selected, it is possible to change a few, but core choices are difficult to change. Care thus has to be exercised in selecting devices. The set of devices used to match risks creates a structure of often largely irreversible commitments and creates a set of constraints that limit future possibilities for action, especially the ability of the project to respond to events that are impossible to anticipate.

The results shown in table 5.3 are interpreted to mean that the scope of strategic systems using a range of devices to deal with risks is more important than seeking to identify silver-bullet strategies or uncover a few ideal best ways. In other words, strategizing under conditions of risk means using a variety of devices simultaneously to create a strategic system with the scope to face expected adverse circumstances.

6 Building Governability into Project Structures

Roger Miller and Serghei Floricel

The overarching problem for sponsors is to coordinate their actions over time with pertinent organizations in such a way that both long- and short-term project issues are resolved. Sponsors develop reasoned approaches to matching knowable risks with appropriate strategies. To deal with potential but unknowable risks, sponsors of successful projects artfully infuse governability—the capacity of project participants to steer through unexpected turbulence—into project structures.

Turbulence

Turbulence and the Failures of Strategies

As IMEC's research proceeded, the recurrence of turbulence became clear. Strategies implemented to deal with anticipated risks were not necessarily effective in dealing with unexpected events; in fact, they often hampered the capacity to deal with them.

Turbulence is a surprise to decision makers, who usually base their actions on conceptual frames, or knowledge structures, that they have individually or collectively constructed. Most events appear normal against the background of such structures. Events that do not occur as anticipated, however, heighten attention, threaten, or pose puzzles.

Surprises introduce discontinuities—deeply felt differences between the future as it was imagined and the present reality. Both exogenous and endogenous events cause surprises. For instance, the manager of an American utility told IMEC researchers, "Market risks were not an issue when this project started. Now, of course, the situation is very different. We all thought that deregulation would be a slow process, but all of a sudden, we found ourselves in a deregulated environment." Unexpected inflexion points in price trends or sudden changes

Table 6.1
Examples of turbulent events affecting projects

Type	Example
Exogenous events	
Sociopolitical and macroeconomic	Financial crises (country or world)
	Major legislation (unexpected)
	Abrupt changes in input prices (oil, gas, etc.)
Unexpected natural events and discoveries	Bad weather, unforeseen geology
	Discovery of valuable natural resources
Direct opposition to project	Court challenges by pressure groups
	Organized community opposition
	International opposition
Sovereign behavior	Rule changes by regulator
	Refusal to grant permits
	Expropriation battles
	Granting of competing concessions
Endogenous events	
Coalition unraveling	Withdrawal or bankruptcy of major partners
	Opportunistic moves
	Difficulties experienced by one partner
Uncontrollable interactions	Unexpected consequences of strategies
	Social deadlocks
	Accidents, strikes
	Complementary work not ready
	Contractor bankruptcy
	Problems with new technology, site, etc.
Ramp-up	Forecasts proven wrong
	Expropriation

in public and political attitudes are other examples of surprises that cause turbulence. Table 6.1 gives examples of unexpected turbulent events in the IMEC research that temporarily stopped projects, required reassessments of viability, or demanded restructuring.

Sponsors of projects deal with anticipated risks, constraints, and issues by creating strategic systems with scope. In spite of their best efforts to design what they believe to be rational matches of project risks with strategies, however, failures occur. Here are a few vivid examples.

Sponsors overestimate their competencies. Buoyed by the euphoria of the late 1980s, numerous private parties were ready to take sponsorship risks because they expected the efficiencies of private ownership to compensate for such risks. Many concessions brought large losses to investors, however, because long-term risks contained too many surprises. Basic rules concerning the value of additional information were overlooked, and major irreversible choices were made because of the illusion that private sponsors knew best. As a consequence, winner's curse set in.

Firms are hungry for work. Concessions to build roads, tunnels, or subways often are proposed by government agencies without complete information on markets, physical conditions, or legislative risks. Sponsors bid to gain volume and assume major risks with the knowledge that they are operating on information that may prove to be false. Commitments made under conditions of ignorance often lead to big surprises.

Alliances between partners fail. Leaders of alliances discover that their partners cannot accept their share of sudden cash shortfalls. Cost overruns, combined with lower-than-forecast market revenues, cause cash binds. Bankers who have loaned on the basis of high debt-equity ratios suddenly go without payments. Policy disagreements between partners arise, covenants cannot be adjusted, and the absence of adjustment options leads to bankruptcy.

Regulators are uncooperative. Many projects experience failure because laws and regulations shift as they are being built. Regulators force renegotiation of agreed-upon projects, allow competing projects that cut market projections, and change rules midcourse after substantial sums have been spent. For instance, the Indiantown power project in Florida was built because regulators wanted to encourage power projects that did not depend on imported fuel. PURPA regulations were used to force utilities to sign PPAs with IPPs. Because of unexpected drops in fuel costs, the project now operates at 50 percent of capacity and survives only because Florida Power is obliged to honor its contractual obligations.

The Tendency of Projects to Disintegrate

The most striking phenomenon observed by IMEC was the tendency of projects facing turbulence to enter spirals of disintegration. Events combine with strategic inaction to trigger feedback processes that sponsors try to stop, but in the absence of solid governance and without the capacity to face difficulties, disintegration ensues.

South Trunk (a fictitious name) is an independent power project, built to burn waste coal from a nearby pile. The project performed very poorly, experiencing repeated difficulties in the coal- and ash-handling systems. Participants started blaming each other: the owner blamed the turnkey contractor for incompetence; the contractor, in turn, blamed the owner for delivering coal not as specified in the turnkey contract. The operator also blamed the coal-pile owner for not meeting fuel specifications. South Trunk's technical problems resulted from planning errors, but mostly from misallocation of risk and responsibility about the testing of waste coal. Moreover, the coal-pile owner had an exclusive, noncancelable contract with no incentive to blend the coal.

All managers interviewed agreed that a surprising reversal in coal prices killed the project; technical difficulties became merely a pretext. The unexpected downward trend, which made the project, as it was structured, essentially unprofitable in perspective, had not been predicted in spite of the fact that both the owner and the bank had used simulations, forecasts, prognosticators, and other methods. The project did not survive this surprise because the lack of cohesion in its organizational system precluded joint problem solving: the "blame game," formalism, and "positioning for arbitration" overtook all participants.

The turnkey contractor asked the owner to pay for changes that were, it claimed, imposed by the fuel nonconformity. The owner, a small entrepreneurial company, turned to the bank for an additional loan: the latter, in turn, wanted substantial changes to finish the project. The owner refused and threatened to declare bankruptcy. The bank agreed to purchase the project and revive it. Thereupon, the turnkey contractor asked the bank to pay for the changes. The bank refused and told the contractor to leave the site; the latter, in turn, put a lien on the project. The bank finally sold the project to the client utility for 25 percent of the original cost; the utility operated the project for one year and shut it down, arguing that it did not need the additional capacity.

The Tunnel Project (also a fictitious name) was hailed as a novel approach to solving urban traffic congestion and rejuvenating decaying parts of a large town. The innovative aspect of the project lay in its being a partnership among a regional government, two large EPC firms, and a group of banks. It became a privately financed concession after negotiations had produced what was believed to be a low-cost, effective solution. Front-end expenditures made by the regional government for access roads, embankments, and so forth made it possible for the project to operate as a concession: tolls paid for loans and promised to make the equity investment profitable.

Immediately after the tunnel opened, opposition by motorists to tolls and forced entrance points triggered challenges that could not be stopped, especially when it became public knowledge that the concessionaire was asking the regional government to increase its contribution. With the decision by the concessionaire to raise tolls because of cost overruns, public outcries emerged. Opponents of the project, who had reluctantly accepted it, suddenly realized that the public purse would have to pay to ensure "private profits." The head of the regional government then declared that tolls would be reduced and concessionaires would have to face up to their business risks.

The concessionaires then filed a suit against the regional government, claiming that unexpected geological conditions not specified in the contract had been found. As each successive group denied responsibility over a seven-year period, the project went from euphoria to a degenerative nightmare. Every bulwark that could have stopped this process of disintegration gave way in the face of difficulties. After the concession was cancelled by the courts, the regional government assumed responsibility for the project and hired a firm to operate the tunnel. The original private sponsors and banks were left with stranded equity investments and loans. Yet, the project served a need and thus could be restarted with new owners.

In the face of difficulties, participants have a tendency to leave projects and minimize losses, perhaps at the expense of other participants. The inability to counter centrifugal forces leads to failure. Reflecting back with private sponsors on the probable influences at work, it appears that failures occurred because unsuspected risks manifested themselves radically and strategies to deal with them were either absent or ineffective. Only the presence of governance capacity in project structure can provide some protection.

The Governance Capacity of Project Structures

Governance, from a management perspective, is the complex process of steering multiple firms, agencies, and organizations that are both operationally autonomous and structurally coupled in projects through various forms of reciprocal interdependencies (Jessop 1997). Coordination across strategically interdependent organizations often requires "partnership strategies" (Byrne 1998). Governance is a term with many meanings: its rise to prominence stems from the difficulties of hierarchical coordination, either by firms or by the state.

Types of Governance

Narrow. Corporate governance focuses on the control of managers by owners and investors (Aoki and Kim 1995). Institutions, practices, and rules are designed to constrain the generic tendency toward inside control by managers who capture strategic decision making. Efficient equity markets ensure stockholders' sovereignty, and property rights are developed (Alchian and Demsetz 1973; Barzel 1989). Bank-oriented governance, inspired by practices developed in Japan, France, and Germany, controls managerial dominance by having banks as active strategic investors and by the participation of financial intermediaries such as mutual funds, pension funds, and so forth.

Midrange. Economists search for optimal governance structures (Williamson 1992). The hypothesis is that over time, managers will arrive at forms of organization that will cope with opportunistic behavior and bounded rationality. Efficient contractual relations will range from markets for standard products to bilateral governance for recurrent products and hierarchical governance for specific assets.

Students of organizations view governance of networks as being fostered by informal social systems such as collective sanctions (penalties for malfeasance or incentives to conform); cost and gain of maintaining reputation; access restricted to competent players; incentives; and shared expectations and understanding (Jones, Hesterly, and Borgatti 1997). Collaboration counters adversarial relations (Gras 1993; Powell 1990) by pooling appreciations and tangible resources across organizations to solve sets of problems that cannot be solved individually (Ring and Van de Ven 1992).

Networks exist in high technology (DeBresson and Arress 1991; Saxenian 1994), movie production (Baker and Faulkner 1991), regional development (Miller and Côté 1987), financial services (Eccles and Crane 1987) and other sectors. Projects and alliances often fail, but they are nonetheless needed to link the needed complementary competencies (Doz 1993).

Broad. Governance is the integrative and generative force that counters the fragmentation of competencies among many firms, agencies, and bodies. Thus, leadership and systemic thinking are needed to make governance work (Gamson 1968; Jessop 1997).

Stakeholder analysis focuses on social control of business (Freeman 1982). Stakeholders are interest groups that can affect the performance of corporate objectives and are, in turn, affected by the achievement of objectives and by cospecialized parties, upon which sponsors depend for continued survival (suppliers, banks, shareholders). Firms with ethical concerns for stakeholders are said to have competitive advantages (Jones 1995).

The institutionalist approach aims to identify the various governance modes that enable coordination of major actors in society (North 1990). Modes of governance extend far beyond markets to include communities with solidarity, trust, and obligation; networks with voluntary exchange and contractual bonds; associations with closed membership; private hierarchies with asymmetric power, resources, and rules; and the state (through its various agencies), which has the right to use coercive power and develop institutional rules. Each society develops its own architecture, and optimal solutions are hard to identify (Coriat 1998; Hollingsworth and Boyer 1997).

Failures, as Schumpeter (1942) observed, can be positive. In the case of LEPs, however, the problem is not how to get rid of failures but how to transfer already built, useful, but failed projects to new owners. Governance is thus needed to define rules for new forms of ownership and procedures to be followed in case of bankruptcy. In this way, governance rules help to deal with emergent risks, prevent them from spreading, and contain processes of explosive positive feedback.

Project Governance Relationships

Instead of focusing on governance processes, which would lead us down many difficult-to-observe paths, our orientation will be to assess the capacity of projects to trigger governance processes in response to turbulence. Configurations of project structures are unequal in their ability to create value and adapt over time. Yet, the design of project structures can introduce potential governability that will trigger emergent processes to face turbulence: decisions, reactions to risk, codecisions, and cooperation. We need first to understand, however, how governance capacity, or governability, can be instilled into project structures.

Building governability relies on second-order strategic thinking, in which sponsors think through each relationship and organizational device for its ability to trigger appropriate responses should turbulence arise. The objectives sought in building governability are usually contradictory. For instance, long-term agreements are sought to provide security far into the future. Yet, the logical desired or undesired consequence of long-term agreements is inability to adapt. Sharing risks across organizations brings not only joint governance and sharing of returns, but greater adaptability. There are a number of relationships and devices that sponsors deliberately use to build in governability.

The leader's relationships with partners in ownership raise the following issues: whether commitment to adaptive behavior will remain strong; whether ownership interest will be balanced with contractor or supplier interest; whether partners will provide creativity and resources to face crises instead of escaping. Devices to spur owners to respond to turbulence include a strong equity position; integration of ownership and operation; diversity of competencies; alliances; and joint ventures.

Relationships with clients raise the following issues: whether the client will help by renegotiating PPAs or concessions, or will renege; whether the client will rescue the project with temporary cash-flow allocations; and whether individual clients will pressure the project with court challenges. Devices to influence governability include flexible PPAs, guaranteed revenues, and owner operation.

Relationships with banks and institutional investors raise the following issues: whether banks-investors will influence key actors to save the project; whether banks will agree to modify covenants; and whether restructuring will be considered a real option. Various devices will be used, including debt-equity balance, rendezvous clauses, guarantees, project financing, and visibility of lenders such as pension funds.

Relationships with affected parties raise the following issues: whether agreements will be reneged on; whether local and international groups will support the project over time; and whether benefits will be renegotiated. Devices used include negotiated compensation, sustained commitments, participatory approaches, and regional development agreements.

Relationships with contractors raise the following issues: whether contractors will respond with creativity or simply fall back on contracts; whether they will attempt to build the coalitions necessary to finish the project; and whether they will get involved in joint decision making.

Devices with governability properties include turnkey contracts, part-ownership by EPC firms, functional specifications, incentives in target price contracts, and frame agreements.

Relationships with operators raise governability issues during ramp-up, when reality sets in. Will the operator market the project energetically, cope with social crises, and bring efficiency to its optimal level? Devices to trigger the appropriate behavior include self-operation by sponsors, operating contracts with incentives, and concession/BOT/build-operate-own (BOO) arrangements. Most of these devices foster early responsible involvement with a view to the long-term horizon over which the project will be operated.

Relationships with the state raise the following issue: whether, in cases of turbulence, the state will honor its commitments, act as a bulwark, or change regulations. Devices that may enhance governability include formal agreements, direct involvement, and the presence of multilateral or bilateral agencies.

Responses to events provide projects with an almost organic ability to self-organize to face shocks and restructure. When the going gets tough, the tough save the project. Emergent processes to face turbulence consist of reactions to risk, codecision, and cooperation.

The Art of Designing Governability

Many devices can be used to infuse governability; table 6.2 lists twenty-nine devices that were used by sponsors in the IMEC sample with this overt intention. Examples of devices are three partners joined in ownership with balanced equity positions but with a strong leader; financial guarantees provided by a government to support the sponsorship coalition; sponsors with multiple project and revenue streams providing reserves to the project; rendezvous clauses making it possible to renegotiate contracts; integrated project teams with incentive to stimulate creativity; and multiple financing sources diversifying dependencies.

IMEC's inductive study of sixty projects led to identification of six properties that a project's structure can display. Each device can contribute to governability by enhancing bonding for internal cohesion; long-term coalitions; presence of reserves or stocks; flexibility options; generativity; and modularity and diversification. Through the presence or absence of devices, sponsors can hope to enhance the governability of project structures.

Table 6.2
Devices used by sponsors to instill governability

Relationships between leaders and owners	*Relationships with contractors*
alliance of equity owners	number of work packages
diversity of competencies	consortium
leadership of major investor	EPC firms involved in ownership
business linkages (prior)	degree of specification at cutoff
partners' agreement	owner's involvement
Relationships with affected parties	incentives in engineering
negotiation-compensation	incentives in construction
sustained engagement	owner-contractor collaboration
Relationships with clients-markets	*Relationship with the state*
power-purchase agreements	founding contract
tolls-public support	agreement with state
revenue guarantees	involvement of multilateral agencies
client is owner	state participation
Relationships with banks and institutional investors	*Relationships between owner and operator*
strong equity position	owner(s) operate
financial architecture-covenants	contract operator
selection of responsible leaders	
government guarantees	
adaptability protocols	

Bonding for Internal Cohesion

Ownership bonds. Governability is enhanced when ownership provides incentives that trigger the leader and sponsors to group together to develop solutions in times of crisis. Equity participants need to have strong enough stakes to want to resolve crises, instead of walking away.

Sole ownership and network operations lead to a systemic view. Firms that plan, design, finance, operate, and even build projects internally are likely to integrate issues across time and functions. Projects built by owners of large systems are less prone to disintegration, though rigidities may set in.

Integrative ownership and continuity also exist when alliances sponsor projects or when EPC contractors build, own, and operate them. Strong ownership stakes trigger governability because the project can have a substantial impact on investors' future. The Prado

Carenage tunnel in Marseilles, France, is a project-financed concession, linking banks and construction firms as owners. EPC contractors were limited to less than 50 percent ownership to ensure that the project would not take a construction focus only but a long-term operating view. The balancing of sponsorship, construction, and operating interests contributed greatly to the project's success.

A special case is represented by BOT and concession arrangements. Continuity among design, construction, and operation requires the early and full involvement of sponsors, construction firms, and equipment suppliers. Strabag, an Austrian EPC firm, was an equity partner in the Vienna-Budapest highway project. When financial difficulties began to develop, Strabag was compelled to provide additional financial resources to save the project, even though this meant carrying high commitments: in fact, the company's future was at stake. A large part of its net cash flow for a few years had to be allocated to additional equity investments. In contrast, many equipment suppliers became equity partners to sell equipment: their interest was to unload their ownership as fast as possible.

Contracts fostering mutual thinking. Contracts often steer relations toward antagonistic thresholds when projects appear unprofitable in perspective. Turnkey contracts, in particular, can create antagonism on a grand scale. In the IMEC sample, PPAs that were imposed by economic regulation or political expediency often led to antagonistic relationships. As often happened, the evolution of wholesale market prices for electricity made these contracts too expensive: utilities, which were unwilling parties, attempted to exploit ambiguities, omissions, and temporary difficulties to get out of them.

Contracts can be made, however, to provide for mutual thinking and innovation. For instance, Tepco, a Japanese utility, selects contractors a priori by using qualifying criteria because of the fear of being swamped by bids. Project engineers from Tepco and selected contractors then work through the project to build what they believe to be the best path. The contract price is the sum of the expenses entailed in the jointly developed path, but it is only a target. Because their reputation is at stake, contractors continually interact with Tepco's project engineers to better that target price. This process of mutual interaction spreads over many years and leads to cost reduction: maintaining a reputation to do better-than-agreed spurs the process.

Complementarities and interdependencies. The complementarity of nonredeployable assets creates strong bonds between separate companies.

For instance, a power plant that uses syngas from a coal-gasification plant and supplies it with auxiliary power and water is highly interdependent with that plant. In the case of cogeneration plants, technical systems can become highly integrated with those of the steam host. In other cases, power and industrial plants share the water-treatment system, or the wastewater from one plant is used as the water source for the other.

PPAs can be designed to heighten complementarity. The sensitivity of various revenue components can be tied to costs, for instance, by linking the payment received for power to fuel prices and by matching payments for capacity to the debt-servicing, fixed-operations, and management expenses. Lenders can also be reassured by requiring that sponsors increase their proportion of equity in the total financing. In the IMEC sample, many projects at the ramp-up stage were financed up to 50 percent by sponsor equity.

Continuous parallel contracts. These are agreements between two or more participants that extend into the future. Interesting examples are the frame agreements concluded by Norsk Hydro and British Petroleum with respective selected suppliers for the development of innovative low-cost solutions for marginal oil fields in the North Sea. To create incentives for suppliers to contribute their knowledge, firms concluded agreements that guaranteed suppliers business for the following five years, in return for investments in R&D, technology sharing, and joint engineering.

Prior working relationships can lead to the development of trust and knowledge bonds. For example, Alabama Electric Cooperative Inc. partnered with Burns & McDonnell, an independent engineering consultant, with which it had worked in most of its previous projects.

Aligning synergistic interests. Firms often have interests that link them to projects beyond immediate contractual bonds: maintaining reputation, developing competencies, testing technologies, and developing complementarity of interest, experience, and know-how with reputable companies. These synergies may be exploited through exchange contracts.

Leadership to handle ambiguities. Leadership helps in dealing with ambiguities and commitments. For instance, J. Makowsky, an independent power entrepreneur and leading sponsor of the Ocean State power project in Rhode Island, was able to build and maintain an alliance of utilities, suppliers, contractors, regulators, and community leaders.

On the other hand, in many projects, clashes and tensions are not contained by leadership. Centrifugal tendencies are often caused by differences in interpretation. Ambiguities are exploited by parties that want to behave opportunistically. The early definition of expectations and the recording, airing, and enforcement of commitments serve to prevent project disintegration.

Long-Term Coalitions

Coalitions among the sponsor and external parties can save projects in time of turbulence, although their failure can send projects into degenerative spirals. When successful, they play the role of bulwark and safeguard to counteract centrifugal tendencies.

Social, capital, and personal contacts. Such contacts, built during project shaping, are linkages that can serve the project in the face of later crises. Coalitions can continue well into the operation phase through permanent entities such as educational foundations, local hiring and purchasing, and partnership with regional interests. Periodic meetings, an open-door policy, the building of lasting objects such as recreational facilities, and the preservation of historic sites all help to build coalitions.

The Northumberland Strait Crossing project owes its success to two long-term coalitions. The sponsorship coalition—the Department of Public Works of Canada, the Treasury Board, and the concessionaire—helped the project survive legal challenges initiated by a local ecological group called FOTI (Friends of the Island). The execution coalition was engineered by the project manager and included fishermen, farmers, and regional industrial interests. The sharing of benefits and good communications helped to make the project a prized venture.

Legitimacy-building evaluation frames. Public frameworks, such as environmental-impact assessments and participatory decision processes, depending on the processes they foster, either thrust sponsors against affected parties or force them to work together. This is a matter of institutional design.

The selection of public-transport modes in France is an institutionalized process that evolved over fifty years, administered by a department charged with urban and infrastructure development. Cities must study at least three options, such as subways, buses, and tramways; organize a referendum; engage in public bids; and so forth. Following each step allows for participation, voice, and eventually a decision.

Participants thus embark on a structured process that provides legitimacy.

Contractual agreements and the regulatory compact. Enforcement of laws and regulations provides stability. PURPA is the anchor for many independent power projects in the United States. Many utilities attacked PPAs because they were forced under PURPA to conclude such contracts against their will. Regulators stood firm, however, and did not allow utilities to abrogate the agreements.

A structured regulatory system makes disintegration of projects difficult. For instance, the Zimmer project demonstrates how the regulatory framework facilitated the transformation of a 90 percent completed nuclear-plant project into a conventional coal-fired plant. Despite disputes with regulators over costs to be included in the rate base, the conversion was relatively easy to work out.

The application of laws, however, may lead relations between projects and external constituencies to become adversarial. One person or group contesting a permit can cause losses of millions of dollars. When sponsors do not conform to environmental standards with diligence, they can trigger costly adversarial relationships and delays.

Direct government involvement. Such involvement is a necessity in most countries where publicly owned utilities or agencies remain strong players. For instance, a significant proportion of the Wabash River Repowering Project, a technology-demonstrating project, was financed through Round 4 of the Clean Coal Technology Program of the U.S. Department of Energy.

Highway 407 around Toronto was initiated as a concession, but because of the high cost of private-sector financing and the likelihood of opposition, it was sponsored by a public corporation of the Ontario government. Low-cost financing was possible using Ontario's high credit rating. Once built and ramped up, the project was sold to a private consortium of engineering firms and pension funds for operation.

When local communities or publicly owned entities are clients of projects, the potential for disintegration is much higher. We have observed that concession projects in which private sponsors assume public risks are subjected to challenges, legislative changes, or opportunistic behavior. Conditions get worse when the institutional framework has not been fully adapted to the realities of concessions.

The Presence of Reserves

A common practice in dealing with cost and schedule variability is having contingency funds, but such funds are insufficient when successive negative events occur. For instance, the Wabash River Repowering Project, mentioned above, experienced wet weather conditions, major floods, a cold winter, strikes, and unfavorable changes in transportation laws, and obstacles to the transportation of equipment that caused contractor failure. Nonetheless, devices can be used to build reserves.

Callable resources. Reserves can be built into the project through redundancies and slack resources. Important reserves exist when sponsors and partners are able to call on outside networks for resources. Thus, both owners and banks favor a strategy of selecting partners with deep pockets and international reputations.

Blue-chip sponsors. Project financing is, by definition, a low-reserve model from the banks' point of view: there is no balance sheet to fall back on in the event of problems. Therefore, banks tend to favor blue-chip sponsors who are able to refinance projects and are concerned with maintaining their reputation. Sponsors are required to invest a high proportion of equity funding, as opposed to concession projects, for which banks financed most of the projects with loans.

Portfolios of revenue streams. Sponsors operating portfolios of projects, each at different stages in their life cycle, probably offer the best reserves. These sponsors enjoy cash flows from prior projects; should a particular project face difficulties, they can temporarily divert incoming cash flows. In contrast, entrepreneurial sponsors with eggs in only one or two baskets cannot resist major crises and entrepreneurs are often compelled to sell to sponsors with strong cash flows.

Reputation. A significant reserve is the sponsor's reputation with regulators, politicians, and communities. For instance, Suez Lyonnaise des Eaux aims to create a reputation as a developer that cares for the environment and local communities. Similarly, the reputational capital that US Generating Co. built served well during the problems experienced by the Cedar Bay Project, initially developed by an IPP but taken over by banks and assigned to US Generating, first as project manager and then as owner.

Flexibility

Keeping options open provides flexibility. One spectacular case is a power plant built on a barge: in case of political instability in the host country, it can be towed away. Options and flexibility can be built in many ways.

Technical flexibility. Power plants can be designed to burn many fuels. The Bergen power plant in New Jersey can burn both natural gas and fuel oil. To maintain flexibility in gas sourcing, the Alabama Electric Cooperative Inc. built, as part of the McWilliams project, a 42-mile pipeline that ties the plant to a main pipeline and gives access to various gas sources. Many combined-cycle plants have the capacity to function as both combined- and simple-cycle plants, depending on demand.

Flexible financial methods. Faced with the prospect of having to refinance the Indiantown project after ramp-up, US Generating financed construction with a "miniperm" loan. The loan had a seven-year maturity, leaving about four years after the end of construction for refinancing, and gave the developer flexibility on the timing and methods of refinancing. The project obtained an investment grade from rating agencies, and hence US Generating was able to refinance the project on the public bond market, even before construction was finished.

Parallel strategies. Alarmed by the requirements that the Rural Electrification Administration was placing on loan guarantees, Old Dominion Electric Cooperative (ODEC) decided to develop market-financing options for its Clover project. Managers developed relations with Wall Street investment firms, asked for shadow credit ratings from agencies, organized visits for bankers, and so forth. In just a few months, ODEC was able to issue bonds on public markets.

Flexible contracts. The problem of rigid turnkey contracts was solved in the Clover project by creating a contractual mechanism that allowed the owner to change specifications during design up to two months before the start of construction. Technical drawings became specifications only upon approval by the owners, which could request changes, provided that a balance was maintained between additional costs and cost savings to the contractor. Mechanisms were devised to deal with any conflicts that might arise.

Generativity

Project participants must be able to generate adequate responses when crises hit. Issues have to be analyzed, interpreted, and debated. Innovative solutions are triggered by the use of devices that foster the joint capabilities of suppliers, contractors, and sponsors.

Inclusion of cospecialized players. Inclusion strategies bring in firms with different competencies and comparative advantages in facing risks. Various points of view can be brought to bear once joint problems arise. On the other hand, too many participants may hamper creativity, especially when formalism and contractual disputes prevail. The presence of too many owners makes even a simple sale of excess capacity in spot markets problematic, because too many approvals are required. Even when interests converge, an unpleasant personality can turn trust-building relations into hostility.

Voluntary involvement. This process is characterized by a willingness to work together as a team, to offer full information to all parties, and to maintain a policy of openness. In turn, interactions and informal learning lead to trust, understanding, and familiarity. Learning processes result in a gradual improvement of relations, streamlined joint-decision processes, better communications, and increased productivity.

Identification of better practices. Radical innovations changing the nature of LEPs will be rare. A stream of small improvements, however, may lead to radical results, especially when design standards have not been changed for years. Joint work makes possible the identification of practices that are neglected by the sponsor but used elsewhere. Such practices contribute to reducing costs or improving quality.

Site-management committees, commercial-issues teams, and other entities will help with joint problem solving. Partnering among owners and contractors is also useful and results in activities such as collaborating to refine project scope, reviewing costs (using an "open book" approach), and addressing problems.

Sharing benefits. Incentive contracts in which targets are established and eventual savings or gains are shared make innovations feasible. Benefit-sharing agreements specify the explicit or implicit obligations of each party and sketch out potential rewards. Sponsors and suppliers can work together to develop innovative solutions. Furthermore, suppliers can invest in R&D with the knowledge that sustained business activities will allow them to recuperate investments in innovation.

Broad functional specifications. Unlike multiple-contract projects, in which the owner, sometimes with the help of a consultant, dominates technical decisions, turnkey contracts bring a powerful player with an integrative perspective into the project. Functional specifications allow the prime contractor the space to innovate—although, in certain cases, because the contractor bears risks, turnkey contracts may block innovation. A similar phenomenon occurs with project financing, which brings banks, investment advisers, and rating agencies, along with their respective consulting engineers, to the heart of project debates. Their interest may be focused on risk avoidance, however, and this can lead to less creativity.

Modularity and Diversification

Modularity and diversification are passive forms of dealing with turbulence, as they rely on portfolio effects. Projects withstand adverse developments because components do not have a critical role. Sole-source, long-term fuel-purchase contracts reduce diversification. Detailed long-term contracts, such as the PPAs under PURPA, may provide security but are not diversified because the fate of the project is tied to one power purchaser. In contrast, a franchise territory with many toll roads or bridges is more diversified, as it combines multiple revenue sources from existing bridges to new tunnels. An open market, such as a spot power market, appears to be the most diversified.

Project financing as a method is weak on diversification from the investor's point of view, because it is based on the cash flow from only one project. To increase the attraction of project finance, bundling pools cash flows from different projects.

Governability and Performance

Configurations of project structures will be unequal in their ability to face crises and difficulties. There is no obvious optimal project structure: sponsors will build configurations that are appropriate to the project's context. The reductionist dream of finding one or a few organizational devices that can solve governability issues is an illusion, as projects are complex and dynamic systems. Many devices will be thought through and used.

Building governability is an art based on experience and judgment. Each device used to govern a relationship will be studied for its potential to provide responses in times of crisis. For example, sponsors will ask whether pension fund X will provide protection against threats to projects. The same long-term contracts that reduce market and supply risks for independent power producers can block efforts to respond to new market realities. The presence of contradictory requirements is one of the major obstacles that sponsors of LEPs face in achieving governability. Sponsors have to use judgment to decide on the positive and negative contributions of each device to the properties that enhance governability.

A governability index was built for each project in the IMEC sample in the following manner. First, a range of twenty-nine devices was identified by surveying the narratives and questionnaires compiled for the sixty projects. Second, a weighting system ranging from –1 to +2 was established a priori to measure the extent to which each device contributed to enhancing the properties of cohesion, coalition, reserves, flexibility, generativity, modularity, and diversification. Then, IMEC researchers rated all projects independently with the devices used in each project. Finally, ratings were compared, discussed, and adjusted. Very few scores changed. The governability index is a matter of judgment, but the large number of items forming it gave the IMEC researchers confidence as to its robustness and validity. A broad range was observed in the index, indicating that projects truly varied on the governability scale.

Did projects facing turbulence fare better when infused with higher governability? In other words, did governability help in times of crisis? Indeed, for projects facing high turbulence, higher governability scores were associated with good performance. The Pearson chi-square coefficient of correlation between project governability and performance was 6.67, significant at .019, with one degree of freedom. When projects faced low turbulence, the relationship between governability and performance was not significant, indicating that such projects did not gain much from governability properties.

Turbulence—not technical difficulties, external effects, or complications—is the real cause of difficulties in projects. Projects that have built governability in resist turbulence. Instilling governability, however, is never a sure solution. Having imagined the potential for governability and designed each device, sponsors must have faith that parties will respond to turbulence as imagined. Opportunism or omission, however, may dash dreams.

7 Transforming Institutions

Pascale Michaud and Donald Lessard

Institutions influence the delivery of projects and have a significant impact on project performance. The prevailing framework of laws and regulations serves to reduce uncertainty and opportunism in complex project undertakings. In turn, projects challenge and significantly transform laws and regulations, particularly in the current context of transition toward the governance model for the delivery and management of projects.

Prevailing institutional arrangements and the sponsoring of LEPs share an intimate relationship (see figure 7.1). On the one hand, institutions help to anchor projects by suggesting options and by directly influencing the way in which projects are shaped, built, and operated. On the other hand, projects often raise issues that require changes to laws and regulations. By testing the relevance of prevailing practices and norms, they raise questions that require changes in land ownership, financing methods, pricing structures, and so forth. New rules developed for a particular project can become legitimate and diffused, thus creating lasting changes in institutional arrangements.

The Influence of Institutions on Projects

Why place so much emphasis on institutions in project-based activities? A simple answer is that institutions, through the various forms that they take—laws, practices, and regulations—make project shaping and legitimation possible. In fact, the development of institutions is the most important factor in predicting eventual project success. Laws assert, for example, who has the right to own and operate projects, under what conditions, and how behavior that does not conform to rules is sanctioned. Public policies and recourse to socially mediated and legally constructed rules for negotiation and arbitration

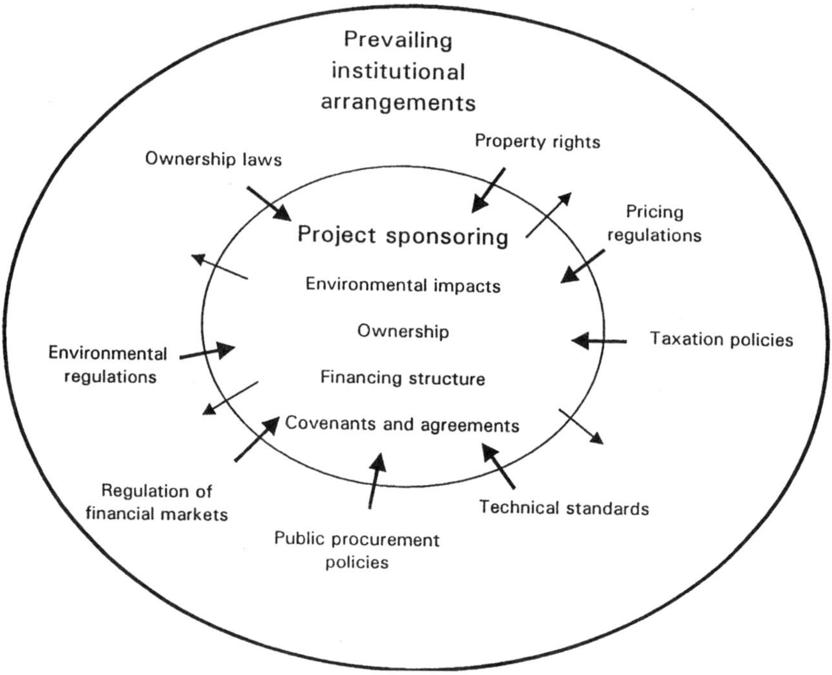

Figure 7.1
The interplay between institutions and projects

are significant in project-based activities. Failures and difficulties in contracts and agreements are often dealt with in the regulatory layer of institutions.

A useful metaphor to describe institutions has been suggested by North (1990), who compares them to rules of the game in a competitive team sport. Institutions are rules by which players in projects interact: they guide, structure, and frame the play, and they bring to bear specific incentive structures and penalties that influence behavior and coordinate action. In other words, institutions shape projects and provide a buffer against the unpredictability inherent to alliances by regulating participants' access to choice opportunities (March and Olsen 1989).

Many options exist to shape and build a greenfield 500 MW hydroelectric project. In a first scenario, one could imagine a network operator taking the traditional way: internally planning, financing, and executing the project, and then operating it. Funds would be secured by loans guaranteed by the utility's balance sheet. The utility could contract out the detailed engineering and construction work through a competitive bidding process. Tariffs could be fixed by a regulatory board.

In a second scenario, the utility could create an independent subsidiary, acting as a profit center, to finance the plant with nonrecourse financing and organize execution of the project on the basis of a large turnkey contract with a consortium. Tariff setting could be guided by competitive principles, with rates charged reflecting user demand and market conditions.

In a third scenario, the utility could form an equity venture with financiers, contractors, and industrial users. The venture would be financed mainly with equity and executed by forming a risk-and-reward-sharing alliance with contractors and suppliers. Operation would be guided by a protocol of electricity allocation among industrial equity partners.

The above scenarios are feasible and were implemented in different countries. The particular path that is selected depends largely on the prevailing characteristics of institutional arrangements: organization of the power sector, accepted ownership structures, the country's regulations and investment policies, and its norms and standards for procurement of work.

The degree of development of the institutional framework in a country, as indicated in chapter 1, has a significant impact on project success. Among the sixty IMEC projects, most of those that performed well were built in countries where the institutional framework was well developed. In contrast, projects more likely to perform poorly were built in countries where the framework was less well developed.

The Impact of Projects on Laws and Regulations

Risks in projects can be managed by anchoring them solidly in the existing institutional framework. Sponsors attempting to anchor a project, however, often find that laws and regulations are incomplete. Managing risks by changing institutions, and therefore destabilizing the prevailing order, reflects the powerful challenge that projects pose.

If laws and regulations were perfect and exhaustive, projects would be relatively simple endeavors to undertake. Transactions between parties with property rights and sponsors would take place rapidly. For example, transactions between bankers and regulators that define how returns on investment are distributed (taxation levels, profit repatriation rules on fixed capital assets, etc.) and project sponsors that wish to gain net returns would be straightforward. In other words, margins of freedom would be known. Since laws, regulations, and contracts are neither perfect nor optimal, however, institutional management is a critical competency of project sponsors. This is especially true in the early twenty-first century, with the shift toward more private sponsoring of projects that is redefining the rules of the game.

Projects are powerful levers of institutional change. Many projects serve to unlock new models of project delivery (for example, the first BOTs developed in the 1980s). Some projects are specifically used to experiment with and eventually implement policy changes (for example, the Tennessee Valley Authority experiment).

Stretching the Limits of Institutional Frameworks

Sponsoring projects under governance arrangements clearly highlights the incompleteness of the prevailing stock of institutions. IMEC's research shows that laws and regulations are indeed highly incomplete and often need to be reshaped to manage the risks inherent to projects. To facilitate investments, governments accept new templates such as BOT, nonrecourse financing, and other fast-track devices, but often without fully understanding their institutional implications.

One-third of the projects analyzed by IMEC required at least one change in laws and rules. Concession rights, property rights, economic regulations, or foreign-investment rules needed to be modified. More than one-fourth required or accompanied changes in property rights: land rights, water rights, monopoly rights, and so forth. More than one-third required the development of or improvements to BOT and concession frameworks. Changes to laws and regulations in capital markets were also frequent. A few projects called for new environmental frameworks.

These statistics indicate that sponsors spend tremendous effort, in both time and money, to understand institutional environments within the geopolitical boundaries where their project is undertaken, so that they can align their strategies to this context, assess risks related to institutional change, and develop strategies to act upon them. Understanding prevailing institutions enables sponsors to assess the margins of maneuver they have for undertaking a particular project.

The game of institutional change among sponsors, government agencies, and regulatory bodies is a difficult one. Sponsors put their efforts into acquiring the most rights at the lowest cost. Regulatory agencies aim to control opportunism; impose effective limits and sanctions to control prices efficiently; and manage entry, profits, and environmental impact. Sponsors may even feel obliged to play the role of regulatory agency by responding to voids and uncertainties in the institutional framework to save their projects.

Three broad approaches were observed by IMEC in projects that transformed institutions: incremental changes in the traditional model; stretching the market; and building public–private partnerships. Projects built with only incremental changes involve low risks, while the other two approaches are usually associated with higher levels of risk.

Incremental change. The majority of projects were built under stable laws and regulations; marginal changes, such as new environmental standards, changes to tariff structures, or modifications to settlement rules with affected parties, were required. These changes did not significantly affect or require modifications to ownership, rights, and governance structures. Rules of the game changed slightly, but the game remained the same.

Stretching the market. This approach uses market theory to modify institutions significantly. Such changes, promoted by international agencies such as the IFC or the IMF, are based on a strong belief that private initiative, disciplined by competitive market forces, can deliver LEPs with superior efficiency. The creation of competitive market forces is supported by the unbundling of activities in which scale effects are not viewed as important, such as power generation, and by eliminating regulatory barriers to entry. There is also a strong belief in the minimization of monopoly forces, reduction of government guarantees, and a reliance on nonrecourse project financing. Because such models require changes in prevailing institutions, projects may require many years of work and the expenditure of several million dollars with a high probability of dysfunctional effects.

Public-private partnerships. Partnerships, as opposed to market models, blend private initiative with public accountability, rather than push all complex problems related to projects to the market. They are based on the design of state-chartered private companies that are granted concessions: franchises stipulate pricing structures, price escalation, standards of construction and maintenance, and so forth. Concessions often include agreements to spur regional economic development. Uncertainty of revenues is generally taken into account by government actors providing land grants (for example, to capture a portion of land-exploitation revenues), subsidies, or guaranteed prices or revenues.

Managing Institutional Changes

Institutional management capabilities then become an issue for sponsors. These capabilities include the ability of sponsors to understand the scope of institutions constraining their projects, manage their way around rules that are obsolete or inefficient, and influence the paths to be taken by new institutional arrangements (such as BOT frameworks or concession laws) so that projects can succeed.

Triggering Institutional Changes with Shaped Breaker Projects

Projects often become radical institutional breakers; these represented approximately one-fifth of the projects in the IMEC sample. Vivid examples include publicly supported private investments such as the Hub power project in Pakistan or the Confederation Bridge in Canada; market endeavors submitted to powerful public management, such as the Second Severn Crossing in the United Kingdom; and market arrangements negotiated between sponsors and industrial users, such as the Igarapava power plant in Brazil. These projects departed radically from prevailing ways of doing things and required sponsors and partners to take important roles in setting up new rules such as the creation of economic or environmental regulatory frameworks. Also required were the opening of local capital markets to private project financing, the development of new guarantee mechanisms and special funds or trusts, the reversion of concession rights, significant alterations to tariff structures, or renegotiation of prevailing procurement agreements.

Some sponsors enter these difficult projects deliberately. For instance, Mitsui, Mission Energy, and GTM Entrepose developed comprehensive strategies for managing risks and uncertainties in breaker projects. Others live through them as painful experiments, such as some of the construction companies that formed Eurotunnel and embarked on the Channel Tunnel project.

The Paiton power project in Indonesia. Mitsui and its partners worked with law firms in the United States to organize protocols, conventions, and contracts with the government, the local utility, and financiers. Front-end expenditures turned out to represent almost 25 percent of total project costs. Sponsors found ways to recuperate some of these costs by turning them into expertise fees and obtaining tax exemptions when they created the concession company. Mitsui aims to increase its activity in breaker projects, especially in emerging countries. It is looking at ways to improve its capabilities as an operator (acquisition of IPPs) and its ability to negotiate detailed power pricing structures to lead the interface with economic regulators on future projects. Thus, Mitsui is deliberately choosing to become an owner-operator.

The Igarapava power project. Unable to borrow to finance the Igarapava hydroelectric project in Brazil because of a government decision, CEMIG decided to look for partners, creating a sponsoring alliance with energy-intensive and construction companies. The reframing of project ownership forced changes to institutions in at least three ways: a decree authorizing consortiums to enter the power-generation business had to be issued; the transfer of the territorial concession from the utility to the consortiums also needed to be authorized by decree; and an extension of the concession for thirty more years had to be formalized. Authorizing a business consortium to undertake the Igarapava project was a first step toward the design of a general concession framework for Brazil.

The Pangue power project. The sponsors of Pangue, the first BOT undertaken in Chile following privatization of the power sector, demanded the creation of an environmental regulatory framework to ensure the project's legitimacy. As the project was being financed on a nonrecourse basis with the participation of foreign investors, many issues were raised. To manage risks and meet the requirements of powerful stakeholders, such as the IFC and local ecological groups, the power utility Endesa asked Chilean government officials to develop a comprehensive environmental management and monitoring plan. The Pangue project was thus submitted to a voluntary assessment process to meet the concerns of funders. The assessment framework later formed the basis for Chile's environmental laws.

The Confederation Bridge. This project required the passage of two enabling pieces of legislation: an amendment to the Canadian Constitution Act of 1982, because local pressure groups argued that the project violated the 1873 Terms of Union with Prince Edward Island about communication between the island and the rest of Canada; and the Northumberland Strait Crossing Act, to authorize the private undertaking of the project through a subsidy agreement and the imposition of tolls.

From Breaker Projects to Realignment and Stabilization

Breaker projects, by forcing changes to rules of the game, yield results that are sometimes unpredictable, such as stricter regulations, changes in standards, or entry of new players. External forces, such as currency devaluations or financial crises, also influence the trajectory taken by these projects. Yet, breaker projects eventually lead to a process of alignment and stabilization of institutional arrangements and help to forge new business models. Finally, institutional arrangements are developed in detail, opening the door to standard solutions, and projects are executed in series. Repeated projects become "commoditized" solutions.

Research in economics, sociology, and management emphasizes six basic ways in which institutions change (see March and Olsen 1989): (1) adaptation as a result of competition of institutional models and survival of the fittest; (2) rational choices between alternatives (between the choice of a Keynesian economic regime, for example, and a Thatcherist one); (3) experimentation (trial and error); (4) conflict (confrontation and bargaining); (5) contagion (imitation and emulation of other institutional models); and (6) turnover and regeneration of participants.

An emerging institutional arrangement is therefore the result of innovative actions by public and private parties that seek new models and policies with which to attain their goals and therefore to govern rights and obligations related to projects. IMEC found that international concessionaire/developers often choose projects that break institutions to reap the benefits from shaping new arrangements. Some arrangements mature very rapidly—that is, they are short-lived (such as the TVA experiment in the United States, an innovative model of regional economic development that was not repeated)—while some may prevail for many decades (such as the private power monopoly model in the United States).

As innovations survive, patterns are reinforced and legitimized. Institutional arrangements grow from specific contractual relations to rules for negotiated deals, structured relations, and social compacts.

The first BOT experiments in rapidly developing countries in the 1980s and 1990s were individual agreements between government and firms. Then, questions about their legitimacy were raised: the ways in which private companies obtained rights and privileges; the profits that firms made; inefficiency of the bidding process; and so forth. Breaker projects are often renegotiated.

In early stages of shifting institutional arrangements, the phenomena of leapfrogging, imitation, and emulation take place. Diffusion of blueprint BOT legal and regulatory frameworks went around the world at an amazing speed between 1986 and 1995, with select investment banks and law firms promoting their "BOT deal" templates. Many countries leapfrogged the normal process of institutional design to make it possible for the private sector to finance, build, and operate projects rapidly. Early BOT deals were templates that played a significant role in building the legitimacy of the BOT concept.

In reality, the degree of development of the legal system and the administrative capabilities of a government severely limit the importance and relevance of such templates. Countries facing problems of discretionary power by regulators and arbitrariness of government agencies need rules to limit the scope of authority. The adoption by Indonesia of the British PFI model, without much adaptation, is a case in point. Development costs of BOT projects in Asia often reached over 20 percent of total project costs in the IMEC sample. Ill-adapted rules force complex and costly negotiations of front-end processes. Expensive advisers often act as substitutes for clear and realistic institutional frameworks.

Tracing the Birth of an Institutional Arrangement: Cofiroute

In 1968, six French EPC firms that had successfully built underground parking lots in Paris decided that they could also build highways. They approached Albin Chalandon, the minister of public works, to propose a concession framework. In 1969, Chalandon decided to accelerate the French highway-construction program. By May 1970, a decree allowing the private sector to sign highway concessions was issued.

A first call for proposals to build, own, and operate 450 kilometers of highway (Paris–Poitiers and Paris–Le Mans) was set up. The call focused on roads with expected high traffic. Functional, rather than prescriptive, specifications were used.

The new institutional framework was legitimized by three factors: Chalandon's fierce determination to build a strong highway network rapidly and at low cost; a willingness on the part of highway planners to distance themselves from the Ministry of Finance, which blocked infrastructure expenditures; and a desire to spur the profitability of the Sociétés d'économie mixte. The existence of legislative and regulatory systems for private concessions, developed in the nineteenth century for railroads, opened the way. The EPC entrepreneurs' determination to design, build, finance, and operate roads also called for rapid decisions.

The bidding process was put on the fast track, but there was room for negotiation once the winning concessionaire was chosen. Cofiroute won by proposing highway construction at a cost 25 percent lower than the standard, essentially by cutting down on overspecifications, setting up an organization that carefully divided its ownership and contracting roles, and creating two separate construction groups to build in a competitive frame of mind. A small operating firm was established with only key specialists (ex-civil servants and financiers) to monitor the work of the construction companies.

The state kept a strong planning and supervisory role, but maintained the same rules and regulations during the four years it took to construct the 450-kilometer highway. Stable conditions helped Cofiroute implement its innovative engineering and construction proposals (thereby reducing its costs) by adjusting norms and procedures pertaining to road quality.

To compensate for the risks taken by the private sector, the state provided soft loans and sovereign guarantees on debt. Tariffs were to be set by the concessionaire for the first ten years, and were thereafter to follow a formula to take inflation into account. The state did not keep its promise, however; after 1975, tariffs were subjected to government approval following the oil shock. Three other private concessions were created between 1970 and 1972 to build and operate highways in France, but only Cofiroute survived.

Once Cofiroute succeeded in building the first 450 kilometers of highway, the state requested that it undertake the construction and operation of 300 additional kilometers, forecast to be less profitable than the Paris–Poitiers and Paris–Le Mans corridors. These additional mandates gave a new direction to the company: long-term owner-operator of highways rather than single-concession contractor. Cofiroute refused some of the additional concessions proposed by the state because they represented too high a risk for the company, even though they would have brought in construction work. This shows that the company had a clear focus on its owner-operator role despite the fact that the main shareholders were construction companies. By 1997, Cofiroute owned and operated 15 percent of the French highway network.

Competency to Transform Institutions

Sponsors that decide to shape projects at the early stages of emerging institutional models need high levels of competency and a willingness to take high risks. Many BOT projects are organized as unique, secret, self-contained endeavors: institutional gaps and voids remain, especially in rapidly developing countries. To compensate for such voids, sponsors develop safeguards.

For instance, the PPA signed for the Paiton project with the national utility PLN is structured to hedge inflation, fuel prices, and regulatory risks. It contains provisions that allocate currency risk to PLN and provides for the full recovery of project capital and operating costs, including debt service. Furthermore, PLN's contract obligations are backed by a letter of support issued by the Republic of Indonesia. In spite of tight contracts, PT Paiton Energy Ltd. is having difficulty with PLN, which filed a lawsuit to renegotiate the PPA, claiming that it was paying too much compared with its other suppliers.

The shaping of breaker projects is extremely difficult. Companies should enter this field only if they intend to grow as owner-operators and can accumulate enough resources to negotiate with governments. Sources of added value include land concessions, a portfolio of projects in the region or country, local operating subsidiaries that export (hard currency providers), and stable alliances with local corporations and with powerful financiers such as investment banks and export credit agencies.

Project developers should also choose where they want to play this game. Some countries will have weak institutional structures for many years to come, such as Vietnam, Burma (Myanmar), and China. Unless sponsors are able to maintain strong international and local alliances that have the power and financial capability to negotiate with governments, they should focus on countries where institutional structures are transparent.

Facing the Difficulties of Transforming Institutions

In many countries, BOTs and concessions are used because of severe public finance crises. Change brought with insufficient preparation creates uncertainty and confusion, therefore increasing projects' economic cost and probability of failure. Many difficulties need to be resolved.

Rigidity and opposition are particularly important in the case of breaker projects. Preset ideas nourish the mental models of policymakers and civil servants. Changing rules for project ownership and governance raise questions among powerful stakeholders.

The Birecik project in Turkey was blocked for four years by that country's constitutional and supreme courts. It was the first BOT in Turkey and it challenged existing ways. The legal environment within which private projects could be undertaken and project financing used was, in large part, nonexistent. The Turkish constitution required that all concession-like contracts be submitted to the court, leaving the government with no legislative power to approve concessions. The Constitutional Court was to be the final judge in the case of contractual disputes, thereby closing recourse to international arbitration for foreign developers. The situation created a dead end. The government aimed to get projects in motion rapidly and passed a BOT law specifying that contracts with the private sector be considered commercial contracts rather than concessions. The Constitutional Court, however, opposed the scheme. After years of negotiations and pressures, the Supreme Court finally cleared the Birecik project as a commercial contract, requiring, however, that all subsequent projects be reviewed separately.

New regulatory environments often impel governments and firms to behave in ways that are broadly inconsistent with efficient resource allocation. Special guarantees are given by governments to attract sponsors when risks and costs of project development are high. The design of a deficient competitive structure by policymakers may lead projects to be inefficient yet profitable. The ways in which competition is organized for the sector, for new project investments, and for substitute products have a tremendous influence on project performance.

States create property rights to enhance the public good, but uncertainties remain as to the incentive structures at work. Property rights are protected by the country's constitution, but some countries, especially those with communist traditions, do not fully recognize private ownership. Amendments to a constitution do not guarantee that new owners will be able to exercise their rights (for example, the right to use or extract value from the land or to draw economic benefits from ownership). Uncertainty about ownership rights affects private investments.

Governments often respond to pressures by locking in rapidly on fashionable concepts—for instance, favoring IPPs to build thermal-power plants when it could exploit hydroelectricity. Only a strong owner-operator, managing a portfolio of projects, can respond to future requirements and embrace complex projects. A planning framework has to be put in place to ensure that project ideas are debated and analyzed in terms of a least-cost planning perspective that will benefit the country.

Changes to institutions may create problems. For instance, the current PFI in the United Kingdom has bidding requirements that force developers to bear high front-end costs that can be only partly recuperated by the winner. PFI is perceived as a procurement path to force the private sector to finance public investments and carry public risks. It requires bidders to present detailed technical and financial proposals to permit the government to compare innovative low-cost solutions, pick the best proposal, and negotiate an improved version with any of the contestants. Construction companies in the United Kingdom are unhappy about both unclear terms of the PFI and the legislative risks that they are obliged to assume.

Three simple conclusions emerge from our research.

The development of a sector, or industry, is a cumulative process that requires complex projects, which, in turn, affect institutions. Institutions are powerful instruments, for both sponsors and governments, for regulating business and fostering investments in new capacity. Rules determine or largely influence the degree of competition, ownership structures and property rights, tariffs charged to users, and monopoly privileges.

Smart institutions and regulations are a true public good, encouraging economic development. Smart governments and regulatory agencies try to design efficient arrangements. Intelligent leadership and policies can create laws and regulations that make private action efficient and contribute to the public good.

Transforming institutions is possible. A limited number of firms, however, have the competencies and the resources to play institutional and regulatory shaping games. Sponsors' strategies need to be carefully aligned with their real competencies and capabilities.

8 The Financing of Large Engineering Projects

Richard Brealey, Ian Cooper, and Michel Habib

The allocation of risk is one of the most important aspects of the management of LEPs. Indeed, it is viewed by investment bankers and lawyers involved in project financing as *the* central consideration in securing financing. As noted in chapter 3, the overall risk of an LEP should be split into its constituent risks, and each risk should be allocated to the party that is best able to control or bear that particular type of risk. Direct and complete allocation, however, may not always be feasible. Some risks will emerge that are large, difficult to foresee, and not contractible. The contracts allocating risk will, by necessity, be silent or unclear as to the consequences of some events that may occur, or they might not be appropriate were these events to occur. There will therefore be the need to renegotiate initial contracts.

The thesis developed in this chapter is that the financial architecture of a project—as represented by its use of debt, equity, recourse, and guarantees—has the dual role of allocating risk and making effective renegotiation possible.

To illustrate this dual role, consider an IPP. The sale of a large equity stake in the IPP to an operator serves to allocate much of the operation risk to that party, thereby providing it with the incentive to operate efficiently. For example, National Power of the United Kingdom owns 27 percent of the equity of Pakistan's Hub power project, of which it is the operator. Similarly, the sale of a large debt stake in the IPP to a major commercial bank or a multilateral institution such as the World Bank serves to allocate much of the risk of expropriation of the IPP to that institution, thereby providing it with the incentive to resist any attempt on the part of the host government to renegotiate to its own advantage the terms of the agreements entered into by it and the IPP. An example of such renegotiation is arguably provided by the ongoing negotiations between the government of Pakistan and the

World Bank about the Hub power project. The World Bank is a subordinated debt-holder in the project and a guarantor of senior debt against political risk.

The financing of large projects therefore involves not only the traditional goal of obtaining the cheapest funds possible but also strategic goals such as structuring of ownership and control and the organization of governance to allocate risk and make effective renegotiation possible. These are achieved through the choice of financial architecture for the project.

Modern corporate finance holds the view that financing choices such as the amount of leverage in a project cannot be separated from incentive and control considerations. For instance, the amount of leverage affects the incentives of managers; the structure of ownership provides the setting for renegotiation; and the type of debt affects the level of risk in the project. The choice of financial architecture, therefore, is complex, multidimensional, and dynamic. A variety of solutions and goals are sought: to allocate risk; to provide incentives; to design an effective governance structure; to set the stage for efficient renegotiation; and to obtain the cheapest funds possible. Some of these goals may conflict. Others may be somewhat ambiguous. In particular, what exactly are "cheap" funds and how is risk priced?

Financial Architecture: The Potential for Strategic Effects

Sponsors of large projects seeking to raise capital often appear to be of the view that bank debt is cheaper than equity and frequently bemoan the difficulty of raising the desired amount of debt. Yet, the classic work by Modigliani and Miller (1958), which provides the basis for the modern analysis of capital structure, states that debt is not intrinsically cheaper than equity. Although equity requires a higher return than debt does, it also bears a greater amount of risk. Once return is adjusted for risk, the returns to debt and equity effectively must be the same in a well-functioning capital market.

As an example, compare the interest rate on debt with the return on equity required by investors in infrastructure projects. The former rarely exceeds 12 percent even for highly leveraged projects, whereas the latter is 18 to 25 percent. A simple comparison of these two rates however, is, misleading, for the greater return required by equityholders is compensation for greater uncertainty about the cash flows that they will receive: the payments to debt-holders are contractually fixed, whereas those to equity-holders are not.

Furthermore, an attempt to exploit debt's presumed cheapness by increasing a project's reliance on debt financing would likely be ineffective, for the concentration of much of the risk of the project on a reduced equity base will increase the return required by equity-holders. The high rates of return required by equity-holders in highly leveraged infrastructure projects are therefore simply the consequence of that degree of leverage. Indeed, Modigliani and Miller show that the increase in that return will be exactly such as to leave the project's overall cost of capital—that of debt and equity—unchanged.

Modigliani and Miller's argument has much wider applicability than the choice of leverage alone. Any financing choice that is made in a competitive market and that does not change a project's cash flows and risks cannot change its value and cost of capital. Ultimately, the overall cost of capital of the project reflects the risk that must be borne by the parties financing it. Simply reallocating risk among these parties does not reduce the total risk that must be borne and therefore does not reduce the overall cost of capital. This is true of debt financing, which simply reallocates risk to equity-holders, and of government financing, which reallocates risk to taxpayers.

The ability of a government to finance a project entirely with debt, which is often raised at close to the risk-free rate, is at times contrasted with the private sector's need to raise both debt and equity at rates that are generally well in excess of the risk-free rate, and leads to the conclusion that the government has a lower cost of capital than the private sector does. The government is therefore sometimes argued to have an advantage over the private sector in financing large, capital-intensive projects. For example, the government of Ontario chose to finance what became North America's first electronic toll highway through direct provincial borrowing rather than have the project consortium finance the project. The government reasoned that its lower borrowing costs would make lower toll payments possible than if the project were financed by the consortium.

Such a view is mistaken, for it ignores the cost of the guarantee provided by taxpayers to lenders. It is this guarantee that allows the government to finance a project entirely with debt and to raise such debt at close to the risk-free rate. To illustrate the value of this guarantee to lenders and its possible cost to taxpayers, imagine that construction of the English Channel Tunnel had been financed by government borrowing rather than by the shareholders and debt-holders in Eurotunnel. The huge losses that were and continue to be incurred would then have been borne by French and British taxpayers rather than Eurotunnel's hapless shareholders and bankers. Properly accounting for the cost of the guarantee reveals that the government need not have a lower cost of capital than the private sector (Brealey, Cooper, and Habib 1998).

Modigliani and Miller's argument thus provides a benchmark for thinking about the financial architecture of large projects. It states that simply reallocating a fixed pool of cash flows and risks among various parties does not, in general, create value or lower the cost of capital. But it admits that financing choices can affect value and affect the cost of capital if they have one or more of the following effects: they exploit sources of finance that are subsidized or not fully priced given their risk; they reduce the taxes paid by the project and its owners; they improve the operating performance of the project by improving incentives; they lower the expected cost of future renegotiation.

The first effect applies when a government is willing to guarantee or subsidize a loan for political reasons. As an example of the second effect, corporate taxes introduce a preference for debt. This is because corporate interest payments are tax-deductible in most jurisdictions, as interest is paid out of a project's pretax income, whereas dividends are paid out of its aftertax income. The desire to exploit the tax advantage of debt may provide a partial explanation for the use of project financing in the United States. American power utilities are prohibited from having debt-equity ratios in excess of one. Such a constraint however, may, be circumvented by having a power utility enter into a PPA that commits the utility to buy the electricity produced by an independent power project, with the IPP having a debt-equity ratio as high as nine. The extremely high leverage of the IPP is made possible by the security provided by the PPA, and the tax shield it provides is reflected in the price paid by the utility for the electricity it has committed to purchase. But the view of corporate taxes as introducing a preference for debt ignores the personal taxes paid by investors in the project (Miller 1977).

The last two effects of financial architecture—on incentives and on renegotiation—are the focus of this chapter. To place this analysis in context, we first present the dimensions of financing and categorize the risks that are to be allocated and controlled.

The Potential for Transferring Risk

A sponsor that is considering a new project can proceed along many dimensions in financing this project. It must choose the proportion of debt and equity that it will use. While the sponsor, as equity-holder, will bear most of the risk of the project, some risk will nonetheless be borne by the project's debt-holders, which would stand to lose at least part of their investment if the sponsor were unable to service the debt it has raised, either from the project's revenues and assets or from those of its other operations.

Debt therefore provides a sponsor with the ability to transfer at least part of the risk of a project. The extent of this transfer can be increased by raising debt in a nonrecourse form, which limits the revenues and assets that are used to service the debt to those of the project alone; this denies the project's debt-holders recourse to the revenues and assets of the firm's other operations, even in the case of failure to service the debt. The extent of the transfer of risk, through either recourse or non-recourse debt, will evolve over time in line with the changing debt-equity ratios of the project and the sponsor. This reflects changes in the values of the project and the sponsor, and in the face value of the debt as old debt is repaid and new debt is raised. The repayment of all debt ends this particular form of risk transfer.

The sponsor need not limit the external financing of the project to debt. It can, for example, undertake the project jointly with another firm, thereby transferring part of the risk through equity. As in the case of debt, neither the terms of the transfer nor the transfer itself need be permanent, for the shares of the partners may evolve over time and the joint venture may eventually be dissolved.

Whether done in the form of debt or of equity, financing may involve numerous other parties. Debt may be raised from a syndicate of lenders rather than a single lender. Similarly, equity stakes may be sold in a project company set up for the specific purpose of undertaking the project. At the limit, debt and equity may be raised from a large number of investors through publicly traded bonds and shares.

The sponsor can further decrease the fraction of the risk of the project that it bears by entering into a variety of contracts. It can hedge its currency and interest-rate exposure, enter into long-term purchase or supply agreements, require guarantees, and purchase various forms of insurance. Although such contracts are not true forms of financing, they nonetheless have a bearing on the choice and terms of financing available. Lenders to an IPP, for instance, generally will not finance the project in the absence of a PPA. Furthermore, some such contracts can essentially be transformed into financing contracts. For example, the expected revenues from a long-term supply contract can be securitized, enabling the sponsor to receive the present value of these revenues at the outset, thereby decreasing its initial financing requirements. Finally, the transfer of risk through contracts need not be permanent and may involve a large number of parties, as do exchange-traded contracts.

Sources of Risk

The preceding discussion has noted the use of financing and contracts in transferring risk, but it has not specified the nature of the risks that would thus be transferred. In large infrastructure projects, these are construction risk; operation risk; demand and supply risk; regulatory, institutional, and political risk; and macroeconomic risk (see chapter 3 for a description of these risks).

Regulatory, institutional, and political risks are often of overriding importance. They may delay the completion of a project, compromise the operation of the project and its profitability, or result in de jure or de facto expropriation of the project. A government may expropriate investors in a project either directly through nationalization or indirectly through regulation that lowers prices to the extent of precluding investors from recovering their initial investment.

Thus the Hub power project in Pakistan was delayed by the Gulf War and by uncertainty over the conformity of its financing structure with Islamic Shariaa law; the Dhabol power plant in the Indian state of Maharashtra was delayed by the coming to power of a party that was committed to renegotiating the contract signed by the previous state government; and the construction of highways and railroad lines in England is bitterly opposed by environmental activists and, in many cases, local residents. Similarly, accusations of corruption made by the government of Pakistan against managers of the Hub power project have thrown the future of the project into doubt, and changes made to the regulatory framework of privatized utilities in the United Kingdom have decreased shareholders' returns below what they might have expected at privatization given the then prevailing framework.

Macroeconomic risk is related to demand risk, in that dramatically changed economic conditions such as those brought about by the Asian crisis will surely affect demand for the products and services provided by a project. But macroeconomic risk is more general than demand risk. For example, a devaluation of the local currency would increase the cost of servicing the project's foreign debt even in the absence of any change in demand.

Risks matter because they affect a project's cash flows: the initial investment (construction risk; regulatory, institutional, and political risk), operating costs (operation risk; regulatory, institutional, and political risk), and revenues (demand risk; regulatory, institutional, and political risk; macroeconomic risk). The project's success therefore depends on controlling these risks. This, in turn, depends of the allocation of the risks.

Direct and Indirect Allocation of Risks through Financial Architecture

The general principle for allocating risk in LEPs is that stated in chapter 3: a given risk should be allocated to the party or parties that can best control or bear that particular type of risk, which provides the incentive to do so. Thus, construction risk should be allocated to the contractor of the project, operation risk to the operator, and political risk to a government or a multilateral institution. This last consideration may explain why political risk insurance is generally provided by the public sector. It is important to note, however, that the party that can best control a given risk is not necessarily the same as the one that can best bear that risk. This is perhaps best illustrated by the tale of mid-nineteenth-century railroad contractor-promoters such as Thomas Brassey and Samuel Morton Peto. These contractors provided much of the financing needed for the construction of new railway lines through borrowing or by relying on their own funds. The resulting overexposure to a relatively limited number of projects led to Peto's collapse in the crash of 1866 (Barker and Savage 1974). Risk-bearing considerations alone suggest that a given risk should be divided among a large number of parties each of which would each bear only a small fraction of that risk.

Such fragmentation is in direct conflict with the need to induce the parties to control the risk, because a party that bears only a small fraction of a given risk has a correspondingly small incentive to control that risk. There is therefore a trade-off between the control and the bearing of risk that is of fundamental importance to the overwhelming majority of financing and risk-management choices. Only in the case of a risk that cannot be controlled is there no trade-off. Such a risk should be divided among a large number of parties. For example, the risk of freely floating currencies should generally be borne by banks or by the futures and options markets.

In contrast to chapter 3, where the direct allocation of risk through contracts is discussed, we consider the indirect allocation of risk through financial architecture. Admittedly, financing arrangements are contracts in their own right; however, their object is an entire project rather than a specific aspect of the project, as is the case for contracts. Contrast, for example, the claim for payment by an investor in a project to that by the project's contractor. The former is a claim on the *general* payoff of the project, whereas the latter is a claim on the *specific* facility or plant that the contractor has built.

The need for the indirect allocation of risk exists when contracts that would allocate risk directly cannot be written, perhaps because of the complexity of the task involved. For example, it may be difficult to describe in meaningful contractual terms what the efficient operation of a project entails. Furthermore, some manifestations of political risk, such as revolutions and civil wars, likely imply the inability of the government to enforce contractual agreements. Nonetheless, the desired allocation of risk may be achievable through financial architecture: by the operator in the first case and by the government in the second. Both the operator and the government have a stake in the success of the project.

The allocation of risk through financial architecture also sets the stage for renegotiation, which is made necessary by the incompleteness of both the direct and the indirect initial allocation of risk, and by changes in circumstances that may make the initial allocation of risk no longer appropriate. Financing implies ownership and ownership generally entails control. Control clearly affects renegotiation. Financing should therefore be provided by, and ownership and control should reside with, the parties whose importance to efficient renegotiation is greatest.

Part of the ownership of a major infrastructure project should reside with a large bank or multilateral institutions whose considerable clout likely would deter an attempt at opportunistic renegotiation on the part of the host government. Four elements of financial architecture are now discussed, with particular emphasis on their capability to cope with risk and renegotiation.

The Choice of Ownership Vehicle

The first important decision that a sponsor considering an LEP must make is whether to do so through a special-purpose vehicle such as a joint venture, consortium, or project company or as a wholly owned, integral part of the sponsor. Clearly, the entire equity of the project is provided by the company in the last case, and there can therefore be no transfer of risk through equity. There is also little transfer of the risk of the project through debt, as lenders have recourse to the revenues and assets of the company's other operations. Any transfer of risk in the case of a wholly owned project is therefore limited to that which can be achieved through contracts. This suggests that a project will be wholly owned when a single party—the project's sponsor—can best control and bear all of the risks of the project or when they can be transferred through contracts.

In contrast, when there is a need to rely on financing to transfer risk, a project will be undertaken through a special-purpose vehicle for only in such cases is the transfer of risk through financing possible. Such a vehicle makes it possible for the parties to which risk is to be transferred through equity to acquire equity stakes in the project alone, and for the parties to which risk is to be transferred through debt to make a loan to the project alone.

An example of a wholly owned project is the Nanko power plant, built and operated by Kansai Electric Power in Osaka, Japan. IMEC research noted that Kansai was observed to possess "all the competencies to do the project from early planning to operation—except for equipment manufacturing." This suggests that Kansai was the party best able to control the entire risk of the project. With stable technologies, it is arguable whether equipment manufacturing is truly part of the project. In any case, such risk appears to be satisfactorily allocated through contracts for equipment that uses tried-and-tested technology. There was therefore no need for the transfer of risk, either through contracts or through financing, and the plant was financed entirely through retained earning and traditional, full-recourse debt.

The Navotas I power plant in the Philippines was undertaken though a special-purpose vehicle. The equity in the project company was shared among Hong Kong's Hopewell, the operator and majority shareholder; Citibank; the Asian Development Bank; and the IFC. The debt was provided in the form of nonrecourse financing by Austria's Osterreichesche Landerbank; France's Indosuez and Credit Lyonnais; Girozentrale; the IFC; and the Asian Development Bank. A PPA committed National Power Corporation (Napocor) of the Philippines to make fixed-capacity-charge and variable-energy-charge payments to the project company. Napocor further committed to supply fuel to the plant. These contractual obligations were guaranteed by the government of the Philippines.

Comparison of the Nanko and Navotas I projects raises the question of why two seemingly identical projects should have been structured and financed in such different ways. The answer relates to the allocation of risk and incentives. A number of financial and organizational constraints combined to make Napocor reliant on private infrastructure providers such as Hopewell for the generation of electricity. Hopewell's majority stake in the project company provided it with the incentive to perform that task efficiently. Transmission and distribution, however, remained Napocor's responsibility. This implied that, in the absence of any contract between Napocor and the project company, demand risk for the power produced by the project would be borne by investors in the project, whereas control over that risk, to the extent that such control is possible, would reside with Napocor. This was especially true as the plant was intended for peak-load operation, with plant dispatch determined by Napocor. The PPA was therefore necessary to transfer demand risk to the party that could best appraise and control that risk—Napocor.

The guarantee provided by the government of the Philippines was intended to provide it with the incentive to hold state-owned Napocor to its contractual obligations. Financing of the project company in the form of nonrecourse debt by multilateral institutions and commercial banks was, in turn, intended to provide these parties with the incentive to hold the government of the Philippines to its own contractual obligations. Their involvement was desirable because of their greater clout, compared to Hopewell, in renegotiation with the government stemming from their ability to cut a defaulting borrower off from all credit.

Renegotiation of the terms of the contract was a distinct possibility in the case of Navotas, for the project was a high-cost power plant built at great speed to remedy acute power shortages. This high cost was the price to be paid for speedy completion, but Napocor may have no longer been willing to pay this price once new, lower-cost plants had been built, yet before investors in Navotas had recovered their investment. None of the above issues existed in the case of Nanko (see Trujillo et al. 1998).

The Choice between Debt and Equity: Upside and Downside Risks

The role of financing in allocating risk has been discussed, but not whether a risk that should be allocated through financing should be allocated through debt or through equity. Thus, to return to two types of risks that have often been referred to, operation risk and expropriation risk, note that we have not justified the assertion that the former should be allocated through equity, whereas the latter should be allocated through debt. Why not allocate both through equity, or through debt, or allocate the risk of expropriation through equity and that of operation through debt?

To answer these questions, and more generally to provide guidance for choosing between debt and equity when allocating risk through financing, we need to introduce some grouping of the risks discussed here. In particular, we wish to distinguish between upside risks and downside risks. Both operation risk and expropriation risk, for instance, affect the value of a project. There are therefore benefits to controlling both, but there is a difference in the benefits to controlling each. There is no upper limit to the benefit of controlling operation risk: the more efficiently the project is operated, the more valuable the project. In contrast, there is an upper limit to the benefit of controlling expropriation risk: the value of the project can be no greater than its intrinsic value, absent any risk of expropriation.

The incentive to control expropriation risk therefore resides in the desire to preserve the value of the project, whereas the incentive to control operation risk resides in the desire to maximize the value of the project. In other words, the concern of operation risk is the upside of the project, whereas that of expropriation risk is the downside of the project.

The other types of risk fall between these two extremes. Thus, construction risk is likely to be partly upside risk and partly downside risk; it is upside to the extent that better, more timely, and more cost-effective construction increases the value of a project or makes feasible a project that was hitherto considered to be uneconomical. For example, innovative construction techniques and forms of organization for development of marginal oil fields in the North Sea have yielded substantial capital-cost reductions (Lascelles 1996). Construction risk is downside for construction projects for which there is little scope for innovation, in which case the primary concern is the avoidance of delays and cost overruns. The same holds true for demand and supply risk; regulatory, institutional, and political risk; and macroeconomic risk; although these are probably more in the nature of downside risk as their control is necessary not so much to increase the value of a project as to avoid jeopardizing that value.

The differing characteristics of upside and downside risks suggest that these should be allocated through different forms of financing—equity and debt, respectively. Like the benefit of controlling upside risk, the payoff to equity has no upper limit. Like the benefit to controlling downside risk, the payoff to debt does have an upper limit: the sum of principal and interest. Any increase in the value of the project above that limit accrues to equity-holders in its entirety, while any shortfall below that limit is borne by debt-holders in its entirety. This suggests that equity-holders will be induced to control upside risk and debt-holders will be induced to control downside risk. Indeed, we find that among the main equity-holders in project companies are operators, contractors, and, to a lesser extent, suppliers. We find that among the main debt-holders are commercial banks (naturally), multilateral institutions, and export credit agencies. The latter two often provide debt financing indirectly in the form of loan guarantees rather than directly in the form of loans.

As upside risk is allocated through equity financing and downside risk through debt financing, the relative importance of these two types of risk should be a major determinant of a project's leverage. Projects with a high ratio of tangible to intangible assets will tend to have high leverage. Such projects present greater downside risk than do projects with a low ratio of tangible to intangible assets, for tangible assets are at greater risk of being expropriated than are intangible assets. Similarly, projects with low operation risk, such as bridges, will tend to have higher leverage than do projects with higher operation risk, such as power plants. Indeed, the project company that operates the Northumberland Strait Crossing between New Brunswick and Prince Edward Island in Canada has 81 percent leverage, whereas the project company that operates the Novatas I power plant has 73 percent leverage.

There are other determinants of a project's leverage: taxes, the ability to bear risk, and regulations all play an important role. We have already mentioned the regulatory constraint that limits the leverage of power utilities in the United States. For an example of a regulatory constraint that has a diametrically opposite effect, consider the Third Dartford Crossing in the United Kingdom. The terms of the concession preclude any dividend payment to equity-holders. Not surprisingly, the project has been financed with near 100 percent debt.

We have also mentioned the need to trade off the ability to control risk with the ability to bear risk. This provides one explanation for the allocation of downside risk, such as construction risk, to commercial banks through bank debt. Risk-control considerations alone would dictate that this risk be allocated to contractors, and risk-bearing considerations alone would dictate that it be shared among a large number of investors through bond financing. Naturally, changes in the relative importance of risk control and risk bearing will be reflected in changes in the source and form of financing. Thus, completion of a project and the consequent decline in the need to control construction risk suggest that risk-bearing considerations should increase in relative importance, thereby accounting for the frequent replacement of much bank debt by bonds following completion.

Changes in the source and form of financing also reflect changes in the relative importance of upside and downside risk, or in the identity of the party than can best control a given risk. Thus, the project company that operates the Northumberland Strait Crossing increased its leverage following completion of the project since construction risk that had been allocated through equity no longer existed. Similarly, transfer of project ownership from the project company to the host government in BOT schemes may represent an admission on the part of project investors of their inability to control expropriation risk indefinitely in the absence of wholesale privatization. More generally, the maturity of the form and the source of financing will be determined by the period of time over which the risk allocated by the chosen form of financing is to be controlled by the chosen source of financing.

Recourse versus Nonrecourse Debt

As noted above, lenders to a project may have full recourse to the total assets and revenues of the firm that has undertaken the project, or they may have recourse limited to the project's assets and revenues only.

They may also have loan guarantees, which are a form of recourse. The question then arises as to whether a project's debt financing should be provided in the form of recourse or nonrecourse debt.

It is clear that debt should be nonrecourse if the project's debt-holders are also the parties that are best able to control the project's downside risk. Only nonrecourse debt will be effective in inducing these parties to control downside risk, for only in the absence of recourse will the loans made by the parties be jeopardized by their failure to control that risk.

But the debt-holders of a project are not always the parties best able to control the project's downside risk. For example, in a case where the choice of leverage has been driven primarily by tax considerations, the parties best able to control downside risk may well be equity-holders in the project rather than debt-holders. Providing debt-holders with recourse to equity-holders induces the latter to control both downside and upside risk. Similarly, in a case where the government has been prevented by budgetary or other considerations from becoming a major debt-holder in the project in spite of the importance of political risk, recourse from debt-holders to the government in the form of loan guarantees induces the government to control that risk.

The Role of Government and Multilateral Agencies

As noted, governments and multilateral agencies may be an important source of debt financing, for such debt provides them with the incentive to control regulatory, institutional, and political risk and to see to the success of the project. Such incentives are in addition to that provided by tax revenues. Financing by a government or multilateral agency need not take the form of the direct provision of debt financing; it may be in the form of loan guarantees, guaranteed rates of return, or grants and subsidies. These are used especially in the presence of important externalities or in the case of what are essentially social projects, such as infrastructure projects intended to serve small and isolated communities. Thus, the bonds issued to finance construction of the Northumberland Strait Crossing are guaranteed by the government of Canada, for the bridge, like the ferry service it replaced, is explicitly political in nature and would not be viable in the absence of government subsidies.

The presence of guarantees arguably controls the risk that the government may reduce or terminate the subsidies, for an attempt to do so would likely precipitate default of the project company, leaving the government to indemnify bondholders. In contrast, the third Dartford Crossing was financed without any government guarantee. The agreement that the concession would last until all debt incurred in building the bridge was repaid precluded any "creeping" expropriation by the government. (Strictly speaking, the concession period is to be the shorter of either twenty years or the period needed to repay the debt.)

Financing by a government or multilateral agency may also help lend legitimacy to a project, especially in the case of institutions such as the World Bank or the European Bank for Reconstruction and Development, which are known to decline taking part in the financing of projects that do not satisfy relatively stringent environmental and social conditions. Thus, the three oil companies that are considering developing the Doba oil field in Chad have, in the face of fierce criticism by environmental and human rights groups, made their project conditional upon World Bank participation in the project. Interestingly, the bank's participation is to take the form of a US$115 million loan to the Chad and Cameroon governments, enabling them to acquire a 3 percent equity stake in the project (Corzine 1997).

Designing a financial architecture with instruments such as equity, debt, covenants, recourse, government guarantees, and the participation of bilateral and multilateral agencies is much more than bringing money to a project. In fact, a well-thought-out financial architecture will allocate risks to parties with comparative advantage, provide incentives to respond to events in the appropriate manner, and ensure that a project is governable enough to survive crises by restructuring. The contention here is that the allocation of risk should be such as to maximize the value of the project and to minimize the costs of renegotiation.

9 Partnering Alliances for Project Design and Execution

Brian Hobbs and Bjorn Andersen

Early in the IMEC research, it became obvious that some projects were being developed and executed in a traditional fashion, with a large organization internalizing project identification, selection, and development activities. Other projects, however, were being managed using approaches that differed considerably. All of these involved some form of relationship among participants that allowed several parties to influence the way projects were designed and executed. As the IMEC program developed, more of these innovative or nontraditional projects became apparent.

Configurations of Project Development and Execution

The more novel ways of structuring a project all present notable contrasts with the traditional approach. The way the front end is organized can have a profound impact on how the EPC phase is structured, especially if parties that have an important role in executing EPC activities are heavily involved in project development.

Use of the governance approach during the front end does not necessarily lead to such an approach during the EPC phase. Likewise, the selection and development of the project using a traditional approach does not preclude the use of relational approaches during the EPC phase. But in each case, the way the front end is structured will influence, to a large extent, the players and their roles during the EPC phase. Based on these distinctions, four very different configurations of project development and execution can be identified (see figure 9.1). In (1) traditional sponsorship, the front end is internalized by a sponsor and managed by using approaches that emphasize project selection. In addition, the EPC phase is managed by using arm's-length contracts with executing firms. In (2) the "partners in ownership" con-

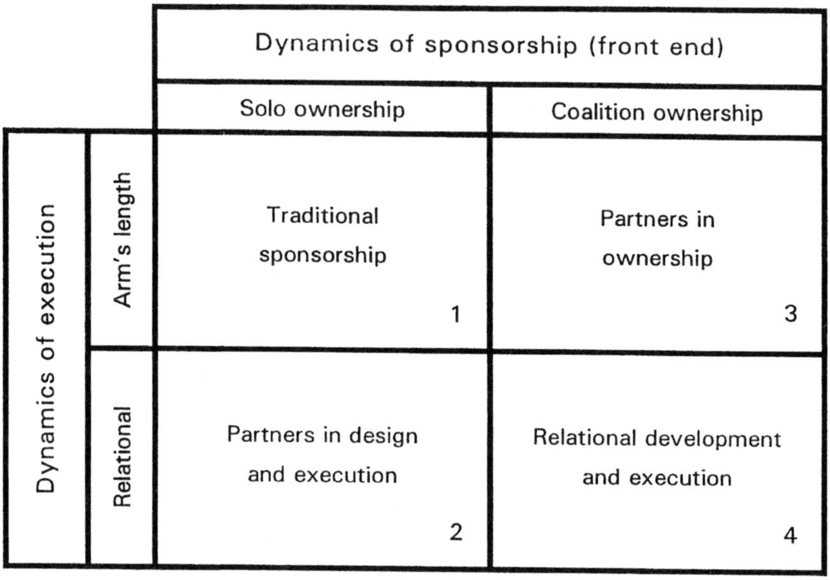
Dynamics of sponsorship (front end)
Solo ownership
Coalition ownership
Dynamics of execution
Arm's length
Relational
Traditional sponsorship
1
Partners in ownership
3
Partners in design and execution
2
Relational development and execution
4

Figure 9.1
Configuration of project sponsorship and execution

figuration, the front end is jointly managed by a coalition of firms, but the EPC phase is again managed through arm's-length contracts with executing firms. When there are (3) partners in design and execution, the project is selected using a traditional approach, but many organizations, including the owner-developer, influence and participate in the EPC phase. With (4) relational development and execution, some of the firms that will be involved heavily in the EPC phase are also members of the coalition of firms that sponsored the project during the front end.

Arm's-Length Contracts

All of the projects in the configurations in the top half of figure 9.1 are structured around contractual relations, in which suppliers are awarded contracts through a competitive bidding process, to provide prespecified goods and services at a predetermined price. The competitively bid, fixed-price contracts introduce a cutoff point in the project life cycle, before which the suppliers have little opportunity to influence project development (their involvement would corrupt the competitive bidding process), and after which the owner-developer has limited ability to influence further development. What is to be supplied is largely determined by the sponsors. How it is to be provided is largely at the discretion of the supplier. After signing the contract, the sponsor has little opportunity to exert influence without fundamentally changing the nature of the contractual relationship.

An important dimension of contract strategy is the degree of detail that the design reaches before arm's-length contracts are competitively bid. At one extreme, the bidding takes place early in the design process. This typically leads to a turnkey, performance-based contract being let out by the sponsor. The supplier is often a consortium of firms that takes responsibility for designing, building, and commissioning an artifact to meet the sponsor's need as specified. Sponsors seek to ensure that the supplier does in fact deliver the artifact by rigorous selection methods, requiring guarantees, and doing due-diligence analyses prior to contract award. At the other extreme, the sponsor internalizes the conceptual design process. The artifact to be built is fully specified, broken down into several contracts, and allocated to different suppliers through competitive bids. In this way, the sponsor maintains tight control.

The two contract strategies described above have in common the existence of cutoff points at which control of project content passes from sponsor to supplier; these cutoff points allow for little joint definition of project content. This contrasts sharply with projects in the bottom half of figure 9.1, in which mechanisms have been put in place to allow sponsors and firms that are active in the EPC phase to define project content jointly. In projects in the bottom left-hand quadrant, there is a clear distinction between sponsoring organizations and the firms involved in the EPC phase. In projects in the bottom right-hand quadrant, several of the firms involved in the EPC phase are also members of the sponsoring coalition.

Traditional Sponsorship

Many projects are still sponsored and executed under the dominant control of an owner. In these projects, the selection process is based on elaborate and formal criteria and is largely internalized. In the case of oil-extraction projects, several firms share ownership, but one firm, the field operator, is responsible for evaluating the field and proposing a project to exploit it. In fact, the need to have the project sanctioned by the other owners makes selection even more formal and rational that it otherwise might be.

Several characteristics of the traditional sponsorship process contribute to the creation of value. Rigorous selection ensures that the project is viable. In fact, the selection process goes beyond the selection of single projects to include portfolios of projects. Capital allocation requires that the market the project is to serve be thoroughly investigated. As sponsors are often network operators, there is the opportunity to integrate operational concerns in conceptual designs.

Large sponsors have developed considerable technical knowledge over the years, because of the vast experience they have acquired through the development and execution of many projects. Effort is expended to develop technology through participation in R&D projects, by keeping abreast with technical developments outside the firm, and by conducting studies to learn from previous projects. Technical departments develop and store this knowledge. Some of the accumulated knowledge is codified in technical standards and in managerial procedures and practices, while some is held by the technical staff in the form of experience.

The sponsor's technical departments are thus in a position to continue to dominate project development through the EPC phase. Typically, the sponsor will let out many contracts to specialized external suppliers, many of which will be competitively bid, often on a fixed-price basis. The sponsor may retain overall responsibility for project integration and coordination, or it may let out a contract for these services to a specialized firm. This organizational arrangement creates value through the use of specialized suppliers and the economic pressures of competitive bidding and fixed-price contracts. It also allows the sponsor to control project content by progressively letting out contracts, while maintaining tight control over the quality of execution.

Although the traditional way of structuring projects can and does lead to good results, it has drawbacks. Previous research (Miller, Lampel, and Floricel 1995) has shown that electrical utilities with large technical departments introduce few innovations in their projects. The codification of knowledge in standards brings rigidities that inhibit the search for innovative solutions. Standards also increase project costs, as they inhibit the search for designs that are "fit for purpose"—that meet the specific requirements of individual projects at least cost. Firms' standards are idiosyncratic from the supplier's point of view. Adhering to standards effectively limits the supplier' ability and opportunity to contribute its ideas and knowledge. Standards thus contribute to the isolation of those who make design choices from those who bid to execute these choices.

Partners in Design and Execution

Projects in quadrant 2 of figure 9.1 are characterized by some form of relational contracting between firms involved in the EPC phase and a sponsor. The organizational arrangements described here represent experiments initiated by owners as a means of overcoming the limits of the traditional approach. Often, sponsors had reached situations that rendered established practices less than acceptable: necessity became the mother of invention.

The most dramatic and best-documented situation was that in the oil-extraction sector in the North Sea, both in Great Britain and in Norway. The Cost Reduction Initiative for a New Era (CRINE) in Great Britain and Norsok, its equivalent in Norway, documented the need for new and better ways of developing the remaining, less lucrative oil fields. A change in the relationships among oil companies and firms providing goods and services to projects was seen as part of the solution to the industry's problems.

The construction industry, particularly in North America, has been plagued with poor performance and adversarial relationships between sponsors and contractors. The popularity of partnering can be explained by the unsatisfactory results produced by traditional approaches. Considerable variety is found among the project structures used to support relational contracting with a dominant sponsor.

The term *partnering* is used, in fact, to refer to two quite different sets of practices. First, it is an arrangement between a sponsor and contractors after contracts have been competitively bid. Second, it refers to long-term, multiproject relationships among sponsors and suppliers of engineering and/or construction services. Here, the expression *frame agreement* is used to refer to the latter relationships and the term *partnering* to refer to the former.

Partnering. The partnering relationship is instituted after the construction contract is competitively bid. There is therefore no opportunity for the contractor to have input into the design process. Partnering approaches, however, put in place mechanisms that reduce some of the undesirable side effects of traditional contractual relationships.

After the contract is awarded, the sponsor's project-management staff and the contractors get involved in team-building activities to improve communications during execution. Team-building activities usually involve joint training sessions in leadership and team management, and they may also involve project kickoff meetings during which each participant's expectations are clarified and documented. Team-building activities are often facilitated by an outside professional and costs are usually shared.

Improved communications are at the heart of joint problem solving. Better management of change requests is a key concern. Projects that use partnering show significant improvement on cost, schedule, quality, change-order management, and litigation. Such effects remain limited to management of the construction phase, however, leaving potential gains in the design phase untapped.

Frame agreements. These are long-term contractual relations between a sponsor and a supplier that cover a range of goods and/or services to be provided over a number of projects. Within the context of large capital projects, these types of relationships can cover EPC and equipment supplies.

Frame agreements reduce the number of supplier interfaces. Sponsors seek to make better use of the potential available in the supplier organization, especially human resources, skills, and knowledge. In selecting the firms with which they wish to enter into frame agreements, sponsors evaluate their competencies. Selection also includes an evaluation of the compatibility of the respective organizational cultures, and of their approach to quality management and innovation. Managers involved in these relationships all stress the importance of trust; to some extent, sponsors are placing themselves in a position of dependency on suppliers' competencies and good will.

Frame agreements lead to gains in operational efficiency. Suppliers become familiar with the owner's site, personnel, and management practices. In addition to avoiding costs and delays by not using the competitive bidding process, familiarity and early involvement make for a smoother and more efficient start-up of each phase of project execution.

Suppliers have an obvious interest in entering into frame agreements: they acquire priority access to a larger and a steadier volume of business as well as prestige. Sponsors expect that in return, suppliers will invest in developing and maintaining the technologies and resources required by their projects and in adapting their administrative systems. As the two organizations become integrated, each will have access to information in the other's information systems.

Sponsors hope that engineering and construction-management resources acquired through frame agreements will be more flexible and cost-effective than internal resources. Outside suppliers can balance variations in the sponsor's requirements with work from other clients and should be able to provide human resources in areas of specialization that the sponsor's own volume of engineering work would not justify.

Many of the frame agreements that IMEC investigated were set up by sponsors with the sole aim of acquiring access to specialized resources. They looked upon the work that they were letting out through frame agreements as contracts. The relationship was still thought of as having a cutoff point before which the supplier was not involved rather than having an extended period of joint project design and development.

Some of these relationships evolved over the years, however, to include a period of joint development. Two scenarios were observed. First, some suppliers proposed alternative concepts that were radically different from sponsors' ideas yet seen as having the potential to be significantly better. This led to an opening up to suppliers for contributions of ideas and knowledge. Second, suppliers gradually became involved in projects earlier on and were in a good position to make suggestions.

Respect for suppliers' competencies and knowledge opened the door for earlier involvement in conceptual design. In many cases, the relationship evolved to the point where the ideas, knowledge, and points of view of both the supplier and the sponsor were used. Joint activities created the opportunity to improve concepts significantly through more questioning of basic assumptions and integration of the supplier's perspective into the early conceptual design. Value-engineering workshops were one mechanism used to support joint design activities.

One-off integrated project teams. On some occasions, sponsors of projects in the IMEC sample opted for teams of suppliers that came together for a specific project. In each case the project had been thoroughly researched by sponsors, but feasible concepts were not found. The dead end compelled sponsors to find a different way to structure the project or to abandon it. From the point of view of large multinational firms, this was not necessarily a serious problem because investment opportunities existed elsewhere. But from the point of view of national organizations, the inability to develop a feasible project meant that investment possibilities became limited. In this context, necessity was definitely the mother of invention.

At the outset of the EPC phase, the sponsor had an unworkable concept. It also had documented normal cost targets, devised a schedule to be met, and set levels of technical performance. It assembled a design team, bringing in many of the specialized suppliers that would be required to execute the project. Design teams were centered on an engineering firm but included construction contractors, equipment manufacturers, fabricators, installers, owners of process technologies, and operators. Each was brought in very early to contribute ideas, information, and knowledge to the search for a feasible design.

The project manager and several technical specialists were from the sponsoring organization. Their role was to provide a bridge between the project team and the owner's technical departments. Yet, the sponsor's personnel and standard practices did not dominate the team. Standards were questioned and were retained only if it could be shown that they added value in the specific context of the project. The design criteria were very clearly "fit for purpose."

During the presanction phase, the sponsor assumed all the risks. Suppliers were paid under cost-reimbursable contracts, with or without a provision for normal profit. The risk that a sanctionable project would not emerge was always present; if a basic conceptual design was not found, the sponsor would pull the plug early.

Once a feasible design and project plan had been produced and approved, contracts were let out for execution. These were either fixed-price contracts or cost-reimbursable contracts with a guaranteed maximum price or both. Some form of incentive was often included in the contracts; incentives for reducing cost, accelerating completion, or technical performance above that foreseen in the project as sanctioned. On some projects, the integrated team was maintained during execution.

Projects that used integrated teams showed good performance. Previously unfeasible projects became doable. New designs, however, explained only part of the improved performance. These projects showed that it is possible to produce greatly improved performance by making better use of well-known technologies. Finally, projects structured as one-off integrated project teams allowed the longest period of joint search for a feasible design, involving the greatest number of participating firms.

Sticky informal networks. Less formal arrangements that fostered joint design and execution were also observed among the IMEC projects. The development of these practices was highly influenced by the history and the culture of both the country and the industry in which they were observed.

Networks of informal and preexisting relations among the participating organizations had an impact both on the way the projects were structured and on how they unfolded. This situation presented itself in what appear to be widely varying national contexts, especially in the French and Japanese construction industries. In each case, relationships were based on informal exchanges and expectations, not on enforceable contracts. These included the norms that the dominant sponsor would treat its suppliers justly and fairly, and it would compensate suppliers for their efforts and contributions.

Sponsors expected suppliers to make contributions and commitments that go beyond those of a normal business relationship as conceived of in Anglo-American culture. The suppliers fully expected to be compensated for their efforts and for the risks they assumed. The sticky informal network thus created some of the same conditions seen in the frame agreements and integrated project teams previously described. It would be difficult, if not impossible, however, for a foreign firm to participate in these structures. Likewise, it would be difficult for French or Japanese firms to transpose these informal networks into projects with several foreign participants.

Partners in design and execution developed high levels of collaboration and mutual influence. Nonetheless, sponsors were still in a dominant position. As one executive put it, "It's a partnership, but we all know who the boss is."

Partners in Ownership

Projects in quadrant 3 of figure 9.1 were sponsored by alliances of firms, but the owners opted for an arm's-length contractual strategy for the EPC phase. The archetype of this project structure is an IPP in which the sponsoring coalition has created considerable value through the deal-making process. The coalition's objective for the EPC phase is to purchase a reliable technical solution and minimize risks.

Quite often, such projects were financed by limited recourse loans. Completion and technical performance risks had to be reduced to a minimum and transferred to third parties. A fixed-price, turnkey contract with a reputable and creditworthy supplier covered detailed design, construction, and start-up. The sponsor made a call for proposals based on a well-established technical solution, and the contractors had to provide a detailed conceptual design of the system to be built. They had to guarantee both the project's completion and its technical performance. The proposal of the chosen supplier, often a consortium of equipment suppliers and engineering and construction firms, was then subjected to a due-diligence analysis by independent experts, after which a third party often provided a performance guarantee. Progress, quality, and performance were monitored during execution by an independent firm that reported to the sponsor, lenders, and parties providing performance guarantees.

In turnkey approaches, there is both the opportunity and the incentive for the firms within the supplier consortium to work together in preparing their bid and during project execution. A joint project office is set up to facilitate collaborative effort. The traditional barrier between the engineering design team and the construction contractor is thus removed, allowing them to work closely and collaboratively during project design and execution. Nonetheless, a consortium's ability to improve on what is already established as industry standards is limited.

Relational Development and Execution

Projects in quadrant 4 of figure 9.1 are characterized by the heavy involvement of some of the same firms in both the front-end development and EPC phases. Typically, this configuration is structured around an alliance of firms that form separate companies or joint ventures through which they both sponsor and execute large capital projects. EPC firms and/or equipment manufacturers are thus members of the ownership group that plays the role of sponsor.

The archetype of this configuration is a joint venture to build and operate transportation infrastructure under a concession framework with a government agency that brings EPC firms into project sponsorship and design. There is no significant period of project development prior to the involvement of firms that not only possess important competencies in project execution but that will do the work during the EPC phase. The securing of the concession agreement and of financing typically signals the end of the front-end phase and the start of the EPC

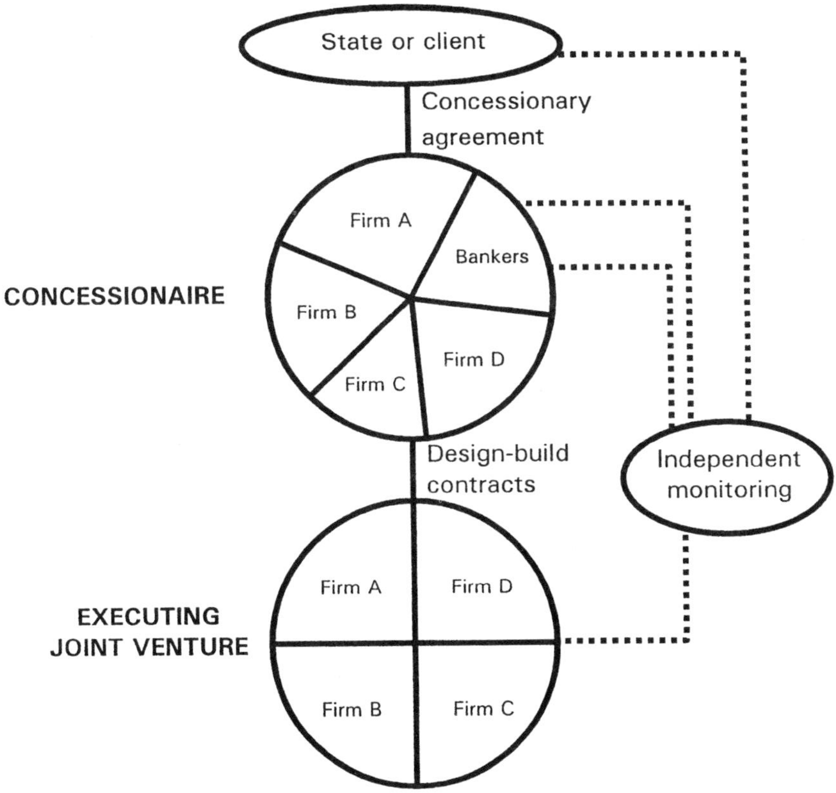

Figure 9.2
Structure for relational development and execution

phase. Turnkey contracts can be let out directly to firms participating in the sponsoring coalition; more typically, groups of firms will form temporary joint ventures through which they will assume responsibility for executing the entire project or large portions of it. This basic structure is presented in figure 9.2.

The viability of such projects rests quite heavily on the ability to achieve substantial performance improvement in project design, construction, and operation above what normally could be expected. The performance that the public sector normally would have been able to deliver if it had managed the project in a traditional manner is often used, implicitly and explicitly, as a benchmark against which the private concession's performance is judged. For example, in the IMEC sample, several road-concession projects were developed on the basis of a 25 percent reduction in construction costs compared to public practice.

Demonstrable increases in efficiency in designing, building, and operating play the dual role of contributing to the project's legitimacy in the public eye and providing incentive to the private parties. Indeed, several projects investigated here would not have been viable without superior performance in the EPC phase, notably in capital-cost reduction. An analysis of projects in this quadrant identified four sets of factors that contributed to producing the superior performance.

Projects subjected to intense scrutiny. Certain mechanisms heighten analysis. First, projects are subjected to scrutiny by government agencies and pressure groups: the promoter must demonstrate to a variety of audiences that the private concession is a viable option in the public interest. Several government departments, agencies, and pressure groups, not all of them supportive of private participation in public infrastructure, will have the opportunity to scrutinize and either block or delay the project.

Government agencies therefore acquire in-depth knowledge of the project's technical and commercial content and are in a position to use this knowledge to monitor the project effectively—particularly to ensure compliance with its many requirements. In addition to having an agency responsible for the project, the government will often mandate an independent firm to monitor the project.

Concessions must be financed, at least in part, by private lenders and investors other than the executing firms. These participants, which have considerable skill in evaluating commercial viability, tend to be risk averse. Their presence pushes the coalition to analyze thoroughly many worst-case scenarios that are often neglected by enthusiastic and optimistic project developers. Investors and lenders will insist that risks be laid off through a fixed-price turnkey contract. Independent monitoring of project execution will be established to ensure that project execution is in line with the established plan.

Scrutiny is also increased by the presence of several executing firms within the ownership group. Having work validated by peer firms with similar knowledge and experience can be more demanding than meeting the requirements of an external client. Parameters will thus come under considerable scrutiny until all are convinced that the firms will be able to meet targets and make reasonable profits.

One of the projects in the IMEC sample, Cofiroute in France, had an unusual but effective mechanism for ensuring scrutiny. The ownership coalition was composed exclusively of construction firms that divided themselves into two equivalent groups of firms, each group building a section of road. Precise descriptions of the work, cost, and schedule were developed for each section. Once this had been accomplished to the satisfaction of all firms, the two sections of highway to be built were allocated randomly to the two groups. This unusual structure ensured that the combined knowledge of the whole group was drawn upon in the preparation of the plans for each section and that each was prepared under the informed scrutiny of the entire group. The concessionaire structure and its mix of participants thus provide several checks and balances through which the project can be subjected to intense scrutiny.

Alliances of firms must run the concession as a business and integrate the dual incentives of the owner and contractor. The concessionaire must seek both to reduce design and construction costs and to produce a project that will be economical to maintain and operate. The concessionaire's design and planning team is thus in a position to make appropriate trade-offs between these often conflicting concerns.

In an integrated business perspective, the concessionaire has overall responsibility for the design and construction process and is thus in a position to make decisions about construction strategy. It can make better use of capacity, alternative construction methods, standardization of components, or adaptations to seasonal variations and site conditions. In several of the projects IMEC studied, innovative technologies were introduced. The fact that firms worked together, rather than separately, allowed them to exploit possible synergies.

Taking a life-cycle perspective, the concessionaire may decide to schedule investments progressively. For example, on projects for roads on which traffic volumes are expected to increase over several years, planning to improve road surfaces or add additional lanes as required can reduce initial investments.

Under traditional contract strategy, the public authority dominates the critical design stages. Probity considerations in the bidding process prevent firms from contributing to the conceptual design decisions. Integration into the early design process of the ideas, knowledge, and differing perspectives that the executing firms provide as a significant source of improvement is impossible.

The design and construction strategies developed during the design phase are better because of incentives to improve performance and the intense scrutiny and early involvement of executing firms. Plans are easier to execute because their presence in the design process has brought in considerations of constructibility and choice of efficient construction methods. Second, the concessionaire facilitates project start-up. Firms are often already familiar with the plans and can avoid the learning curve.

During project execution, there is less conflict of interest between the sponsor and the contractors since the contractors are owners. More open and frank information sharing replaces the games of "cat and mouse" and "cops and robbers" through which each party attempts to gain access to or hide information.

Projects in this quadrant are quite often politically driven which can either accelerate or stall a project. Accelerating a project may be necessary to capture a window of opportunity, while political constraints may impose a slower pace in, or even a halt to, project development. In the IMEC sample, examples of the effects of acceleration included short bid-preparation periods that resulted in hasty analysis, and politically determined and supported in-service dates that were not necessarily technically optimal.

Firms participating in projects of this type can either win or lose, both as owners and as contractors. This can produce four scenarios of project performance: (1) lose as both owner and contractor; (2) win as owner, lose as contractor; (3) lose as owner, win as contractor; (4) or win as both owner and contractor. The only way that a firm can protect itself from the devastating effects of a lose-lose scenario is to minimize its exposure to risk and to spread the risk over a portfolio of assets, including many other projects. The firm that is unable to diversify this risk may be in a precarious position. Projects in which a private party is seen as making unreasonable profits while providing a public service are particularly vulnerable to risk.

These findings call into question the current trend in the project-management literature that seeks to identify "best project-management practices." There is no best way of structuring all projects; furthermore, a "best practice" in one quadrant of figure 9.1 could well be totally counterproductive in projects from another quadrant. Project sponsors and developers must first decide on the best strategic approach and structure for each project in its specific context. They can then identify practices that contribute to good management of projects within this general approach. The variety of practices found within each quadrant, however, makes the identification of best practices somewhat problematic.

Projects that use some form of relational approach become successes because there are many ways to conceive, design, and build a project, and some of these lead to better results than current practice. The safe way to undertake a project, seen from the sponsor's perspective, is to do it as it has always been done by applying the standards and specifications developed through decades of fine-tuning the approach. Petroleum companies, electrical utilities, and departments of transportation have been producing projects for decades within the confines of traditional approaches. As long as there are no compelling reasons to change, firms are unlikely to discover the rich possible futures that are available to them.

Questioning standards and well-established project models is threatening and creates anxiety and complexity. When this complexity is mastered, however, one realizes that it can bring alternative solutions. At the beginning of these projects, their futures are not yet known, but promises of great results are apparent. The positive results of mastered complexity can be tremendous.

10 Rising to the Challenge of Evolving High-Stakes Games

Roger Miller and Donald Lessard

The paradox observed in LEPs is that planning in a traditional sense has little to do with success or failure, yet successful sponsors expend much greater resources on planning activities than even a traditional model suggests. Planning that seeks to reduce projects to a sequence of prespecified activities does not work because the future is often turbulent. Massive, integrative strategic models do not solve the problem either, as they cannot readily accommodate the continuous shaping actions that are required as the future evolves.

This does not imply, however, that raw intuition and improvisation take the fore. The commitment of large sums in irreversible and indivisible assets cannot be made lightly. Due diligence requires research studies, simulations of future interactions with governments, influence attempts, and so forth. Not only are decision-support tools popular for assessing risks, but the sponsors in the IMEC projects were heavily involved in risk seminars, simulations, and impact assessments. Planning obviously means something different to sponsors.

LEPs as Systemic Innovations

LEPs involve systemic innovations that are highly vulnerable and difficult to shape. They require the coordination of many autonomous actors over time, each controlling a part of the puzzle (Miller et al. 1995).

Goals are ambiguous. Multiple parties and distinct evaluation criteria are at work. Trade-offs are inescapable, but projects must meet basic criteria on each dimension. Few technical options or initial project configurations are clear winners from the start and across the board. Juggling a multidimensional project concept until it is accepted is an art form that rewards the design of novel solutions.

Sponsors are tied by dependencies. Agreements are needed from clients and bankers, affected parties and government agencies: many complementary organizations can make or break the project. Birth and infancy are full of dangers for the young project: it is more likely to be abandoned than to survive. Projects can be killed by refusal to cooperate or by failure to make or honor commitments. The consequence of strategic interdependencies is the need to engage in extensive transactions and negotiations that entail front-end strategic expenditures.

The harder the better. Successful projects are not necessarily the easy ones, but those whose real value can be created by hard creative work, leverage at the right moment, and influence on the right groups. Using the mountain-climbing metaphor, value is created not so much in easy-to-climb hills but rather in hard-to-face mountains that open up to further chains of hard-to-climb value peaks. Difficult but value-creating opportunities require heavy planning expenditures.

In response to the paradox of planning and within the context of systemic innovation, effective sponsors have developed a dual repertoire of mechanisms that combine creativity and discipline and engage the various parties in the mutual shaping of the project. They develop scripts to identify issues, allocate risks, rehearse collaboration, and work through technical options, and successful scripts carry over from project to project. At the outset, they behave as imaginative prospectors trying to configure novel concepts. At other moments, they apply the discipline of investing to creative ideas and concepts to extract economic value.

Effective sponsors have developed the core competencies of proposing a vision, marshalling resources, combining multiple views, and formalizing sets of tests as projects move from concept to commitment, construction, and launch. Sometimes, exceptional individuals combine creativity and discipline; much more progress is achieved when sponsoring firms, and the legal and financial advisers they employ have established processes to make discipline possible through decision points or gates.

During the front-end period, creative ideas need to predominate; nevertheless, projects must periodically be submitted to multiple tests. Without this discipline, erroneous commitments may be made or projects may be abandoned prematurely. Worse, the wrong project may be built efficiently. Successful sponsors create internal debates to distinguish among the roles of promoters, analysts, and investors. Prospectors are executives whose task is to identify potential projects, while promoters act as internal champions to ensure that opportunities are moved forward. Analysts from the financial, engineering, and legal spheres inside or outside the sponsors' firms take a fresh and independent look at these proposals and turn them into investment options. Then, investment executives examine these options with yet another independent perspective and assess the proposals as a function of alternatives in a portfolio, exposures to risk that may derail project, the project's ability to survive crises, and other factors. Before a project idea is committed, many iterations and episodes take place.

Discipline during the front end is achieved by matching venture ideas with due diligence practices. In fact, the implementation of disciplined methodologies follows scripts that force both sponsors and specialists to face up to potential difficulties ahead. Here are a few examples.

Review gates at the end of each shaping episode call for decisions either to abandon or to search for additional partners, which will make it possible to create further value. Here, sponsors behave very much like venture capitalists that proceed by rounds of investments: only projects that truly create value progress across rounds.

Risk seminars in which the leading sponsor and its investment banker invite partners and affected parties to identify likely negative futures. Once potential exposures are identified, risks are allocated directly or indirectly to competent players through devices that rely largely on corporate interests, the need to protect reputation, and the desire to maintain credibility.

Stress testing of collaborative arrangements. Alliances, joint ventures, and coalitions certainly serve to share risks and pool resources, but their main purpose is to help rescue projects should difficulties arise. Rehearsals of potential behaviors in crisis scenarios must be conducted. Sponsor, lawyers, and partners thus engineer stress testing of collaborative arrangements through the imagination of future negative events, the passing of judgment on likely behaviors, and the formal commitment to behave in desirable fashion.

At the collective level, discipline is exercised by creating institutional conditions that facilitate the coordination of communities, affected groups and opponents during front end, construction, and ramp-up. Institutional frameworks that provide for hearings, debates, and discussions allow stress testing not only among interested players but also with affected parties with minimal real interests in the project.

Theories to Support the Shaping of Projects

Project-choice and project-management theories point to the need for and possibility of planning. They are helpful in providing tools for discipline, especially during the engineering and construction phase. Unfortunately, many authors fall into the trap of over-optimism by thinking that success can become both predictable and controllable (Cooper 1993).

An alternative set of theories stresses that innovations are due largely to entrepreneurial actions and that planning adds little or no value. The idea of intuitive and fluid decision making rose to prominence in the early 1980s, as environments turned increasingly dynamic and chaotic. Forecasting, it is agreed, cannot extend far into the future: flexibility, innovation, and continued adaptations are thus needed. The management process is focused on creative adaptation.

Entrepreneurship theories value the meritocratic selection of bright, innovative project ideas. The premise is that good ideas get selected naturally by efficient markets, not by planning (Alchian 1950; Alchian and Demsetz 1973). Sooner or later, it is argued, markets recognize merits and reward firms, technologies, and entrepreneurs accordingly. Superior technologies or projects are destined to succeed, while weak ones are bound for the garbage heap (Schumpeter 1942). Theories concerned with innovation rarely stress the need for planning. Yet, LEPs are rarely selected only because they represent the brightest option as viewed by markets. Instead, projects are shaped under conditions of turbulence, indeterminacy, and opportunism, and planning expenses are required to test and implement the various strategies that make a project feasible. As sponsors respond to events, they gradually commit to irreversible and socially acceptable investments.

In line with what we have observed among successful sponsors, strategic governance theories that combine innovation and discipline have emerged in recent years. Their common characteristic is that they focus on real time rather than a "frozen" set of likely futures. We will briefly sketch three perspectives.

The prospective-scenarios perspective emerged with systems thinking in the 1950s, evolved into well-designed methodologies in the 1960s and 1970s, but waned in the early 1980s as doubts were cast on the effectiveness of planning. The recent revival of scenario planning is due largely to high levels of uncertainty and the need to innovate in the face of threats. The main tools for design scenarios are industrial dynamics simulations, scripts of plausible multidimensional stories, seminars to identify likely future events, and articulation of mitigation measures in decision trees.

Prospective scenarios help to build rich views of the future and imagine strategies to shape them while recognizing their basic indeterminacy (Lesourne 1991). In scenario building, sponsors consider well-researched stories to bring forward surprises. The process starts with the past and explores divergent paths using trends and drivers. Thinking through scenarios results in high-level conversations that reveal assumptions, likely behaviors, and potential innovations (Schwartz 1996). The main advantage of scenarios is that they foster distinct views and avoid the dominant thinking that rapidly converges on one view of the future.

The real-options approach took form in the decision-analysis perspective as the value of investing in additional information to better frame a problem (Urban and Hauser 1980). The finance field developed it further based on the fundamental insights of Black, Scholes, and Merton on the valuation of financial options (Amram and Kulatilaka 1999; Dixit and Pindyck 1995). The central contribution of the real-options perspective is that it introduces both time and flexibility by allowing the possibility of delaying investments, accelerating them, or breaking them into components. Dissatisfaction with discounted cash-flow techniques that did not allow for future decisions led managers to look for better-suited perspectives. Real options offer a way to recognize the modular, groping, path-dependent nature of capital investments and to highlight the strategic value not only of pertinent new information but also of both bold commitment and flexibility. The challenge is no longer to optimize a unique, heroic decision, but to work through a sequence of interrelated moves within a complex and evolving ecology of endogenous and exogenous factors. Having thus created real options, decision makers can exercise them if conditions to invest are favorable.

A contribution of the IMEC program has been to spell out the notions of risk unbundling, risk strategizing, and bold actions to break indeterminate situations. Sponsors gain comparative advantages not only through core competencies but also by embracing the risks over which they can achieve some degree of control by internalizing (endogenizing) them. The perspective of risk strategizing assumes that there is an essential difference between risky situations, in which the future is fully framed by probabilistic states of nature, and evolving high-stakes games, in which indeterminacy reigns and strategic leverage can make new futures possible.

Strategizing in situations of high uncertainty has the goal of identifying windows of opportunity where sponsors can exert influence to internalize the sources of high uncertainty. Control is achieved not by shifting risks to others for a fee but by endogenizing them through alliances, contracts, partnerships, coalitions, credible commitments, renegotiations of agreements, and so forth.

Progressive issue resolution looks for points of leverage where influence can be exerted. At the beginning, the project concept to be shaped is ill formed. In a first round, initial decisions are made and policies formulated, until some form of resolution has been achieved. Then, at the appropriate moment, which the sponsor knows by being there, leverage can be exercised as turning or bifurcation points and new payoff structures appear. It is rare that project shaping is completed the first time around. Only innovations in the recasting of issues, the involvement of new participants, and the formulation of new hypotheses can achieve some progress. Closure is achieved when enough progress has been made to confirm the sponsors' hypotheses.

Strategic-governance theories foster the concept that increased investments in planning for shaping projects are necessary to test novel shaping hypotheses as long as sponsors have the subjective conviction that value can be created. Eventually, investments in planning reach a plateau of marginal or even declining productivity. The management process is messy because innovations are needed to respond to shifting events, but managers use disciplined tools to assess returns, estimate impacts, and decide where strategic leverage has potential.

The value provided by strategic-governance approaches are rehearsed decisions, shared understanding, and development of strategies in advance of, as well as in line with, emergent turbulence. The criteria used to select strategies include the ability to break indeterminacy and reduce uncertainty, the sharing of risks, the building of coalitions, and the capacity to exert influence.

Golden Rules for Evolving High-Stakes Games

The golden rule of project management indicates that sponsors ought to eliminate, or at least reduce, uncertainty by gathering as much information as possible before committing large sums and shifting as many of the remaining risks as possible to other stakeholders. Only when risks have been brought down substantially can amounts at stake be allowed to rise, thus keeping exposures under control. Yet LEPs entail many transactions that cannot be specified or controlled in advance of their execution. Projects are constructed and agreements negotiated over time in the context of risks and interdependencies. An improved version of the golden rule, drawing on insights from real options, is that it is still better to stay flexible and uncommitted until as late as possible (Olleros 1991). When the future cannot be influenced, whatever the causes of uncertainty, the rule of thumb is usually to diversify, stay flexible, and minimize the level of irreversible commitments.

LEPs cannot progress, however, without commitments that rapidly become irreversible. Without bold moves at critical points, few agreements can be made and few projects can take off. The golden rule is certainly applicable when forecasts can be made and decision models built. LEPs, in contrast, are often characterized by turbulence, indeterminacy, positive and negative feedback loops, and other factors, all of which create difficult and irreversible decision-making situations.

Dilemmas arise in LEPs because the autonomous strategies pursued by interdependent players, affected parties, and even regulators can become inconsistent with value creation. The rational choices pursued by parties often contradict each other and can yield results that become irrational and even harmful. Fortunately, moves also create conditions of indeterminacy that can be used to create new futures. To resolve these dilemmas, sponsors need to do more than reduce risk; they must act decisively to break indeterminate situations and create advantage. Otherwise, projects are likely either to wither away due to lack of action or to be aborted because of conflict.

Sponsors succeed in shaping projects by recognizing the dilemmas involved and adopting new strategic principles to cope with the contradictions involved. In fact, it can be said that effective sponsors transform dilemmas into strategic principles (see table 10.1).

Planning for the Journey Rather than Planning the Journey

If the future could be adequately predicted, contracts could be designed to lock in on the most rational option, and strategies would be developed using logical analyses. Unfortunately, the future is often unknowable in advance. Commitments lock in to long-term horizons, but planning systems cannot forecast far into the future. Unforeseen contingencies, outside events, and internal difficulties arise over time.

The longer the development time, the higher the likelihood that projects will be affected by turbulence. Conditions do not remain sta-

Table 10.1
Project dilemmas and strategic principles in evolving high-stakes games

Project dilemma	Strategic principle
The forecasting dilemma	Planning for the journey rather than planning the journey
Strategic interdependency	Embracing interdependency and shared governance
Irreversible, indivisible exposure	Avoid locking in too early or too late
Dormant innovations	Unlocking latent solutions through trust-based relationships
Underinvestment in worthy projects	Tailoring public-private partnerships to internalize benefits
The dilemma of time	Stretching the front end and squeezing the back end
External effects	Seeking win-win solutions to accommodate stakeholders' interests

ble for the long period needed to bring projects to fruition. If events are unchecked by the timely actions of sponsors, degenerative processes may ensue. The dilemma is thus how to plan and contract when it is impossible to make deterministic forecasts.

Effective sponsors recognize explicitly that projects are not once-and-for-all decisions but journeys characterized by multiple decision episodes. They are not selected once and for all; rather, they are shaped progressively from an initial concept by the dialectical interactions of views. Similarly, contracts are not complete, but are contingent on various events and rely on the underlying incentives of parties to work through circumstances that cannot be prespecified. The initial idea is at best a hypothesis about a future that guides a sequence of episodes in which sponsors decide on the feasibility of the project, negotiate its legitimate integration into the society and institutions within which it operates, secure financial commitments, and so forth.

During the front-end period, the role of the sponsor is first to foster multiple perspectives by enlarging the boundaries of groups participating in the project and shaping moves to break indeterminate situations. As uncertainty reveals itself, leverage can be applied to make desired futures happen; reasoned commitments are thus made and contingent contracts are drawn up among parties.

The forecasting dilemma is substantially reduced during engineering and construction. A more predictable future has been created by prior decisions: a view of the future has been taken. At this stage, a variety of decision tools to assess risks using Monte Carlo techniques can identify possible interactions and help develop strategies. Technologies such as decision trees, simulations, and subjective utility scaling are useful. Nonetheless, the forecasting dilemma may reappear with a vengeance at the ramp-up period if projections do not materialize.

Embracing Interdependency and Shared Goverannce

A common notion presents large projects as the result of a clear strategic vision that the sponsor imposes on the other stakeholders. In reality, sponsors cannot build projects alone or impose a view: they need complementary, interdependent firms such as investment banks, debt holders, equipment suppliers, and EPC firms. Primarily, however, they need the consent of regulators and governments with interests and agendas of their own. The strategic principle that has emerged to cope with strategic interdependency is the design of business arrangements based on shared governance.

During the front-end period, the alignment of interests requires negotiations, deals, and commitments. Sponsors build coalitions of firms with specialized expertise, allocate risks, and organize incentives to form a coherent pack. A variety of interorganizational relationships, such as alliances, partnerships, and joint ventures, are used to cope with the risks of opportunistic moves. Sponsors, however, rarely start from scratch because they often work with experienced firms that know scripts and modes of interactions. Shared governance agreements become the basis for financial engineering.

Governance becomes the coordination of flows of interactions, materials, work packages, or activities during the engineering and construction phase. Unless major crises erupt, existing project-management tools are applicable. Gains can be achieved by reducing time lost in scheduling and work activities. Again, Monte Carlo risk simulations can be very helpful in identifying coordination difficulties in advance (Levitt and Kunz 1998). When assumptions fail to materialize during the ramp-up period, shared governance issues again rise to the forefront.

Avoiding Locking in Too Early or Too Late

As sponsors, partners, and external parties commit to a project, they lose degrees of freedom and increase their exposure to potential losses, but they also lock in their claims on eventual rewards. Effective sponsors are cautious in making irreversible commitments, but they recognize that, eventually, they must make such commitments. They select partners with complementary competencies who can bring creativity and innovation to the task of joint problem solving, but at some point they also act to force commitment by these parties.

During the front-end shaping period, sponsors must avoid making irreversible commitments until they gain enough knowledge to make reasoned choices. Yet, they cannot remain flexible indefinitely: eventually, cascades of moves must be made. Effective sponsors recognize the value of taking bold actions and committing large investments at the appropriate moment: others wait or commit too early.

In contrast, the engineering and construction phase is concerned with committing as fast as possible to build and operate the project, thus generating flows of revenue as early as possible. Flexibility at this stage will not usually make sense unless the project can be broken up into components: full commitments are necessary for dams, nuclear plants, bridges, subways, or urban roads. At the ramp-up stage, projects become totally vulnerable and rely helplessly on sponsorship coalitions, institutional structures, and governability arrangements to protect them if assumptions fail to materialize.

Unlocking Latent Solutions through Trust-Based Relationships

Cost-reducing ideas and value-enhancing solutions often remain dormant because innovators believe that they will have difficulty appropriating the eventual benefits that result from their ideas. Contractors, suppliers, and bankers are unwilling to share ideas with sponsors because mechanisms to capture benefits are inoperative. In the absence of incentives and mechanisms that value and reward innovation, parties will not foster innovative solutions. Effective sponsors foster generative relationships that unlock these latent innovations. They establish trust among participants that they will benefit if they add value, and they reinforce this trust by fostering relationships that extend over many projects.

The creation of value through innovative ideas is the most important issue during the front-end period. Sponsors know that competent specialists, through interactive problem solving, can help to create rich futures. Generative relationships build on the advantages of sharing views and exchanging information on issues, technologies, and plans.

Debates in which parties jointly deliberate, elucidate problems, and elaborate novel solutions create higher value in projects.

By the engineering and construction phase, the rules of the game have largely been set. The establishment of a climate of collaboration and trust makes it possible for ideas to flow and achieve the potential set by the incentives framework. During the ramp-up period, involved parties will come to the rescue if their own interests are at stake. Incentives thus need to be set up in such a way that regulators, bankers, and constructors lose more by walking away than by working to save the project.

Tailoring Public-Private Partnerships to Internalize Benefits

Many projects with high social utility have limited private potential due to shaping difficulties and limits on the appropriability of revenues. A good proportion of LEPs in urban transport, water, roads, and so forth cannot hope to generate enough direct revenues to pay back the required investments. Although a project to solve specific urban-transportation problems may cost US$2 billion, for example, the present value of the tolls that can be collected from users may be, at best, US$950 million. Without public contributions that reflect some of the project's indirect benefits, such as reduced congestion and pollution, socially useful projects would be stalled, built inefficiently by governments, or simply abandoned. Privatization of LEPs is possible only when revenues from the markets of these concessions can match all costs, including normal profits. Effective sponsors of such projects tailor private-public partnerships that allow them to internalize enough of the benefits to justify the investment required.

IMEC research revealed a number of new patterns of interactions among sponsors, bankers, regulators, and governments at the front end of difficult projects. Innovative sponsors engaged in path-breaking projects through concessions, BOTs, or mixed-economy corporations, in which the costs and benefits of a socially valuable project were shared by sponsors, concessionaires, and governments. Private financing justified by future tolls must be supplemented by private financing secured against public commitments to provide subsidies, pay for complementary investments, and share in risks in the future. In some cases, this involves direct government support; in others, it involves the "securitization" of future government support enable private financing.

Confronted with unrealized value, political leaders need to develop innovative approaches to allow for the emergence of truly superior solutions. Effective public entrepreneurs are not so much those who build visible monuments but those who create the public good by adapting institutional structures and setting new patterns of interactions. During the design and construction phase, concessions or BOTs that create private incentives for efficiency can reduce costs substantially. During the ramp-up period, public-private partnerships are put to the test.

Stretching the Front End and Squeezing the Back End

The saying that "time is money" suggests that the longer the period required to imagine, design, and construct the project, the higher its cost—and, hence, the lower its value. Effective sponsors recognize that time is both friend and foe.

During the front-end period, the passage of time is a friend of appropriate decision making and value creation. The front-end period is usually long because uncertainty can reveal itself only over time; effective solutions are generated over time by interactions among sponsors, specialists, and stakeholders in response to events; and the exercise of real influence and leverage inevitably takes time. If a sponsor can shorten the elapsed time while maintaining flexibility, learning, and the building of trust among the parties, it will gain a competitive advantage. Top sponsors are able to accelerate learning by bringing the accumulated experience of many projects to bear and by creating group simulations in which partners and stakeholders jointly learn and develop trust. This ability to substitute accumulated experience and skill for time is a key competency of top sponsors and world-class specialists, particularly law firms and investment banks. If a given set of stakeholders is new to the game, however, no amount of "virtual time" can substitute for their learning and building of trust. Thus, effective front ends inevitably involve considerable time. Too long a front end, however, may induce competitors to do better. Sponsors thus have to take the necessary time with diligence.

During the engineering and construction phase, where little knowledge of flexibility is gained by waiting and expenditures mount rapidly, time erodes value. The faster the project is built, the faster revenues flow in. Speed from design to revenue generation is of the essence.

Seeking Win-Win Solutions to Accommodate the Range of Stakeholder Interests

Projects generate gains for some parties but losses for others. Sponsors are faced with competing claims. Affected parties often lack the necessary information to understand the issues involved and thus prefer antagonism. As a result of the countervailing influences of positive and negative external effects, optimal choices are difficult to reach. Parties whose consent is needed often use contradictory evaluation criteria to assess projects. At best, what can be achieved is satisfactory utility, not optimality. Sponsors must take into account a variety of value criteria and creatively seek solutions that are seen as win-win.

Effective sponsors seek to understand affected parties' values and power; otherwise, their actions will trigger unexpected reactions. External effects are best dealt with through explicit recognition of the rights and prerogatives of affected parties. Consent will also be gained through redesign of projects, negotiation, and compensations. Sponsors will obviously incur costs, but internalization will build legitimacy. Effective sponsors assume that they can solve the problems of external effects by recognizing the legitimate rights of affected parties to valid information and honest compensation. The dangers are hubris, diktat, and the failure to see the power of negotiation to develop mutual-gains solutions.

During engineering and construction, sponsors have to manage the delivery of positive external effects and reduce the impact of negative ones. They have to honor commitments and live up to promises. The success of many projects observed in IMEC was due to unrecognized public-affairs managers who delivered what was committed to. In contrast, spectacular failures occurred when public affairs were neglected in the front end and erupted during construction or ramp-up.

Traditional prespecified planning does not work because the future is often turbulent and solutions require the interaction of many parties. Reductionism in planning looks for "silver bullet" solutions, but singular strategies and practices that are justifiable in isolation can generate dysfunctional dynamics. Engineers like to look for plannable, practical solutions and substantively rational decisions, but this can cripple projects.

Strategic-governance approaches, in contrast, view management as guided by procedural rationality, which recognizes both the need for innovation and the need for organizational discipline to ensure that creative ideas meet the tests of economic feasibility, social acceptability, and political legitimacy. Shaping a project is a messy process, but players become rational by following scripts and self-imposed discipline in decision sequences over time.

Appendix A: Short Description of the Sixty Projects Studied in the IMEC Program

Hydroelectric Projects

Bakun	A partly built 2,400 MW hydroelectric plant in Sarawack, Malaysia. The sponsor was Ekran Berhad, a Sarawack firm. The project was stopped during the Asian financial crisis.
Birecik	A 672 MW hydroelectric plant and irrigation system on the Euphrates River in Turkey. The sponsor was a consortium of European firms led by Gama Endustri of Turkey. The total cost was estimated to be 2.3 billion DM.
Caruachi	A 2,160 MW hydro dam being built by EDELCA on the Caroni river in Venezuela. The project's total cost is US$2.13 billion. It is expected to be in operation in 2003.
Freudenau	A 172 MW hydroelectric dam on the River Danube in Vienna, Austria. The sponsor was Donaukraft of Austria. The cost was US$1.230 billion.
Igarapava	A 220 MW river-flow power dam built by the CEMIG consortium on the Rio Grande in Brazil. The project was built at a cost of US$293 million.
ITA	A 1,450 MW hydroelectric dam built on the Uruguay River in Brazil. The project was built by a consortium led by Oderbrecht with Electrosul as operating partner. The project cost was US$1.354 billion.
Kazunogawa	A 1,600 MW pumped-storage peak-power plant linking two dams. Located near Mount Fuji. The sponsor was Tepco of Japan. The effective head is 715 meters. The cost was ¥370 billion.
La Grande 1	A 1,400 MW hydroelectric project that is part of the 30,000 MW Baie James complex in Quebec. Hydro-Québec was the sponsor. Cost was CA$2.8 billion.

Lambach — A small-flow-of-the-river power project sponsored by OKA on the Traun River near Lambach and Stadl-Paura, Austria. The cost was SCH500 million.

Machadihno — A proposed 1,200 MW hydroelectric dam sponsored by Electrosul to be owned in partnership with industrial users of electricity. The dam is located on the Uruguay River in Brazil.

Old ITA — A partly built 1,450 MW hydroelectric dam on the Uruguay River in Brazil. The sponsor, Electrosul, has delayed the project for ten years.

Pangue — A 450 MW hydroelectric dam on the Bio Bio River in Chile. The sponsor was Pangue S.A., a subsidiary of Endesa. It was built at a cost of US$360 million.

Pehuenche — A hydroelectric dam in Chile completed in the early 1990s at a cost of US$450 million. The sponsor was Pehuenche S.A.

Ralco — A proposed 570 MW hydroelectric dam on the Bio Bio River in Chile, forming a system with the Pangue project. The sponsor is Endesa of Chile.

Tucurui — A 4,000 MW hydroelectric plant on the Tocantins river in the Brazilian Amazon. A major project to serve cities and aluminum producers, built in the mid-1980s at a cost of US$6 billion. The project is to be extended to 8,000 MW.

Thermal- and Nuclear-Power Projects

Bergen — A 650 MW repowering of an original coal-fired plant in Ridgefield, New Jersey, to use natural gas or fuel oil. The sponsor was Public Service Electric and Gas Co. of New Jersey, and the cost was US$400 million.

Civaux — Two nuclear-power plants built in Civaux, France, producing 2,900 MW. Part of a long series of plants built by EDF and technology suppliers. The cost was 19.5 billion FF.

Clover Power — A 440 MW coal-fired thermal plant built in the early 1990s and sponsored by Old Dominion Electric Cooperation of Richmond, Virginia. The cost was US$1.2 billion.

Gazmont — A small peaking power plant built at a cost of CA$50 million using gas from a dump in Montreal, Canada. The sponsor was a group of firms led by Novergaz of Montreal.

Hub	A 1,300 MW oil-fired power plant located in Hub Chowki in Pakistan, costing US$1.8 billion. A BOT project sponsored by National Power International of the United Kingdom and Xenel Industries of Saudi Arabia.
Indiantown	A 330 MW pulverized-coal cogeneration qualifying facility sponsored by U.S. Generating Co. under PURPA regulations. The plant is located in Martin County, Florida. The cost was US$825 million.
Lambdon	The repowering in the mid-1990s of a 2,100 MW thermal-power plant in Sarnia, Ontario, by Ontario Hydro at a cost of CA$410 million.
McWilliams	Repowering from coal to gas of a 150 MW power plant located in Gant, Alabama, at a cost of US$70 million. The sponsor was Alabama Electric Cooperative.
Nanko	A 1,800 MW liquefied-natural-gas thermal-power plant built in the late 1980s by Kansai Power in a residential area of Osaka Bay, Japan. The cost was ¥260 billion.
Navotas I	A 200 MW gas-turbine power plant in Manila, the Philippines, completed in the late 1980s. The project was sponsored by Hopewell Holdings Ltd., of Hong Kong, at a cost of US$55 million.
North Branch	A 80 MW coal-fired power plant located in West Virginia. Built under PURPA as a qualifying facility, the project was sponsored by Energy America Inc. and cost US$150 million.
Ocean State Power	A 450 MW power plant built by Makowsky and Associates in the early 1990s in Rhode Island. The fuel is natural gas from Canada. Cost was US$450 million.
Paiton	A 1,230 MW thermal-power plant built in East Java, Indonesia, by PT Paiton Energy Ltd., sponsored by Mission Energy, Mitsui & Co. Ltd., and PT Batu Hitam Perkasa. The cost of the project was US$2.43 billion.
Port Dickson	A 440 MW IPP thermal project built in Malaysia in the late 1990s by a consortium led by SIME Darby, at a cost of RM 700 million.
Subic Bay	A 116 MW thermal-power plant in Subic Bay, Freeport, the Philippines, costing US$128 million. The sponsor was Subic Power Corp., 50 percent owned by Enron of Houston, Texas. The project has been operational since the mid-1990s.

Sumatra — A proposed mine-mouth 300 MW coal-fired power plant in Indonesia to sell power to Malaysia. The sponsor was a Malaysian engineering entrepreneur. The project was a victim of the Asian crisis.

Wabash River — A 200 MW repowering of the Wabash River generating station from coal to synthetic fuel gas. The project is a joint venture between Destec Energy and PSI Energy. It is located in West Terre Haute, Indiana. The cost was US$400 million.

Urban Transport

Ankara Metro — A first-phase subway in Ankara, Turkey. The sponsors were SNC Lavalin, of Canada, and Gama and Guris, of Turkey. The cost was US$650 million.

Hopewell — A partly built elevated-rail system in Bangkok, Thailand, sponsored by Hopewell Holdings of Hong Kong under a concession from State Railways of Thailand. The project's future is in doubt.

MRTA — A proposed subway system in Bangkok, Thailand, sponsored by the Metropolitan Rapid Transit Authority of Bangkok.

Orlyval — Development, in the early 1990s, of a link between Orly airport and the RER public transport near Paris, France. The sponsor was MATRA and the cost was 1.74 billion FF.

Tannayong — An elevated-rail system in Bangkok, Thailand, sponsored by Thai and European engineering firms. The cost was US$1.65 billion.

Toulouse Métro — An extension of the Toulouse subway in France. The sponsor was MATRA and the local public network operator. The cost of the extension was 1.5 billion FF.

Roads, Tunnels, and Bridges

BNPL — A recent road and tunnel system around the city of Lyons, France, built by a group of European engineering firms and banks at an expected total cost of 6 billion FF.

Cofiroute — A network of toll highways built by Cofiroute, a road developer owned by six engineering and construction firms in France. Construction started in the early 1970s, but new roads are still being built. The Paris-Poitiers segment cost 1,379 billion FF.

Highway 407 — A toll-highway project near Toronto, built at a cost of CA$1 billion by a corporation of the Ontario government and later sold to a consortium of engineering firms, banks, and road operators.

M1–M15 — A toll highway between Vienna and Budapest. The concessionaire was a group of European engineering firms and banks. Estimated cost was US$440 million.

Mexico Road Program — A partly built network of toll roads covering Mexico. The government of Mexico granted concessions to a number of engineering and construction companies.

Muse — A network of underground roads in and around Paris, France. The project was sponsored by two engineering firms and the regional government, but it has been abandoned.

Northumberland Strait Crossing — A 13 km toll bridge linking the mainland to Prince Edward Island, Canada. The BOT concessionaire was SCI, a developer group including GTM International, Ballast Neddam, and Strait Crossing of Canada. The cost was CA$750 million.

Prado Carenage — A tunnel built at a cost of 1.2 billion FF in the 1990s in Marseille, France, sponsored and operated by a consortium of French engineering firms and banks.

Second Severn Crossing — A road bridge linking England and South Wales. The sponsor was a joint venture led by John Laing with GTM Entrepose. The project cost was £536 million.

Third Dartford Crossing — A third road bridge link over the River Thames, between Kent and Essex counties. It was built in the early 1990s as a BOT at a cost of £200 million. The sponsor was a consortium led by Trafalgar House.

Oil Projects

Andrew — A fixed oil platform with ten production and gas-reinjection wells in the North Sea. The leader and operator was BP Exploration. Production started in 1996 and the capital cost was £290 million.

Copan — Offshore platform to exploit the Cohasset and Panuki oil fields in Nova Scotia, Canada, built in the early 1990s. The

	sponsor was Nova Scotia Resources Ltd. with LASMO Nova Scotia Ltd. The project cost CA$915 million.
Njord	An offshore platform to exploit an oil field located on the Norwegian continental shelf near Kristiansud, Norway. The sponsor was a consortium led by Norsk Hydro. The project cost was 5.9 billion NOK.
Vigdis	An offshore platform to exploit the Vigdis field on the Norwegian Continental Shelf, 150 km west of Flor, Norway. The sponsor was a consortium led by Saga Petroleum. Eight production wells, four injection wells, subsea production system, and other investments at a cost of 4.9 billion NOK.

Technology and Other Projects

Boston Harbor cleanup	A massive US$5 billion project to rebuild the sewage-treatment facilities of municipalities around Boston Harbor. The sponsor was an independent authority created by the State of Massachusetts.
CAMSIN	A software-hardware system for managing air traffic in Canada and over the North Atlantic. The sponsor was Transport Canada.
Euralille	Redevelopment in the late 1990s of railroad land into an urban complex in Lille, France. The sponsor was a partnership between the municipal government and major French banks. Estimated cost was 2 billion FF.
Gardemoen	New airport near Oslo, Norway, sponsored by the Ministry of Transport and Communications, to be completed in 1999. Estimated cost was 22.3 billion NOK.
Lambdon FGD	A flue-gas desulphurization project to serve the Lambdon coal-fuel thermal-power plant built in the mid-1990s. The sponsor was Ontario Hydro and the cost was CA$537 million.
Service Ready Plane	Recent parallel design of planes, training programs, and flight simulators to accelerate commercial use. Collaboration between regulators, plane designers, training centers, and flight-simulation firms was necessary.
Telerobotics	A recent line-maintenance-robot project sponsored by EDF and Hydro-Québec. The contractor was CAE Electronics of Canada.

Thames Water Ring Main	Water-distribution system completed in the mid-1990s at a cost of U.S.$500 million. The sponsor was Thames Water in London, England.

For those interested in having access to summaries of the sixty projects we have studied, please refer to the Hydro-Québec/CAE Chair in the Management of Technology web site at the following address:

www.er.uqam.ca/nobel/r34670

Our e-mail addresses are:
Miller.roger@uqam.ca
dlessard@mit.edu

Appendix B: Attendees at the IMEC Forums in Montreal, Poitiers, and James Bay

Raymond Bachand, President
FTQ Capital Fund, Montreal, Canada

Chris Benjamin, Executive Director
Major Projects Association, Oxford, England

Eric Blanchard, Finance Director
Cofiroute, Sèvres, France

Thierry Chambolle, General Manager
Suez Lyonnaise des Eaux, Paris, France

Michel Clair, Executive Vice-President
Hydro-Québec International, Montreal, Canada

Graham Corbett, Chief Financial Officer
Eurotunnel, London, England

Marcel Côté, Partner
Groupe SECOR, Montreal, Canada

Armand, Couture, President
Hydro-Québec, Montreal, Canada

Torstein A. Dahl, Project Coordinator
Royal Ministry of Transport and Communications, Oslo, Norway

Dennis De Melto, Service Industries and Capital Projects Industry Canada, Ottawa, Canada

Marc Deschênes, Director, Business Development
Export Development Corporation, Montreal, Canada

François Dionne, Vice-President and General Manager
SNC-Lavalin, Montreal, Canada

Pierre Dufour, Executive Vice-President
SNC-Lavalin, Montreal, Canada

Gus Ezers, Project Manager
Ontario Hydro, Toronto, Canada

André Filion, Planning and Business Strategies
IREQ, Varennes, Canada

Ian Gillespie, President
Export Development Corporation, Ottawa, Canada

Pal Gjierso, Vice-President
Saga Petroleum AS, Sandvika, Norway

Eric Jennett
Project Management Institute, Pennsylvania, United States

Jean Lamothe, President
Capital International CDPQ Inc., Montreal, Canada

Serge Lapalme, Acting Vice-President
Hydro-Québec, Montreal, Canada

C. Fausto Levy, Vice-President
Newcourt Capital, Montreal, Canada

Pierre Lortie, President
Bombardier Regional Jets, Montreal, Canada

Hervé Machenaud, Associate Director
Électricité de France, Paris, France

George F. Montalvan, Senior Evaluation Officer
Inter-American Development Bank, Washington, D.C., United States

Philippe Mora
SNC-Lavalin, Montreal, Canada

Ken-ichi Morijiri, International Affairs
Tokyo Electric Power Company, Tokyo, Japan

Knut Erik Nordby, Project Control Manager
Oslo Lufthavn AS, Gardermoen, Norway

James P. O'Brien, Partner
Baker & Mackenzie, Chicago, United States

Denis Pelletier, R&D Director
IREQ, Varennes, Canada

Bernard Poulverel, Project Director
Électricité de France, Paris, France

Jean-François Poupinel, General Manager
Cofiroute, Sèvres, France

Patrick Rich, Chairman, IMEC
Geneva, Switzerland

Richard Riley, Assistant Director
Department of Trade and Industry, London, England

Jean Saintonge, Export Adviser
Government of Quebec, Quebec City, Canada

Tetsuya Sekiya, Construction Management Group
Takenaka Corporation, Tokyo, Japan

Erik Siegel, Executive Vice-President
Export Development Corporation, Ottawa, Canada

Maurice Simony, Vice-President
Groupe Systra, Paris, France

Havard O. Skaldebo, Project Management
Norsk Hydro, Oslo, Norway

Peter Sorensen, Project Leader
Northumberland Strait Crossing
Charlottetown, Canada

Henri Souquières, Vice-President
Export Development Corporation, Ottawa, Canada

Robert Tessier, President
Gaz Métropolitain, Montreal, Canada

Paul Tétreault, Vice-President
Bombardier, Kingston, Canada

André Vallerand, President
EDI World Institute, Montreal, Canada

Paul Wolfe, Director
Alcan, Montreal, Canada

Yusuke Yamazaki, Deputy General Manager
Shimizu Corporation, Tokyo, Japan

References

Abrahamson, E. 1996. "Management Fashion." *Academy of Management Review,* 21: 254–85.

Alchian, A. A. 1950. "Uncertainty, Evolution and Economic Theory." *Journal of Political Economy,* 58: 211–28.

Alchian, A. A., and Demsetz, H. 1973. "The Property Rights Paradigm." *Journal of Economic History,* 33: 16–27.

Amram, Martha, and Kulatilaka, Nalin. 1999. "Uncertainty: The New Rules for Strategy." *Journal of Business Strategy,* 20(3): 25–29.

Aoki, M., and Kim, Hyung-ki. 1995. *Corporate Governance in Transitional Economies.* EDI Development Studies. Washington, DC: World Bank.

Argyris, C., and Schon, D. A. 1978. *Organizational Learning: A Theory of Action Perspective.* Reading, MA: Addison-Wesley.

Baker, Wayne E., and Faulkner, Robert R. 1991. "Role as Resource in the Hollywood Film Industry." *American Journal of Sociology,* 97(2): 279–310.

Barker, T. C., and Savage, G. I. 1974. *An Economic History of Transport in Britain.* London: Hutchinson and Co.

Barzel, Y. 1989. *Economic Analysis of Property Rights.* Cambridge: Cambridge University Press.

Bennis, W. G., and Sheppard, H. A. 1956. "A Theory of Group Development." *Human Relations,* 9: 415–37.

Bergara, M. E., Henisz, W. J., and Spiller, P. T. 1998. "Political Institutions and Electric Utilities Investment: A Cross-Nation Analysis." *California Management Review,* 40(2): 18–35.

Bettis, A. Richard, and Hilt, Michael A. 1995. "The New Competitive Landscape." *Strategic Management Journal,* 16: 7–19.

Black, Fischer, and Scholes, Myron. 1974. "From Theory to a New Financial Product." *Journal of Finance,* 29(2): 399–412.

Boyer, R., and Saillard, Y. 1995. "Introduction." In R. Boyer and Y. Saillard, eds. *Théorie de la régulation, l'état des savoirs,* 9–17. Paris: La Découverte.

Brealey, R., and Myers, S. 1997. *Principles of Corporate Finance.* New York: McGraw-Hill.

Brealey, R., Cooper, Ian, and Habib, Michel. 1996. "Using Project Finance to Fund Infrastructure Investments." *Journal of Applied Corporate Finance*, 9(5): 25–38.

Brealey, R., Cooper, Ian, and Habib, Michel. 1998. "Valuation in the Public and Private Sectors: Tax, Risk, and the Cost of Capital." Working paper, London Business School.

Bromiley, P. 1988. *A Time Series Study of Corporate Risk and Performance*. Discussion paper 92, Strategic Management Research Center, University of Minnesota.

Brown, Shona, and Eisenhardt, Kathleen M. 1997. "The Art of Continuous Change: Launching Complements Theory and Term-paced Evolution in a Relentlessly Shuffling Organization." *Administration Science Quarterly*, 42: 1–34.

Bryson, John M., and Bromiley, Philip. 1990. *The Planning and Implementation of Major Projects*. Working paper 135, Strategic Management Research Center. University of Minnesota.

Buck, S. J. 1913. *The Granger Movement*. Cambridge: Harvard University Press.

Burger, T. 1976. *Max Weber's Theory of Concept Formation*. Durham, NC: Duke University Press.

Burt, R. S. 1992. *Structural Holes: The Social Structure of Competition*. Cambridge: Harvard University Press.

Byrne, David. 1998. *Complexity Theory and the Social Sciences: An Introduction*. London and New York: Routledge.

Callon, Michel, Larédo, Philippe, and Mustar, Philippe. 1995. *La gestion stratégique de la recherche et de la technologie: l'évaluation des programmes*. Paris: Économica.

Caron, F. 1997. *Histoire des chemins de fer en France*. Paris: Fayard.

Chandler, A. D., and Salisbury, S. 1965. "The Railroads: Innovators in Modern Business Administration." In B. Mazlish, ed. *The Railroad and the Space Program: An Exploration of Historical Analogy*, 127–62. Cambridge: MIT Press.

Chapman, O. B., and Ward, S. C. 1994. "The Efficient Allocation of Risk in Contracts." *Omega, International Journal of Management Science*, 22: 537–52.

Clelland, David I., and King, William R. 1988. *Systems Analysis and Project Management*. New York: McGraw-Hill.

Conway Data Inc. 1999. *Superproject Information*. Special inquiry.

Cooper, Robert G. 1993. *Winning at New Products: Accelerating the Process from Idea to Launch*. Reading, MA: Addison-Wesley.

Corbin, J., and Strauss, A. 1990. "Grounded Theory Research: Procedures, Canons, and Evaluative Criteria." *Qualitative Sociology*, 13(1): 3–21.

Coriat, Benjamin. 1998. *Modes de coordination et de gouvernance*. Working paper, IMEC Research Programme, Montreal.

Corzine, Robert. 1977 (October 27). "Bank Role Urged in Chad Oil Plan." *Financial Times*, 5.

DeBresson, Christian, and Arress, Fernand. 1991. "Network of Innvovation." *Research Policy*, 20: 363–79.

Diehl, Ernst, and Sterman, John. 1995. "Effects of Feedback Complexity on Dynamic Decision Making." *Organizational Behavior and Human Decision Processes,* 62(2): 198–216.

DiMaggio, P., and Powell, W. W. 1983. "The Iron Cage Revisited: Institutional Isomorphism and Collective Rationality in Organizational Fields." *American Sociological Review,* 48: 147–60.

DiMaggio, P., and Powell, W. W. 1991. "Introduction." In Walter Powell and Paul DiMaggio, eds. *The New Institutionalism in Organizational Analysis,* 1–38. Chicago: University of Chicago Press.

Dixit, Avinash K., and Pindyck, Robert S. 1995. "The Options Approach to Capital Investment." *Harvard Business Review,* 73(3): 105–16.

Dosi, G. 1982. "Technological Paradigms and Technological Trajectories: A Suggested Interpretation of the Determinants and Directions of Technical Change." *Research Policy,* 11(3): 147–62.

Doty, H. D., Glick, W. H., and Huber, G. P. 1993. "Fit, Equifinality, and Organizational Effectiveness: A Test of Two Configurational Theories." *Academy of Management Journal,* 36(6): 1196–1250.

Doz, Y. 1993. *Managing Technology Alliance.* Montreal: UQAM Hydro-Québec chair.

Eccles, Robert G., and Crane, Dwight B. 1987. "Managing through Networks in Investment Banking." *California Management Review,* 30(1): 176–96.

Ellis, H. 1954. *British Railway History.* London: George Allen and Unwin.

Energy Information Administration. 1996. *The Changing Structure of the Electric Power Industry: An Update.* Washington, DC.

Floricel, S., and Lampel, J. 1998. "Innovative Contractual Structures for Inter-organizational Systems." *International Journal of Technology Management,* 16(1/2/3): 193–206.

Forrester, Jay W. 1987. "Nonlinearity in High-Order Models of Social Systems." *European Journal of Operational Research,* 30(2): 104–10.

Forrester, Jay W. 1992. "Policies, Decisions, and Operation Sources for Modeling." *European Journal of Operational Research,* 59(1): 42–64.

Freeman, Christopher. 1982. *The Economics of Industrial Innovation.* 2d ed. Cambridge: MIT Press.

Gamson, William A. 1968. *Power and Discontent.* Homewood Illinois: Dorsey Press.

Giddens, A. 1984. *The Constitution of Society: Outline of the Theory of Structuration.* Berkeley: University of California Press.

Glaser, B. G., and Strauss, A. L. 1967. *The Discovery of Grounded Theory: Strategies for Qualitative Research.* Chicago: Aldine.

Granovetter, M. 1985. "Economic Action and Social Structure: The Problem of Embeddedness." *American Journal of Sociology,* 91(3): 481–510.

Gras, Alain. 1993. *Grandeur et Dépendance: Sociologie des macro-systèmes techniques.* Paris: Presses Universitaires de France.

Hage, Jerald. 1980. *Theories of Organization, Form, Process, and Transformation.* New York: John Wiley and Sons.

Hirschman, Albert O. 1975. *Exit, Voice, and Loyalty.* Cambridge: Harvard University Press.

Hirsh, R. F. 1989. *Technology and Transformation in the American Electric Utility Industry.* Cambridge: Cambridge University Press.

Hodgson, Geoffrey M. 1993. "Introduction and Conception and Evolution in Economics? Three Twentieth-Century Theorists." *Economics and Evolution: Bringing Life Back into Economics,* 1–52, 121–185. Cambridge: Polity Press.

Hogue, C., Bolduc, A., and Larouche, D. 1979. *Québec: un siècle d'électricité.* Montreal: Libre Expression.

Hollingsworth, J. Rogers, and Boyer, Robert, eds. 1997. *Contemporary Capitalism: The Embeddedness of Institutions.* Cambridge: Cambridge University Press.

Hughes, Thomas P. 1987. "The Evolution of Large Technological Systems." In Wiebe E. Bijker, Thomas P. Hughes, and Trevor Pinch, eds. *The Social Construction of Technological Systems,* 52–81. Cambridge: MIT Press.

Hughes, Thomas P. 1998. *Rescuing Prometheus.* New York: Pantheon.

Hunt, Sally, and Shuttleworth, Graham. 1996. *Competition and Choice in Electricity.* Chichester: John Wiley and Sons.

Illinitch, A. Y., D'Aveni, R. A., and Lewin, A. Y. 1996. "New Organizational Forms and Strategies for Managing in Hypercompetitive Environments." *Organization Science,* 7(3): 211–19.

Ingram, G., et al. 1994. *Infrastructure and Development.* World Bank Report. Washington, DC: World Bank.

Innis, Harold A. 1970. *A History of the Canadian Pacific Railway.* Toronto: University of Toronto Press.

Jessop, B. 1997. "The Governance of Complexity and the Complexity of Governance: Preliminary Remarks on Some Problems and limits of Economic Guidance." In Ash Amin and Jerzy Hausner, eds. *Beyond Market and Hierarchy,* 95–128. Cheltenham, UK: Edward Elgar.

Jones, Candace, Hesterly, William S., and Borgatti, Stephen P. 1997. "A General Theory of Network Governance: Exchange Conditions and Social Mechanisms." *Academy of Management Review,* 22(4): 911–45.

Jones, Thomas M. 1995. "Instrumental Stakeholder Theory: A Synthesis of Ethics and Economics." *Academy of Management Review,* 20(2): 404–37.

Joskow, P. L., and Schmalensee, R. 1983. *Markets for Power: An Analysis of Electric Utility Deregulation.* Cambridge: MIT Press.

Katzenstein, P. J. 1985. *Small States in World Markets: Industrial Policy in Europe.* Ithaca, NY: Cornell University Press.

Keeney, Ralph L., Lathrop, John F., and Sicherman, Alan. 1986. "An Analysis of Baltimore Gas and Electric Company's Technology Choice." *Operations Research,* 34(1): 18–40.

Kulatilaka, N., and Lessard, D. 1998. *Total Risk Management.* Working paper, Sloan School, Massachusetts Institute of Technology.

Laffont, J.-J., and Tirole, J. 1993. *A Theory of Incentives in Procurement and Regulation.* Cambridge: MIT Press.

Lampel, Joseph. 1998. *The Strategies of Engineering and Construction Firms.* Presentation to IMEC Forum, Montreal.

Lampel, L., and Miller, R. 1996. "Impact of Owner Involvement on Innovation in Large Projects." *International Business Review,* 5(6): 561–78.

Lanthier, P. 1986. "L'industrie électrique entre l'entreprise privée et le secteur public." In F. Cardot, ed. *1880–1980 Un siècle d'électricité dans le monde,* 23–36. Paris: Presses Universitaires de France.

Lascelles, David. 1996 (June 28). "Oil Industry Rigs Up Way to Cut Production costs." *Financial Times,* p. 8.

Laughton, David G., and Jacoby, Henry D. 1993. "Reversion, Timing Options, and Long-Term Decision-Making." *Financial Management,* 22(3): 225–24.

Lazonick, W. 1992. "Business Organization and Competitive Advantage: Capitalist Transformations in the Twentieth Century." In G. Dosi, R. Giannetti, and P. A. Toninelli, eds. *Technology and Enterprise in a Historical Perspective,* 119–63. Oxford: Clarendon.

Lesourne, J. 1991. *Économie de l'ordre et du désordre.* Paris: Économica.

Lévi-Leboyer, M., and Morsel, H., eds. 1994. *Histoire de l'électricité en France.* Paris: Fayard.

Levitt, Raymond E., and Kunz, John C. 1998. *The Virtual Design Team: Designing Quality into Project Organizations.* Working paper no. 47, Center for Integrated Facilities Engineering. Stanford University.

Lewin, K. 1958. "Group Decision and Social Change." In E. E. Maccoby, T. M. Newcomb, and E. L. Hartley, eds., *Readings in Social Psychology,* 3d ed., 197–211. New York: Holt, Rinehart, and Winston.

Luhmann, N. 1992. *Risk: A Sociological Theory.* New York: Aldine De Gruyter.

Luhmann, N. 1995. *Social Systems.* Stanford: Stanford University Press.

MacCrimmon, Kenneth R., and Wehrung, Donald A. 1986. *Taking Risks, the Management of Uncertainty.* New York: Free Press.

March, James J., and Olsen, Johan P. 1989. *Rediscovering Institutions: The Organizational Basis of Politics.* New York: Free Press.

Meredith, Jack R., and Mantel, Samuel J. Jr. 1995. *Project Management: A Managerial Approach.* New York: John Wiley and Sons.

Merrow, E. W., McDonwell, L. M., and Arguden, R. Y. 1988. *Understanding the Outcome of Megaprojects.* Santa Monica: Rand Corporation.

Meyer, J. W., and Rowan, B. 1977. "Institutionalized Organizations: Formal Structure as Myth and Ceremony." *American Journal of Sociology,* 83: 340–63.

Miller, Merton. 1977. "Debt and Taxes." *Journal of Finance,* 32: 261–75.

Miller, Roger, and Côté, Marcel. 1987. *Growing the Next Silicon Valley.* Lexington, MA: Lexington Books.

Miller, R., Lampel, J., and Floricel, S. 1995. "L'innnovation dans les projets de centrales électriques." *Conférences de la Chaire Hydro-Québec/CRSNG/CRSH en gestion de la technologie* series, Université du Québec à Montréal.

Miller, Roger, Hobday, Michael, Leroux-Demers, Thierry; and Olleros, Xavier. 1995. "Innovation in Complex Systems Industries: The Case of Flight Simulation." *Industrial and Corporate Change*, 4(2): 363–400.

Mintz, J. M., and Preston, R. S. 1994. *Infrastructure and Competitiveness*. Kingston, Ontario: John Deutsch Institute.

Mintzberg, H. 1994. *The Rise and Fall of Strategic Planning*. New York: Free Press.

Modigliani, Franco, and Miller, Merton. 1958. "The Cost of Capital, Corporation Finance, and the Theory of Investment." *American Economic Review*, 48: 261–97.

Morris, P. W. G. 1994. *The Management of Projects*. London: Thomas Telford Publishing.

Morris, P. W. G. and Hough, G. H. 1987. *The Anatomy of Major Projects*. New York: John Wiley and Sons.

Morsel, H. 1992. "Études comparées des nationalisations de l'électricité en Europe occidentale après la deuxième guerre mondiale." In M. Trèédé, ed. *1880–1980. Electricité et électrification dans le monde*, 440–458. Paris: Presses Universitaires de France.

Nelson, R. and Winter, S. 1982. *An Evolutionary Theory of Economic Change*. Cambridge: Harvard University Press.

North, Douglas C. 1990. *Institutions, Institutional Change, and Economic Performance*. Cambridge: Cambridge University Press.

Olleros, Xavier. 1991. *The Innovation Process: Manageable or Unmanageable?* Montreal: Hydro-Québec Chair in the Management of Technology, Université du Québec à Montréal.

Parsons, T. 1947. *Introduction to Max Weber: The Theory of Social and Economic Organization*. New York: Free Press.

Penrose, Edith T. 1959. *Growth of the Firm*. Oxford: Basil Blackwell.

Perrow, C. 1984. *Normal Accidents: Living with High-Risk Technologies*. New York: Basic Books.

Pfeffer, J. 1978. *Organizational Design*. Arlington Heights, IL: AHM Publishing.

Powell, Walter W. 1990. "Neither Market Hierarchy: Network Forms of Organization." In B. M. Staw and L. L. Cummings, eds. *Research in Organizational Behavior*, vol. 12, 295–336. Greenwich, CN, and London: JAI Press.

Powell, W. W., Koput, K. W., and Smith-Doerr, L. 1996. "Interorganizational Collaboration and the Locus of Innovation: Networks of Learning in Biotechnology." *Administrative Science Quarterly*, 41: 116–45.

Power. 1994. "Independent Power: The State of the Market." February, 45–54.

Power Engineering. 1990. "Turnkey Contracts: The Pitfalls and the Benefits." January, 31–34.

Prahalad, C. K., and Hamel, G. 1990. "The Core Competence of the Corporation." *Harvard Business Review* (May–June), 79–91.

Pressman, Jeffrey L., and Wildavsky, Aaron. 1973. *Implementation: The Oakland Project.* Berkeley: University of California Press.

Project Management Institute. 1996. *Project Management Body of Knowledge.* Upper Darby, PA.

Richardson, G. 1992. *Systems Dynamics.* Cambridge: MIT Press.

Ring, P. S., and Van De Ven, A. H. 1992. "Structuring Cooperative Relationships between Organizations." *Strategic Management Journal,* 13: 483–98.

Roger, N. 1998. *Meeting Infrastructure Needs in the 20th Century.* Joint OECD-World Bank workshop, Paris.

Rudolph, R., and Ridley, S. 1986. *Power Struggle: The Hundred-Year War over Electricity.* New York: Harper and Row.

Salisbury, S. 1967. *The State, the Investor, and the Railroad.* Cambridge: Harvard University Press.

Sanchez, R. 1997. "Preparing for an Uncertain Future: Managing Organizations for Strategic Flexibility." *International Studies of Management and Organization,* 27(2): 71–94.

Saxenian, Annalee. 1994. "Lessons from Silicon Valley." *Technology Review,* 97(5): 42–52.

Sayles, L. R., and Chandler, M. K. 1971. *Managing Large Systems.* New York: Harper and Row.

Schein, E. H. 1969. *Process Consultation: Its Role in Organization Development.* Reading, MA: Addison-Wesley.

Schelling, Thomas C. 1963. *The Strategy of Conflict.* Cambridge: Harvard University Press.

Schumpeter, J. 1942. *Capitalism, Socialism, and Democracy.* New York: Harper and Row.

Schwartz, Peter. 1996. *The Art of the Long View.* New York: Doubleday.

Scott, W. R. 1994. "Institutions and Organizations: Toward a Theoretical Synthesis." In W. R. Scott and J. Meyer, eds. *Institutional Environments and Organizations,* 55–80. Thousand Oaks: Sage.

Shapira, Zur. 1995. *Risk Taking: A Managerial Perspective.* New York: Russell Sage Foundation.

Shapira, Zur, and Berndt, D. J. 1997. "Managing Grand-Scale Construction Projects: A Risk-Taking Perspective." *Research in Organizational Behavior,* 19: 303–60.

Silverberg, Gerald, Dosi, Giovanni, and Orsenigo, Luigi. 1988. "Innovation, Diversity and Diffusion: A Self-Organisation Model." *Journal of the Royal Economic Society,* 98(393): 1032–54.

Simon, Herbert A. 1976. "From Substantive to Procedural Rationality." In Spiro J. Latsis, ed. *Method and Appraisal in Economics,* 129–48. Cambridge: Cambridge University Press.

Stinchcombe, Arthur L. 1990. *Information and Organizations.* Berkeley: University of California Press.

Stinchcombe, Arthur L., and Heimer, Carol A. 1985. *Organizational Theory and Project Management: Administering Uncertainty in Norwegian Offshore Oil.* Bergen: Norwegian University Press.

Stover, J. F. 1997. *American Railroads.* 2d ed. Chicago: University of Chicago Press.

Strauss, A. L. 1987. *Qualitative Analysis for Social Scientists.* New York: Cambridge University Press.

Susskind, Lawrence, and Field, Patrick. 1996. *Dealing with an Angry Public.* New York: Free Press.

Swanson, E. B., and Ramiller, N. C. 1997. "The Organizing Vision in Information Systems Innovation." *Organization Science,* 8(5): 458–74.

Swidler, A. 1986. "Culture in Action: Symbols and Strategies." *American Sociological Review,* 51: 273–86.

Tilly, C. 1984. *Big Structures Large Processes Huge Comparisons.* New York: Russell Sage Foundation.

Tolbert, P. S., and Zucker, L. G. 1983. "Institutional Sources of Change in Organizational Structure: The Diffusion of Civil Service Reform, 1880–1953." *Administrative Science Quarterly,* 28: 22–39.

Trigeorgis, L. 1996. *Real Options: Managerial Flexibility and Strategy in Resource Allocation.* Cambridge: MIT Press.

Trujillo, José; Cohen, Remy; Freixas, Xavier; and Sheehy, Robert. 1998. "Infrastructure Financing with Unbundled Mechanisms." *The Financier,* 5: 10–27.

Tversky, Amos, and Kahneman, Daniel. 1986. "Rational Choice and the Framing of Decisions." *Journal of Business,* 59(4): S251–79.

Urban, Glen L., and Hauser, John R. 1980. *Design and Marketing of New Products.* Englewood Cliffs, NJ: Prentice-Hall.

Utterback, James M. 1994. *Mastering the Dynamics of Innovation.* Boston: Harvard Business School Press.

Weber, M. 1930. *The Protestant Ethic and the Spirit of Capitalism.* New York: Scribner.

Weber, M. 1947. *The Theory of Social and Economic Organization.* New York: Free Press.

Wildavsky, Aaron A. 1993. *Speaking Truth to Power.* London: Transaction.

Williamson, O. E. 1975. *Markets and Hierarchies: Analysis and Antitrust Implications.* London: Free Press.

Williamson, O. E. 1991a. "Comparative Economics Organization: The Analysis of Discrete Structural Alternatives." *Administrative Science Quarterly,* 269–296.

Williamson, O. E. 1991b. "Strategizing, Economizing, and Economic Organization." *Strategic Management Journal,* 12: 75–94.

Williamson, O. E. 1992. "Markets, Hierarchies, and the Modern Corporation: An Unfolding Perspective." *Journal of Economic Behavior and Organization,* 17(3): 335–51.

Index